Standing Up

Standing Up

A MEMOIR OF A FUNNY (NOT ALWAYS) LIFE

MARION GRODIN

NEW YORK NASHVILLE BOSTON

The names and identifying facts of certain individuals in this book have been changed.

Center Street
Hachette Book Group
237 Park Avenue
New York, NY 10017

www.CenterStreet.com

Printed in the United States of America

RRD-C

First edition: November 2013
10 9 8 7 6 5 4 3 2 1

Center Street is a division of Hachette Book Group, Inc.

Library of Congress Cataloging-in-Publication Data
Grodin, Marion.
Standing up : a memoir of a funny (not always) life / Marion Grodin. — First edition.
pages cm
ISBN 978-1-4555-1013-9 (hardcover) — ISBN 978-1-4555-1011-5 (ebook)
1. Grodin, Marion. 2. Women comedians—United States—Biography.
3. Television writers—United States—Biography. 4. Screenwriters—United States—Biography. I. Title.
PN2287.G743A3 2013
792.702'8092—dc23
[B]

2013026471

To my parents, Julie and Charles, two of the All-Time Greats.

To everyone who continues Standing Up, no matter how badly they want to lie down.

ACKNOWLEDGMENTS

I want to thank my remarkably insightful agent, Jane Dystel, who, after seeing me do stand-up, turned to columnist Cindy Adams, and exclaimed, "That girl should write a book!"

Miriam Goderich, my other agent, who was so helpful in guiding me through what often felt like the epic process of writing just the book proposal.

I am so grateful to my editor, Kate Hartson, for all her goodwill and support as she guided me through the truly epic process of writing this book, as well as for not actually wrestling the pen out of my hand, as I sat across from her, day after day, rewriting, revising... and then rewriting and revising some more.

I have to thank Lauren Rohrig, editorial assistant extraordinaire, for her mind-boggling patience during the inordinate amount of time it took me to figure out how to color code all my rewrites and revisions.

Marketing director Andrea Glickson's tenacity in making sure I was able to present this book at the Jewish Book Council will always be so appreciated by this particular Jew.

I would not have been able to write this book without Hans

Leon and Keena Washington, and the rest of the kick-ass crew at the Englewood Staples, who saw me through every computer crisis, starting with my laptop being stolen before I'd even finished the proposal.

I need to convey my deep appreciation to my dear friend Danny Cohen, who, as the final deadline approached, lent me the money (which I have since repaid) necessary to stop doing anything but devote myself to finishing this book.

And lastly, to all my friends who talked me off the ledge, whenever necessary, over the two years it took to write this book! I couldn't have done it without you. You know who you are.

STANDING UP

1

"Maybe this wasn't such a good idea," I said, adjusting my Chico's burgundy velvet tunic. "What if I *suck*?" I whispered into my dad's ear as we sat on the side of the stage, watching the cast of *Wicked* belt out one extraordinary song after another in the tent at the Kennedy compound in Hyannis Port, in front of the thousand or so attendees to the annual Kennedy gala. "You'll be the best thing in the show," my dad said, staring straight ahead as he stood up, adjusted his tuxedo, and walked to the middle of the stage.

"Just incredible... really... a couple of those high notes... I couldn't hit them...," my dad said, pretending to try to hit a high note as the cast of *Wicked* exited the stage to thunderous applause. "Our next performer I've known for a very long time—her whole life, actually. She's been on *The View* and *Late Night with Conan O'Brien*; she headlines regularly at Gotham Comedy Club; she's opened for Lewis Black, Colin Quinn, and for Pat Cooper. Please welcome one of the funniest people I know: Marion Grodin!" He hugged me tight as he handed me the microphone.

"You forgot to tell them I starred in *Rapunzel* when I was ten," I whispered into his ear, laughing as I took the microphone from him.

"Next time," he whispered back, kissing the top of my head.

As I looked out at all these beautiful, smiling faces, everyone so sparkly in their gowns and tuxedos, I was overcome with gratitude that on one of the worst days in my forty-two-year life, I got to step into the light and do the one thing I could always count on to pull me out of the dark.

"First, I just want to say how truly happy I am to be here with all of you tonight. You all look *fabulous*! Okay, so...I'd like to *start* by going around the room...and everyone just 'sharing'—*briefly*, because I do want to get to *everyone*—what medications they're currently taking." Big laughs. "...That would take the whole night, right?"

"So...are there any other Jews in the room, besides me?" (A table toward the back claps energetically.) "Okay...okay, good...good...but why in the back, Ethel? Seriously...," I said, smiling at Ethel Kennedy, who was seated right in front of me in a spectacular turquoise-and-champagne-colored ball gown, laughing as she shook her head from side to side.

"So, before I was *married*, y'know, I was really trying to meet someone, and my friend Erin, who works on *The Dating Game*—yeah, it's back on. Y'know, *that* was, like, the first reality show. Anyway, she said I should come on there to try and meet someone. And I said, 'I'm not going on that show, Erin, and you know why? You know who's not on *The Dating Game*? Jews. We are *not* on that show because whenever it's a female doing the picking, it's always the exact same thing. It's always like, *Tammy's from Tarzana, California. She's a speech therapist. She enjoys windsurfing, Rollerblading, and scuba diving. She says she's looking for a man who's not afraid to laugh, and claims she makes an unforgettable sea bass. Come on, Tammy. Come on down....*'" I stop, stare at the audience, shaking my head slowly from side to side. "*That* is not a Jew...that is not one of ours." I make a circling motion toward the Jews in the back. "I'd love it to be one of my tribe: a really neurotic, tortured, broken Jewess, like myself. The profile'd be completely different, like"—I drop my head, letting out a huge sigh—"*Myrna's from a long line of depressed codependents. She says she'd* like *to write a screenplay...it's just* so hard *to get out of bed. She enjoys a high dosage of Zoloft, a variety of twelve-step programs, and sharing the same insights about herself over and over again.... She says she's looking for a man who's willing to pay for some therapy, and one who wouldn't be too put off by public sobbing. Come on down, Myrna. Come on down.* They bring her down on a gurney, with a platter of whitefish and a Barbra Streisand box set....It's a whole other thing. Boy, do I *not* miss dating. Ladies, you ever get with a guy, and he wants you to do something you don't want to do? Not like...the dishes. Nobody wants to do the dishes." I gesture toward the crowd. "Can I talk about sex, is that okay?" Applause, especially from the back. "Oh, sure...the Jews. So, I used to go out with this guy whose favorite position was me on top.

"And when I first got with him, I was thin, so I could pretty much just backflip right up there. But after a while...well, I realized I was very...hungry, and I got heavy. So one day, I said, 'Honey, can we talk? Look, we both know that I am not, remotely, anywhere near that entry-level weight...so by the time I hoist my big, fat ass up there, I'm tired. I'm hungry. I'm frightened and disoriented. Nothing hot is going to happen up here.' I said, 'Look, if you really want me to get up there, give me some kind of incentive... y'know, give me a reason to climb. Suspend, like, a Snickers from the ceiling.... Something for baby...'

"Thanks, thanks," I said during a fairly long applause break. "But thankfully those days are behind me. I'm married now, and actually, we've been trying to have a baby for a while, so every month, I pee on the stick... to see if I'm pregnant, or if I've just had a little too much Mexican that week... and every time I do that, I can never get over the fact that you can find out something that profound by whizzing on a stick. And, honestly, I would love to be able to find out *other* information by peeing on a stick, like... is alternate side of the street parking suspended? I don't even know who to *call* at this point! I get towed like every five days."

As I waited for the crowd to stop applauding, I snuck a glance over at my dad, who was beaming brighter than any of the lights flooding the stage. He shot me an enthusiastic thumbs-up as we winked at each other, and I took a breath, gearing up for my closer.

"But that weight stuff... whew...," I said, exhaling as I dropped my head. "Ladies, can we talk about how *traumatic* that swimsuit fitting room is? I mean, the lights are *so bright*. Look, I'm in there for a *one-piece*, not a colonoscopy. And why are there mirrors everywhere? No, seriously... it's brutal... and I don't know about you, but I get hungry. Honestly, they could offer you a little snack—just slip a little hunk of cheese through the curtain... some guacamole on a chip... *something*. And y'know when you catch a glimpse of yourself that you did not see coming..." Everyone began applauding as Ethel Kennedy and I smiled at each other. "At one point, I'd fallen against the wall, weak from hunger and...*despair*...and I twisted around...and I was like, *No...no...what the hell happened here?!* Because from a certain angle, it looked like someone was hugging me...but it was just *me* in there. And then I got so depressed, I thought, *I wonder if anyone has ever tried to kill themselves right here in the swimsuit fitting room...just built, like, a noose out of thongs and string bikinis.... They come in, they find your big ass hangin'...*" I acted out hanging myself from my neck as I gurgled. As I put the mic back in the mic stand, I threw my arms into the air, waving good night. "Thank you...really! Good night!" I shouted as I continued waving while I exited the stage.

I pulled back the big, heavy curtain and started to walk toward the other side of the stage.

"Omigod, you were soooooo funny," one of the thin, blonde *Wicked* women said as she carted several long, sequined dresses over to the clothes rack in front of me.

"Ah, thanks; you guys were amazing," I said, watching her push the costumes back to reveal a full-length mirror. She squeezed in her dresses just as another *Wicked* cast member ran up, grabbing her arm. "Come on. They're waiting," the woman said, pulling her along. "You were great!" she called over her shoulder as they trotted off.

I turned to look at myself in the mirror. Jesus, talk about catching a glimpse of yourself you did not see coming. I'd just finished a savage year of treatment for breast cancer—surgery, chemo, radiation, steroids. I'd gotten so heavy, and my hair was just starting to grow. It was so short and gray. I looked like a cross between KD Lang and Newt Gingrich...and my husband, my best friend, my partner for the last sixteen years, had moved out that morning, just before I'd left for the airport. As the rest of the cast from *Wicked* raced by, all seeming to know exactly where they were going, I stared at my reflection. Then, after a moment, doing everything I could not to cry...I whispered, *How the fuck did I get here?*

2

Where is he? I wondered for the umpteenth time, twisting around on the stone stoop in front of my building as I craned my neck, trying to see all the way down the block. My block—*the* block—which those of us who were lucky enough to live on knew was the best block in the city. Seventy-Seventh Street between Columbus and Central Park West—the Museum of Natural History block! That's how everyone referred to it. Sometimes when I'd tell someone I lived on the Museum of Natural History block, they'd get that glimmer of recognition in their eye and say, "Oh, you're on Eighty-First Street."

"No, that's the planetarium block. I'm on the Museum of Natural History block," I'd say proudly, certain of *my* block's superiority. I'll tell you why my block was so great: in a city where space is so hard to come by, our street was wider than any block I'd been on in the whole city. It was almost the width of two normal streets. The museum ran the entire north side of the street. It looked like some gigantic medieval castle. It was made of light sandstone and had wide steps cascading up either side all the way to the top, where they spilled out onto a very spacious landing. All of us who lived on *the block* and all our friends who hung on *the block* treated the landing and the steps leading to it like our own spectacular private patio. The top part was also where everyone went to get high. I hardly went up there, since I didn't get high, even though a lot of the older kids were always trying to get me to go up there. But I'd seen that movie *Go Ask Alice*, where the girl—who actually looked a lot like me—starts out just smoking cigarettes and pot, then the next thing you know she's in a mental hospital trying to scratch her face off. They could keep their drugs. I'd keep my face.

On the ground level were more stone steps, only these steps were gray and more modern. They went down to the entrance to the museum and were not *our* steps. They were for civilians. Nobody who lived on *the block* or hung on *the block* ever used those stairs. Wait, that's not true. Once on a school trip with my sixth-grade class, I did go down those steps. Omigod, now I remember. I not only went down those steps, I also made out with this black guy Darnell behind a canoe full of Indians. Didn't love it. Anyway, other than that one time, those stairs were for the never-ending legions of brightly clad, camera-noosed tourists descending on our shores every fucking day. They always reminded me of those rows of neon-colored candies on those sheets of white paper—spots . . . dots.

On street level out in front of the museum sat a stately circular garden that always boasted the most stunning flowers in a greater array of colors than even those spotty, dotty tourists.

And to top it all off, on both sides of the museum were two enormous grassy fields bordered by a black fence. The fence closer to the park, everybody who lived on *the block* had been trying to walk the length of since we were really little. Over the years, a lot of us had made it *almost* all the way down, but then, just when you thought you had it, you'd lose your balance, shoot your arms out to your sides, and shove your belly around like you were working some invisible Hula-Hoop, right before you came crashing down into the field.

As if all of this wasn't spectacular enough, at the end of the museum, at the end of *the block*, was our own personal entrance to Central Park! Lots of teenagers and even some older than teenagers hung out on *the block*, but I *lived* on the fucking thing! My little brick building was directly across from the Museum of Natural History. How lucky was I?!

When my parents split up, I was maybe five. I have no memory of them being married, but when they split up my dad found this apartment for me and my mom and... *Wait, is that him?* A yellow cab was crawling down my block and I leaned so far forward that I came off the stoop, hovering over the ground like one of those Olympic swimmers waiting for the start signal. I bent over, pulling up my left knee sock just as the cab stopped right in front of me.

"Yo, you can settle this," Roy yelled from behind his blue shades as he climbed out of the cab, followed by Evie and Manny. Roy and Manny didn't live on *the block,* but they might as well have; they were always there.

"Please tell me that motherfucker does not wash his cheese," Manny cackled as he turned down "Rapper's Delight" pouring out of his boom box, which was practically the same size as Manny. Manny was *much* older than the rest of us—probably like twenty-five. Roy and Evie were both eighteen. The buzz on *the block* was that Manny had been to prison *at least* once. Manny had thin, yellowish, fucked-up teeth that looked like no one had ever told them we had such a thing as *dentists* on our planet. Both of Manny's pinky fingernails were unusually long—I assumed for the snorting of cocaine. Also he had a long, thin Fu Manchu goatee that he stroked methodically whenever he spoke while one of his long pinky nails peeked out. Manny *always* wore a wife-beater—a disgusting name for a white tank top. Manny would have been one scary motherfucker if it weren't for the fact that he was four foot ten and had the body of a sixth grader. And I happened to know for a *fact* that those wife-beaters he wore every day were from the boys' department at Morris Brothers over on Eighty-Fourth and Broadway. And for some reason I suspected strongly had more than a little to do with all his little clothes, he was always, and I mean *always*, furious. Furious to the point that if everyone on *the block* threw you a surprise party and you walked in and they all jumped out and yelled, *Surprise*, and then Manny came running toward you and stabbed you as he yelled, *Surprise*, you wouldn't be. And obviously, the fact that his name was Manny, as in "tiny man," could not have helped.

"We all watched your dad last night on *Johnny Carson*, and he said he washes his cheese. I said he was jokin'. Manny and Roy said he washes it," Evie said as she leaned over and kissed my cheek. Evie was one my best friends. She lived in 20, the building next to mine. She was Manny's girlfriend. She was beautiful and bore an uncanny resemblance to Elizabeth Taylor, and would have been a total knockout except that she was morbidly obese. She was adopted, and a couple weeks ago she'd told all of us that, through some social worker lady she knew, she'd gotten a quick look at her birth file. So quick that she wasn't sure if the file said she'd been born in Columbia, South Carolina, as in a great place for kayaking, or just Colombia, as in a great place for drug cartels. I knew Evie was searching for way more of an identity than a place known for its kayaking could provide. Within a week of deciding to go with just Colombia, she was speaking with a subtle but definite Spanish accent. And obviously, the fact that her name was Evie, which sounds a lot like "heavy," could not have helped.

"He doesn't wash his cheese," I said, glaring at Manny, still smarting from his referring to my father as *that motherfucker*. "He's very convincing," I said, realizing they were all high as I studied their beady little red eyes.

"Your pops is definitely that. Like when he played that doctor in *Rosemary's Baby*, I was like, *Yo, why you gotta give that nice lady back to the devils?*" Roy said, grabbing the Newport from behind his ear as Manny did the same.

"That shit fucked me up!" Manny cackled/coughed angrily as he lit their cigarettes.

"It really did," Evie chimed in as she took the cigarette out of Manny's hand. "You wanna come with us?" Evie asked as Roy and Manny started to head across the street.

"I'm waiting for my dad," I said.

"Oh, right, that's tonight; come hang out when you get back," she said, as she caught up to Manny in the middle of the street. From the back they looked like the number ten. I knew they were all going up to the top of the museum to enjoy their high and probably smoke some more.

I let out a deep sigh and leaned over, looking toward Central Park. "Still not here, huh?" my other best friend, Marion, said, plopping down next to me. Squinching my face up, I shook my head slowly. "Not yet," I said as we fell against each other. Marion lived in 40, the building on the other side of mine. To our faces, everyone called us Marion G and Marion H, but behind our backs we both knew everyone called us Marion: Good Body—that was her—and Marion: Good Face—that was me. It wasn't that she had a bad face or that I had a bad body, just not as great as our other parts. Marion dug into her jacket pocket for some Bazooka bubblegum while I glanced down at the brand-new shiny black Mary Jane shoes my mother had bought me especially for tonight.

"He will be," she said, handing me a piece of gum.

"Oh, I know," I said, borrowing some confidence from my new shoes as I popped the pink square of gum in my mouth and stuffed the wrapper in the pocket of my outfit, which, by the way, aside from my Mary Janes, I felt *ridiculous* wearing. It had taken me close to a month and several trips to Harry's Shoes on Broadway and Eighty-Third Street before finally convincing my mother to buy me the Mary Janes, and only, *only* after she got me to agree that if she did buy them I had to let her make my outfit for tonight. Three Halloweens ago I'd been a sailor. My mom had found material at the costume store around the corner from our apartment that was navy blue with little anchors, waves, buoys, and sailors all over it. She had yards of it left over, and that's what she'd made today's outfit from. Not only did I feel completely ludicrous in this getup, but no matter how much I tried, I could not seem to adjust the lower part of the culottes to *not* look like there was a little sailor waving from my vagina. The best I could do was just try to cover him with the little tan cape my mother had also made.

My mother hated to spend money on *anything*. I mean, in

fairness to her, we didn't really *have* any, just what my father gave us. So her whole thing was *You know what I could make that for?* Omigod, how much did I *hate* that sentence. We could be out just walking around the neighborhood having a great time on a beautiful Saturday afternoon, and we'd walk by the pizza place. "Hey, it's almost lunchtime. Could I get a slice and a soda?" I'd ask in a thoroughly great mood, just loving our time together.

"Mmmm, how much would that be?" she'd ask.

"I don't know...a couple dollars. Why?" I'd answer, instantly mad.

"*A couple dollars?* I could make you a whole pie for that," she'd say as my great mood took off down the street.

"You're gonna make a whole pizza pie?" I'd say, unable to avoid raising my voice.

"I *could*," she'd say, smiling, while the door to the pizza parlor kept opening as everybody in the world filed out with their slices, pies, and giant sodas.

"You're gonna get the dough, the sauce...the apron...the hat...hurl the thing into the air repeatedly like they do?" I'd say, acting out throwing a pizza into the air over and over.

"How hard could it be?" That was my second least favorite sentence of hers after *You know what I could make that for?* Which always led to me snapping, "Forget it. I don't want it anymore."

For a few feet we'd just walk along side by side, neither of us speaking. Then, after realizing just staring at me lovingly was not going to get me to talk, she'd do something like take my hand in hers and give it a little squeeze. We'd walk another few feet, then she'd loop her arm in mine, saying, "Look, if you really want it...But I really think I could make one...." as she steered us back toward the pizza parlor.

"Omigod," I'd yell, laughing, wondering how the same person could evoke such anger and love from me all in the same moment.

"Wait, is *that* him?" Marion said shoving another piece of Bazooka in her mouth.

"*Is* it?" I said as Marion leapt up, raced over to the curb, grabbed one of the poles supporting my building's canopy, and flung her body as far out into the street as she could, trying to get a better look.

"OMIGOD!" she squealed, swinging around the pole to face me, her eyes stretched to capacity.

"What? What?" I demanded, topping her crazy-stretched eyes with my own. "Omigod, just tell me before we both pop a vein!" I yelled, rubbing my eye.

She lowered her head, making sure I understood the seriousness of what she was about to say. "It's *Lucien*," she said, her eyes stretched so wide she looked like Marty Feldman.

"Get the fuck out," I said, tugging on the sailor living in my vagina, who now appeared to be waving to the boy I dreamt about every night.

"Y'know, everyone still talks about that *kiss*," Marion said admiringly. The kiss she was referring to occurred last summer in the field during an unusually well-attended game of Spin the Bottle. Everybody was there, and by everybody, I mean all of us who lived on *the block* and everyone who hung on *the block*. Marion and I had sat next to each other. On my other side was Roy, who, in addition to his blue shades, always wore a jean jacket, even in the dead of winter, which Marion and I both felt was probably because he did so many drugs that he'd lost the ability to properly gauge weather.

Next to Roy sat Ricky, Roy's best friend, who was also eighteen. Ricky was a totally hot Spanish guy who had sexy lips the color of grape Kool-Aid. Ricky was always on his bike, which he said he needed for his job as an auxiliary policeman. None of us really knew what that was, but anytime we'd try to get an explanation out of Ricky, he'd get very defensive and flash us his auxiliary policeman badge, which Marion and I were fairly certain we'd spotted at the same store where my mother had bought the sailor material.

Next to Ricky sat Shana, a very promiscuous seventeen-year-old Jewish girl with an amazing body and wild curly red hair. She was currently sleeping with Ricky, but I happened to know she had recently slept with Cruz, a nineteen-year-old drug dealer, who was sitting on the other side of her.

On the other side of Cruz in the Spin the Bottle circle was Cindy, his girlfriend. Cindy lived on the block and Marion and I were pretty sure she did not know that her boyfriend, whom she was madly in love with, had fucked her best friend. Cindy was very short and athletic and had the kind of ass on her that Marion and I agreed we'd only seen on black girls. Sadly, not even her athleticism and big ass had proved sufficient to keep Cruz from straying.

Next to Cindy sat Richie, a very handsome Chinese guy who never said much but could frequently be seen off to the side, either practicing his tae kwon do or in a heroin nod. It was never really clear. Rounding out the circle were Evie, Manny, and Kathy. Kathy was Evie's sister—also adopted, but from a different family. Kathy was gay and, like Roy with his jean jacket, no matter how cold it was, always wore shorts.

Okay, now you've met all the players. We were about an hour into our game of Spin the Bottle when Lucien walked over and asked if he could join. I couldn't believe it. I was thrilled and completely shocked, as was everybody, since he'd *never* hung out with us. Lucien was the most beautiful boy I'd ever seen *anywhere*, I mean, even including movies and TV. His building was the fanciest and the last one on our block right before you'd cross the street to get into Central Park, which my mom and I did every day as soon as I got home from school. This was our routine. We'd take her dogs—all four of them—into the park for their long walk and our long talk, where I'd recount my entire day. *Tell me everything!* she'd say as the dogs pulled us along. It didn't entirely make up for *Y'know what I could make that for?* but it definitely helped. And she meant it; she really *did* want to hear *everything*. How many people can say they had *that* growing up? And if something wasn't clear, she'd make me go back: "Wait, was that before or after you fell of the balance beam in gym?" she'd ask intently, shooing the dogs away from something that was either a dead pigeon or a discarded lasagna.

But back to Lucien. His apartment was on the first floor. Marion had found out from one of the building's many doormen that Lucien's bedroom window was the one facing the street with the little white balcony off it. Whenever my mom and I would get to Lucien's window, I'd laugh and toss my hair to the other side of my face just in case he was standing at his window behind a white curtain. And to top it all off, his name, Lucien, meant "light" in French—which to me he was.

All the buildings on my block had doormen, except mine. Mine just had a locked glass door that would open with a key or if somebody buzzed you in through the intercom located next to the door. Lucien's building had more doormen than any of the other buildings on the block, as if the people who lived there were much more important than the rest of us. Like they were really worth guarding, maybe even laying down your life for, if, God forbid, it came to that. Trust me, if a tenant in Lucien's building was kidnapped or murdered, the place would be crawling with police sergeants, detectives, profilers, mediums, and dogs. If someone in *my* building was kidnapped or murdered, we'd get, like, one squad car and the super. But I loved my building. We were the only building on *the block* with black and Spanish people, which to me seemed like more than a fair trade-off for no doorman.

That evening in the field, so far, I'd kissed Kathy *twice*. Definitely a better time for her than for me. It was the last week of summer, and the air was heavenly that night—warm with the softest little breezes that would just tickle and kiss you everywhere. Even a few fireflies (which you hardly ever saw in the city) were hovering inside our circle. Every so often their amber glow would shine like tiny floating lanterns. The sun had just begun its descent, and the sky looked like a beautiful electric bruise—all blue and purple and red.

It was my turn to spin, and at this point I'd given up on ever getting to kiss Lucien. I just hoped I wouldn't have to kiss Kathy again. I shut my eyes tight then placed my opened hand on the bottle and spun it with all my might. Squinting through one eye I watched as the bottle spun around three times fast. It began losing momentum as it neared Roy. Roy smiled at me fiendishly from behind his blue shades as the bottle made its way over to Manny, who began slowly stroking his goatee and smiling at me salaciously, revealing the full extent of the yellow Chiclet museum inside his mouth. As my head screamed *Noooooooo*, the bottle crept toward Kathy, who was wearing a smile almost identical to Manny's. I closed my one open eye, trying to come to terms with the reality that although unintentional, over the past two hours I had apparently become a lesbian. Just as I was preparing myself to kiss Kathy for the third time, the craziest thing happened. A firefly landed on the bottle. It shone its little light and as if it were a tiny generator seemed to give the bottle the energy necessary to move past Kathy's muscular knee to the knee belonging to *the boy of my dreams!*

Are you fucking kidding me?! This cannot be happening! my head shouted as it exploded in ecstasy. *I am actually going to get to kiss the most beautiful boy ever, the boy I've been fantasizing obsessively about kissing for the last two years.* Slowly lifting my eyes from the bottle, I looked up to see Lucien staring at me. Smiles as bright as a sunrise crept across both our faces. Even though neither of us was speaking, there was such volume between us I was barely aware that everyone was clapping, whistling, hooting, and hollering wildly. They all knew how I felt about this kid. Manny stuck his little thumb and index finger in his mouth, whistling so loudly that all the dogs in the field stopped whatever they were doing and shot their heads around. Evie, Marion, Kathy, and Shana were all shaking their heads in joyful disbelief as they chanted, "Ma-ri-on! Ma-ri-on!" I winked at Marion and Evie then took a very deep breath as a little laugh escaped my lips. I leaned forward and began crawling seductively—I hoped—as the craziest smile kidnapped my entire face. I had played this exact moment over in my mind a million times, and now here in the museum field with the help of a firefly, it was about to be *real*. I was almost there—just a few inches away from those eyes, those lips! I could hear everyone still going nuts as I placed my hands on either side of me and, rocking back on them, lowered myself into a sitting position. *Wait...what?* All of a sudden I realized I was sitting in something very warm and very soft. I leaned over onto my right buttock, lifting my left buttock up as the smell hit my nose. *Noooooooooo*, my head screamed as I along with everyone in the circle realized I had just sat down in a big steaming pile of dog shit. A look of utter horror swept over Lucien's face. Turning to look around the circle, I suddenly felt like I couldn't hear anything. Everything was happening in slow motion. Everyone was laughing hysterically, their heads thrown back, their mouths wide open. I felt like Sissy Spacek in that scene from the movie *Carrie*, when she's at the prom in her beautiful dress with the boy of her dreams and a bucket of blood falls on her head. Evie and Marion were each waving their hands in front of their faces as if to say, *So, so sorry, but this is fuckin' hysterical.* And *I* was fucking hysterical! *This cannot be happening!* my head screamed. One minute I was starring in my own *Field of Dreams*, and now I was Carrie with the fucking bucket of blood.

Then I heard Cruz screaming, "That is fuckin' nasty!" He was laughing so hard that he fell on Ricky, who was leaning back kicking his feet into the air and shouting, "Yo, Grodin, you got to go upstairs and hose that shit down!"

"This is one shitty situation," Roy chimed in as he stood up, running back and forth, laughing so hard that every few feet he had to bend all the way over just so he wouldn't pass out.

Even Marion, Evie, and Cindy were unable to stop laughing. "Mar, just go upstairs. We'll hold your place," they screamed. "Mar, you have to go upstairs! You have to go change! Seriously, Mar, it stinks really bad!"

And then everyone started yelling, "We'll hold your turn! We'll hold your turn!"

I thought about it for a moment but as I looked around the circle I thought, *I have come too far to let this motley crew bully me out of my kiss.* Plus I knew that if I did go upstairs, change, and come back down, even if I really hurried, there would be *no turn.* The game would have moved on or maybe even ended. This could very well be the only chance I would ever get in my whole life to kiss *my dream.* At this point, stressful and extremely awkward negotiations ensued, led by Manny, who I guess identified with my underdog status, because he kept yelling, "Yo, let the girl get her kiss!" Eventually, the group albeit reluctantly acquiesced, and I, oblivious to everyone but me and Lucien, leaned forward, dog shit in tow, and kissed the boy of my dreams.

And that has pretty much been the story of my life—reaching for the light, no matter how much shit I'm sitting in.

3

"Saw your dad on TV last night. You look just like him," Lucien said, closing the cab door behind him as he walked toward me, those deep blue eyes of his twinkling up a storm. I opened my mouth to speak, but like how sometimes a cat opens its mouth to meow and nothing comes out—that's what happened.

"Luci," his gorgeous mother called from down the street. Lucien shot me a big smile, ran a few feet toward his mother, stopped, turned around so that he was running backward, and yelled, "I thought my grandmother was the only one who washed her cheese."

"Omigod," Marion squealed, punching me repeatedly in my arm.

"Owwww," I shouted, laughing, as I watched his perfect curls bounce rhythmically down the street. "Something must have happened." I looked toward Columbus.

"See if he called," Marion said as I got up, dragging myself into the outer lobby of my building and leaning on the buzzer.

"*Hello?*" my mother called through the intercom, her inflection strangely coquettish.

"He's still not here," I said into the speaker as I watched Evie, Manny, Roy, Cruz, and Richie, sitting on top of the museum, dangling their legs over the wall.

"He just called. He'll be here any minute. Is the other Marion with you?" my mom asked, returning to her regular voice.

"Uh-huh, why?" I answered, watching Evie pass what I knew was a joint to Manny.

"Her mother just called looking for her. Tell her to go home. Dinner's on the table." My mom clicked off.

"Dinner's on the table," I repeated under my breath, thinking how comforting the sound of that was. My mother was a lot more likely to say *Dinner's under the table* than *Dinner's on the table* after one of her seven rescued animals had swatted my food onto the floor for their own consumption.

"Did he call?" Marion twisted around, yelling from the stoop.

"He's on his way, and your mom just called. Dinner's on the table!" I said, about to laugh till I saw the man.

"Hi," he said familiarly.

"Hi," I said, my stomach flipping as I walked slowly toward Marion and the man.

"Is your mom upstairs?" he asked as I sat back down on the stoop.

"Uh-huh," I said as Marion stared at me, waiting to be introduced.

"Okay, well...thanks," he said, smiling as he trotted up the steps and walked over to the intercom.

I sat there feeling frozen.

Marion leaned all the way over, pressing her mouth right up against my ear. "Who is *that*?" she whispered too loudly.

"Just wait," I whispered back, pulling my head away from her mouth, "I want to hear."

"Hiiiii," I heard him say into the intercom, his inflection just like my mom's when I'd buzzed her before.

"Hiiiii," I heard my mom say as I realized she must have thought it was him before. *Bzzz.* The intercom sounded, letting him in as I twisted back around, staring across the street.

"Who *was* that?" Marion said, her entire face pleading for an explanation

"Nathan Weiss," I said as Marion stared at me, clearly needing more. "Remember, camp two years ago? He was one of our counselors," I said, aware I was holding my breath.

"I thought he looked familiar. Wow. Sexy, right?" she said emphatically, widening her eyes. He was sexy, but that wasn't anything I even wanted to think about. He looked like a Jewish Paul McCartney... with a mustache. My mother, although goyim, had always dated Jewish men. Before she'd married my father, she'd dated Dustin Hoffman and Gene Wilder. And before she started seeing Nathan, she was dating a Black Panther. One day his name was Steve, the next day, Kaleema Ganzel. Seriously.

"But why would he be coming to see your mother?" she asked, her face so close to mine I was inhaling her bubblegum breath. "Mar, why is he coming to your house on a Saturday?" she persisted.

"Well, he's not here for further lanyard instruction," I said, staring at her.

"Oh...," she said softly as she scooted closer to me.

My mom had met Nathan at camp two years ago, when she was also a counselor there.

They'd been having an affair ever since. He was married with two small daughters. He'd told my mom he wanted to leave his wife to be with her, but he couldn't because the wife was severely depressed, and he couldn't leave his girls with her. I remember the day she finally told me. I was sitting... actually... right here on the stoop when she'd buzzed down, letting me know I could come back up. I remember walking into the building just as Nathan Weiss was coming out.

"Have a good night," he said cheerily as he stepped out of the elevator.

"You too," I said, averting my gaze. I stood there holding the elevator door, staring at the empty box he'd just walked out of. After a moment, I took my hand off the door, deciding I'd take the stairs instead. Taking my time climbing the three flights of stairs to my apartment, 35, I couldn't stop thinking how *icky* this whole situation felt. I'd been sleeping in the same bed with my mother my whole life. Ever since I could remember it had just been my mom and me—the two of us. Our relationship was ridiculously complex. We were so many things to each other—all things, really... too many things, it would turn out. There were no boundaries at all, and our roles were always changing and reversing. Sometimes I felt like *she* was the mom; a lot of the time I felt like *I* was. We were definitely best friends—that was a constant. And a lot of the time I felt like I was my mother's partner—almost like her little husband.

I had just turned eleven when Nathan Weiss entered the picture, and not only was I sleeping in the same bed with my mom, but she was still telling me bedtime stories. Well, *her* version of a bedtime story.

They all began the same way. We'd usually have both just taken our baths, so we were warm and cozy. As we lay in bed in our nightgowns, side by side, arm in arm, my mother would say, "Isn't this *great*?" bursting with delight as she pulled me even closer.

"Mmm-hmm," I'd say, chuckling. Her boundless enthusiasm always made me laugh.

"Who loves you more than anyone else in the whole world?" she'd ask, giggling, snuggling, as she rubbed her foot against mine. "I know you think Mrs. Hochberg's so great because she puts all those dinners on the table, but I bet she can't make you laugh like I can. Can she?" she'd demand, grabbing ahold of me and tickling wildly.

"Omigod...stoooooooopp!" I'd finally manage to scream, laughing so hard I was afraid I might pee. "What is wrong with you?!" I'd shout, pretending to be the parent but unable to keep a straight face as I held her wrists so she couldn't get me. Both of us would scream with laughter as we wrestled back and forth. "No, no, Mrs. Hochberg...does...not make me...laugh like you dooooo..." I'd eke out *barely* between bouts of hysterical laughter, kicking my legs out and pushing my feet onto her thighs in an attempt to get some leverage. "Seriously, stoooooopp!"

"Okay, okay," we'd both say after a while, gasping for air like fish on a dock. Once we'd each caught our breath, she'd loop her arm back through mine as we settled in for our story. I'd close my eyes as she wiggled around till she got comfortable. The smell of my mother just out of the bath—her freshly moisturized skin, her damp just-washed hair, her breath—was always so dependably comforting.

"Let's pretend that we're in the back of a wagon and...*we're wounded*...," she'd say, slowly, deliberately.

"Badly?" I'd ask, picking up my cue.

"Well, not so badly that we're in any real pain, except when we go over big bumps...just badly enough that we can't really be expected to do anything...," she'd say, pulling me closer.

"...except lie here in the back of the wagon. What's gonna happen to us?" I'd whisper, smelling her cheek.

"Well, we're just gonna have to hope someone finds us and rescues us," she'd say, resting her head against mine.

Some kids got *Goodnight Moon*. I got *We're Wounded in the Back of a Wagon...Waiting for Someone to Rescue Us*. Now, I'm not saying this is solely responsible for my having lived (or not lived) my entire life as if I'm wounded in the back of a wagon waiting for someone to rescue me...but a little more *Goodnight Moon* couldn't have hurt.

"Mar, I gotta go; my mom's calling me," Marion said, snapping me back to the stoop. "I'm sure he'll be here any minute," she called over her shoulder as she ran toward her mother.

"I'm sure," I yelled. I could feel the temperature dropping. I pulled my cape around me just as a cool breeze sent a shiver up my spine. I looked across the street just as all the museum lights came on, illuminating Evie, Roy, Ricky, Shana, and Manny. Al Green's "Love and Happiness" was pouring out of Manny's boom box, and they were all dancing and laughing. *God, they look free*, I thought, pulling up my knee sock as I contemplated going across the street. I stood up, walked to the curb, and just as I was about to step into the street, a big yellow cab pulled up right in front of me.

4

"Forty-Third and Broadway will be our next stop, driver. Thanks," my dad called through the divider as he put his arm around me. "I am *so* sorry; shit, were you waiting long?" he asked, hugging me so hard that he literally squeezed a little laugh out of me.

"No," I lied, so happy just to be with him.

"I couldn't get off the phone with Harry about *The Tonight Show* appearance. Did you see it?" he asked, grabbing the tiny notebook and black Sharpie he always kept in his shirt pocket.

"Na na na na na-na na-na na na-na..." I sang to the tune of *The Tonight Show* theme, which is what we always did whenever either of us had really great news. "You were amazing," I said, putting my hand on his knee.

"And Mommy told me you got into Stuyvesant; honey, that's so great," he said, humming our song back to me as he motioned for me to move to one of the two metal seats across from us. "Why don't you sit over there so I can see you better," he said, putting his thumb and middle finger around my wrist as he guided me into my seat. We were both laughing, as this was one of the many bits we'd been doing for a long time. From the time I was very little, whenever my dad would take my hand to cross the street he'd hold my wrist between his thumb and his middle finger as if he had me in handcuffs.

I loved riding with him in these big yellow cabs, with their collapsible round metal seats. I don't think I'd ever been in a cab with my mother. And these ones felt so luxurious to me, like Ali Baba and the magic carpet, especially since the driver was usually wearing a very large turban.

"You were amazing," I said again, steadying myself on his knee as the cab lurched forward. "What?" I asked, realizing he was just staring at me.

"No...," he said, seeming suddenly hurt as he stared at my outfit.

"Dad, what?" I asked again, nervously.

"I know we haven't seen each other for a while, but I just thought if you were going to make a decision as big as joining the navy, you would have consulted me," he said. Both of us fought to keep a straight face. "So tell me what you thought of *The Tonight Show*," he said, smiling warmly.

"You were amazing," I said once more, leaning back in my seat.

"Harry's worried when I say stuff to Johnny like *You're not really interested in any of what you're asking me* that people will think I'm serious and I'll come off as being difficult, like I'm giving Johnny a hard time."

Adamantly shaking my head back and forth, I said, "I totally disagree; that's why it's so funny. No one's sure if you're kidding or not."

"You don't think it makes me seem unlikable?" he asked.

"Not at all. That's what's so great. I had three people today ask me if you really wash your cheese!" We both cracked up. "I mean, come on. That's hilarious!"

"I mean, what's the alternative? Talk about how great it is to be in the movies? How excited I am about my new movie? Who gives a shit? I don't. It's all too fucking self-important," he said, staring out his window at a fire truck. "I mean, seriously, you think *those guys* give a fuck about how excited Charles Grodin is about his new movie?" he said passionately.

"I mean, that's who we should be celebrating," he said, pointing at the firefighters. "Not actors. I mean, gimme a break. Those guys are our real heroes," he said emotionally.

I nodded in agreement but thought, *I'm lookin' at* my *hero.*

My dad. God, he was cool. He was very tall—over six feet. When it was cold out, like tonight, he always wore thick-ribbed corduroy pants in a black, brown, or tan color with a dark-colored, very soft sweater and a leather jacket and a cap. He was very handsome; that was obvious. But it was way more than just that. His face was so warm and reassuring, like a thousand pairs of Mary Janes. He was also the funniest person I or anyone had ever met. He could make me laugh so hard with what he said and how he said it that it felt like I was being tickled as hard as my mother would tickle me at night under the covers. And as if all that wasn't enough, he was famous...and rich!

I was in my last year at I.S. 44, the very tough, predominantly black and Spanish junior high school down the block, where a lot of the kids were bused in from some of the roughest neighborhoods in Harlem and the South Bronx. Many of my friends' parents either worked in prisons (i.e., janitors, correction officers, etc.) or were actually *in* prison. My friend Isabella Izu lived in a tenement with her mom and her two sisters, who always had so many hickeys it looked like they were wearing maroon turtlenecks. Her father was in prison; and her mom and sisters were on welfare. In the very back of their apartment was an entire room of pigeons in cages. I was never sure what that was all about, and Isabella never said. But let's just say no matter how many times they asked me I never stayed for dinner. One of my other friends, Lola, was lucky enough to have a live-in, working father. Her dad stood on the corner of 125th Street and Lenox Avenue dressed as a chicken in front of the chicken restaurant, handing out flyers. If you didn't take one, he'd chase you'd down the street, flapping his wings and furiously squawking.

My dad was a movie star! And if that wasn't spectacular enough, he always smelled like he'd just gotten out of the shower, no matter how late in the day it was or even if it was nighttime. His warmth added to the fact that he was so nice and tall and insanely funny, plus that he was rich and famous and the shower thing.... To me he was just magic.

Magic, I said to myself, suddenly aware that my dad was staring at me again. "What?" I said, sensing I was about to get tickled.

"What's going on with *that* sailor?" he said, indicating the little man docked in my crotch.

"Mommy made it; I told her it was too tight down there," I said, rolling my eyes as I tugged on my culottes.

"How *is* your mommy?" he asked.

"She's okay," I said, looking down at the miniature sailor, who wasn't really willing to budge.

My dad looked out the window, nodding his head intently.

"I know she thinks I talk too much, but I don't think she talks enough. She probably says it's because I'm talking, but I tell her whenever she has something she wants to say she should just jump in. I'm always interested," he said, glancing down as he picked a piece of lint off his pants. "I mean, *jump in*," he said softly under his breath.

I smiled at him empathically as I prepared to do my own jumping, right onto that bottom bar in the Olympic sport every child of divorce learns to excel in—the uneven parallel bars, where you swing between the two people you love most in this world, demonstrating your allegiance to one parent while making sure you're not betraying the other. Swinging up onto that top parallel bar, I delicately offered, "I think it's hard for her to jump in. Y'know she's not like us." As soon as the words left my mouth, all I could think was *Jump in? Don't you know you're dealing with the wounded-in-the-back-of-a-wagon, waiting-to-be-rescued woman who most of the time when you call and want me to put her on the phone insists (usually gesturing frantically from the bedroom) that I tell you she was asleep just so she won't have to come to the phone and jump in? There would be no jumping in. Crawling, maybe. Maybe she could crawl in!*

"I always try to get her to talk about herself," he said earnestly.

"I know you do. She doesn't like to talk about herself," I said, swinging around the bars.

"I ask her what she wants to do with her life," he continued.

"She feels pressured," I said softly.

"Because I ask her what she wants to do?" he said so intensely I felt pressured. "Most people would be thrilled to have somebody be that interested in them, don't you think?" he asked genuinely.

"Yes," I replied, wondering what about my mother had ever given him the impression that she was in any way *most people*.

"I mean, jump in already," he mumbled exasperatedly as I leaned forward, resting my hand on his knee. I felt terrible for him. He only ever had her best interests in mind.

"I mean, does she tell *you* what's she's interested in?" he asked, his voice softening.

As I struggled to remember what I was and was not allowed to tell him, I felt suspended in the air, frozen between the bars. Both my parents were extremely private people. Whenever my father would confide in me, he'd always say, *This has to stay in this room*—or at this table or in this cab. Wherever we were...that's where it had to stay. On this porch, in this vestibule. Between the two of them I felt like I was in the CIA. "Birds," I said.

"Birds?" he repeated, staring at me intently as he nodded his head slowly up and down.

"Yeah, she's got these books about all the different kinds of birds living in Central Park. She likes to go into the park with her books and her binoculars and see how many different species she can identify."

"Uh-huh," my dad said so seriously, it made me giggle.

"Macrobiotic cooking," I continued. "That's where you don't use any sugar or meat or dairy. She's started making some dishes. Oh, and antique bird decoys; she's just started collecting them." I smiled at my dad, pretty sure I had exhausted all the subjects I wasn't sworn to secrecy on. Obviously the married camp counselor was off limits.

My dad smiled at me sweetly. I think he knew that I was on the bars. Then he looked out the window as he closed the fingers on his left hand around his thumb, tapping the knuckle of his thumb on his teeth very quickly. That's what he always did when he was trying to figure something out. "What would be the purpose of that?" he asked, again with such seriousness, I had to bite my lower lip not to laugh.

"What?" I said, not sure where this was going.

"Collecting the decoys. I mean, I know how much she loves animals, but…I mean, she'd never try to, like, capture any of those birds, would she? Because I'm pretty sure that would be illegal," he said with such a straight face, I could no longer contain my laughter.

"You're joking, right?" I said, laughing.

"You know she skinned a bear once?" he said, laughing. She had. A long time ago. I'd seen a picture.

"What can I tell ya—the woman loves animals. It's *people* she's not that nuts about," I said, grateful there was at least one other person on the planet who knew her almost as well as I did.

Understand that had anyone else joked that way about my mother, it would have felt condescending, disrespectful, bad. But my dad was the rescuer in our wagon. There was never any doubt about that. So his ability to take the stuff that hurt the most and literally transform it into the stuff that made me laugh till it hurt…Well, that was one helluva magic trick. And one that, having apprenticed under the best, I too would come to master in order to survive the roughest shit life had in store for me.

"You two still sleeping in the same bed?" he asked, hurling me back onto those parallel bars.

"Uh-huh," I said nervously.

"And you feel that's okay?" he asked, giving me power I suspected shouldn't be mine.

"Yeah, I mean, it's not like we're *lesbians*!" I said, wondering instantly if we were in fact lesbians.

"Look, based on your outfit it's not that clear!" He laughed.

"Whadaya think: would we be better off on Ninth?" my dad asked the taxi driver, as we both stared out the window at the bumper-to-bumper traffic.

"Ninth, Seventh, everywhere bad! Too much traffic, my friend! Too much traffic!" the man with the very tall turban said, leaning on his horn as he tried to squeeze into the left lane.

"No fuckin' way," the driver next to us, wearing an even taller turban, screamed out his window.

"Let me get in!" our guy yelled, stepping on the gas.

"Your motherfuck," the other driver yelled, stepping on his gas.

"My motherfuck?! *Your* motherfuck!" our guy shouted so angrily he spit on his steering wheel.

"Let him go. Let him go; it's not worth it," my dad said, trying to defuse the situation. A minute or two later, we could tell our driver was still very upset based on how agitatedly he was mumbling and how frantically his turban was shaking back and forth.

"You got any snacks in there?" my dad said, gesturing toward the driver's turban. "Maybe a Snickers or, like, a Hershey's with Almonds? I know my daughter would really appreciate a Hershey's with Almonds." Thinking my dad was making fun of his turban, the man turned bright red as he glared at us in his rearview mirror.

"He's joking. He's joking with you. He's a famous comedy actor. That's where we're going, to see a movie he's starring in," I said quickly, beaming with pride.

"Ohhhhhhhh," the man said, very impressed, twisting around to get a better look at my dad as he pulled up in front of the theater. "Wait. I just saw you…last night on TV with Johnny Carson!"

"See?" I said.

My dad and I both smiled at the man as my dad handed him a twenty through the divider. I opened the door, scooting out as my dad took the change from the driver, handing him back a tip.

Just as my dad put his right foot on the pavement, preparing to get out of the cab, the driver said, "Can I ask you a question?"

"Sure," my dad said warmly.

"Why so mean to Johnny?" the driver asked, glaring at my dad.

"He was joking. It was a joke," I said just before he drove off.

My dad and I both chuckled as we stepped onto the curb.

"You can't please everybody," I said. Then, slipping my hand inside my dad's as we stared up at the marquee, I gasped, "Omigod!" as I read aloud: "*The Heartbreak Kid*, starring Charles Grodin."

My dad squeezed my hand. "Not bad for a kid from Pittsburgh, huh?" he asked, smiling down at me as we stood there, both of us savoring the moment.

Smiling up at him, I said, "Well, I can think of only one thing to say."

"What?" he asked, tucking both our hands inside the pocket of his leather jacket as we walked into the theater to the sound of me humming *The Tonight Show* theme.

5

I was staring across the room at Woody Allen, buttering a roll, while my dad, resting his hand on my shoulder, chatted with his good friend Paul Simon. We were having dinner at Elaine's, and trust me when I tell you there was no place like it. This was where all New York's biggest and hippest celebrities, writers, and politicos came to hang out and schmooze. I'm talking Al Pacino, Michael Caine, Nora Ephron, Jack Nicholson, Mia Farrow, and plenty more. You could feel the buzz the second you walked in—all these fabulous regal bees in this golden inner sanctum.

"Hey, Chuck, saw you on *The Tonight Show* last night. Tremendous, really," a very tall, very beautiful woman, who was either Cheryl Tiegs or Christie Brinkley, said as she stopped and gave both Paul and my dad a kiss on the cheek. "Thanks, honey," my dad said, then continued chatting with Paul. "You know my daughter, Marion, right?" my dad said as Enrico, his favorite waiter, approached the table.

"I know, she is more beautiful every time," he said, pouring a can of soda into my glass.

"Thank you," I said, blushing.

"I'll take the veal chop, medium well, and french fries, well done. You wanna split those with me?" my dad asked.

"Can I get my own?" I asked, wishing I were as thin as the woman who was either Cheryl Tiegs or Christie Brinkley.

"Get whatever you want. Get my daughter *whatever she wants*," my dad said, squeezing my shoulder. *Whatever I want, whatever I want*. My mind was intoxicated by the thought.

"For the lady?" Enrico, who always impressed me, as he *never* wrote anything down, said. I'd already reviewed all the specials on the menu and wanted to get something I knew I could never have if I wasn't with my dad.

"I'll have...the Cornish hen with well-done french fries," I said, handing Enrico my menu.

"She just starred in *Rapunzel*," my dad said, squeezing my cheek.

"Really?" Paul said sweetly.

"You going to be a famous movie star like your poppa?" Enrico said.

Yes, I plan on going right from my school auditorium the big screen, I thought, amusing myself as I watched Woody Allen telling a story. "Chuck, stop by before you go; I know everyone would love to say hello," Paul said, smiling at me as he turned to go back to his table.

"Go over. I'm totally fine," I said, smiling at my dad as I reached for a roll.

"*Totally?*" my dad playfully repeated in a high-pitched voice.

"Stop," I said, laughing as I watched the two of them walk across the room.

As I went table by table, I realized, *Wait... am I the only kid?* Omigod, how fucking lucky was I, I thought, watching my dad across the room. He was so talented but so down-to-earth. I mean, he's a *movie star*, and he could have easily afforded to move out of where he lived into some fancy shmancy place, but that just wasn't who he was.

He lived on the Upper West Side like me and my mom, only fifteen blocks farther uptown, in one of the places he'd lived all those years he wasn't a movie star, and there were *a lot* of them. His building was called the Windermere Hotel, and you really had to *see* this place to believe it! It was a very old (I mean truly from some whole other time), predominantly Jewish, residential hotel, with furnished apartments on Ninety-Second Street and West End Avenue.

It had an enormous brownish lobby, in the center of which was a sizable sitting area comprised of several old upholstered armchairs that looked like they'd been covered in the same material the carpet covering the lobby was made from. In the middle of the carpet-upholstered chairs sat a low, dark-brownish coffee table. At any time of the day or night, there were always at least a couple of very old people sitting there reading, arguing, sleeping next to their canes, walkers, or caretakers (usually heavyset Jamaican women, all of whom looked like they'd rather be *anywhere* besides perched next to a bitter, bossy, elderly Jew).

On the far right wall was a long, narrow glass case, the kind you'd see at a movie theater, only lower. It contained an impressive assortment of candy bars, licorice, gum, mints, and cigarettes for sale. The woman standing behind the counter looked exactly like Lily Tomlin's Ernestine—y'know: "One ringy dingy, two ringy dingy..." She even had Ernestine's poodle hairstyle on top, with the tucked-in buns on the sides and that bright-red lipstick.

At the far end of the lobby, past both the sitting area and the long candy case, was the hotel's main counter, which was long and dark brownish. About six feet behind the counter towered a vast wall of mail slots, but it was behind the counter in front of the mail wall where all the real action went down. That was where a virtual *legion* of Indian men, all dressed in traditional dhotis (long cotton loincloths) and sandals, could be found shuffling back and forth sorting mail, answering phones, jotting down messages on little pink *While You Were Out* pads. Throughout the day when it was slow you might see them in the back in the small area not covered by the mail wall, *praying* on small Oriental rugs. You might have almost thought you were looking at a scene from the movie *Gandhi* if it weren't for the fact that every single one of these men was wearing a Newport cigarette baseball cap. It was almost as if when these guys came to the US and went through immigration, someone handed them these caps and said, *Look, we understand that you're gonna continue wearing your dhotis and sandals, but we'd really appreciate it if you'd also wear this.* They all knew my dad was in the movies, and they were very impressed, but no matter how hard they tried, they could never get his messages right. Last time I visited him was particularly memorable. We had just gotten back from a matinee of Woody Allen's *Sleeper*, which we were still laughing about, when we walked up to the counter.

"Good afternoon, Mr. Grodin," the head man behind the counter said enthusiastically from beneath his Newport cap.

"Any messages for me?" my dad said as he glanced over at me, scrutinizing my consumption of the Hershey's with Almonds candy bar he'd failed to talk me out of getting at the candy counter.

"Yes, I have a very important message for you, sir," the man said, retrieving the small piece of pink paper from my dad's box and handing it to him.

"Thanks, Abib," my dad said, looking at the little piece of paper.

"*Ha*bib," I whispered. "That's *Habib*."

My dad's eyes darted up, holding my gaze till a smile slowly crept across both our faces.

Glancing back down at what looked like hieroglyphics on the little pink paper, he said, "I'm sorry, *Habib*, I can't make out what this says."

"I am *Abib*; my *brother* is Habib," the man shouted, taking the message from my father, who looked over at me just as I was popping the last bite of my Hershey's bar into my mouth.

"Habib!" Abib yelled, shuffling to the edge of the mail wall as my father and I stared at each other, determined to keep straight faces. Suddenly, from behind the mail wall emerged a veil of steam followed by a large skillet held by a very short fat man who looked to be about as tall as he was wide. The man—*Habib*, I assumed—set his skillet down on the counter as he grabbed the note from *Abib*, laying it down on the counter beside his skillet. The four of us leaned in, studying the note as the steam from the skillet wafted around us. After a moment, *Habib* shouted furiously, "*I* did not write this! This is the handwriting of *Zabib*!" He then grabbed his skillet, shot Abib a dirty look, and shuffled back behind the mail wall.

Habib was so angry I wondered if the same person who had given him his Newport cap had also told him, *In this country indecipherable handwriting automatically gets prison time.*

My dad and I, now both completely immersed in the comedy of the situation, stared at each other, tiny beads of sweat covering both our faces.

"Zabib!" Abib yelled, hanging his head to the side and shaking it apologetically toward my dad as he handed him a box of tissues from beneath the counter.

"Thank you," my dad and I said as we each took a tissue from the box, patting our faces down.

A moment later, two Indian men in dhotis, sandals, and Newport caps emerged from behind the mail wall, each one carrying a small steaming skillet with potatoes and onions. The three men huddled around the note as my dad and I stepped back from the curry sauna.

"Hairy Fissures. That's who called. Hairy Fissures," Zabib said sternly.

My dad and I stared at each other, both biting our bottom lips to keep from laughing. "Hairy Fissures... Hairy Fissures," Zabib said exasperatedly.

"Do you remember *what* they said?" my dad asked using every muscle in his face to keep from laughing.

"We would love you to come to East Hampton for the weekend," he screamed, spitting as my dad stared at him.

I closed my eyes, begging God to please keep incarcerated the uprising of laughter threatening to escape my mouth as I realized what the note said.

"Carrie Fisher?" I said, staring straight ahead.

"What I said, yes, Hairy Fissures," Zabib shouted, shooting Abib a dirty look before he and the other man, along with their skillets, disappeared behind the mail wall as my dad and I stared at each other, trying not to laugh till we rounded the corner.

—

"Cornish hen for Rapunzel," Enrico said, setting my plate on the table with one hand as he poured the rest of the soda into my glass with the other.

"Thank you," I said, inhaling the sumptuous aroma coming off my hen. "Wow, this is incredible." I closed my eyes, chewing away.

You know what I could make that for? a voice in my head intruded.

What the fuck was that? I asked myself in midchew.

What do they get for a Cornish hen? the voice persisted.

Omigod, can you please wait till I get home? I begged my mother's voice in my head. I started to laugh as I suddenly had this image of my mother leaping off a rock in Central Park onto an unsuspecting hen.

Mom, seriously, I'm trying to enjoy myself.

Just tell me what they get for the hen, she demanded.

No, I'm with Dad now. I'll talk to you when I get home, I said adamantly as my dad slid back into his seat.

"How ya doin'?" he asked, looking over at Enrico."I'll take that soda whenever you get a chance."

"Of course, Mr. Grodin!" Enrico said, heading toward the bar.

"I have some *good news*," my dad said, grabbing a roll from the bread basket.

"*What?*" I said excitedly.

"I'm gonna rent a house in LA for the summer. Paul and Artie, Carrie, Penny, and Rob, they're all gonna be out there," he said, buttering his roll. ("Artie" was Art Garfunkel, "Carrie" was Carrie Fisher a.k.a. Hairy Fissures, and "Penny and Rob" were Penny Marshall and Rob Reiner.)

"That's great," I said, putting my fork down.

"What's *wrong*?" he said, leaning in toward me.

"Nothing," I lied, wondering if he'd be back by the time the next Woody Allen movie came out. "Did you see Woody Allen?" he said, lowering his head to my level.

"Uh-huh," I said staring at the table.

"Honey, what's wrong?" he said softly.

"Nothing, I'll just miss you, that's all," I said quietly.

"You're right around the corner," he said.

"Los Angeles to New York? Not really," I said skeptically.

"No, your room in the house in LA. It's right around the corner from mine."

Staring at him as a smile hijacked my face, I screamed, "*Get out!*"

"*You* get out," he said, motioning for me to lower my voice.

"Omigod, does Mommy know?" I asked anxiously.

"Mmm-hmmm," he said, nodding, as Enrico brought over his soda, veal chop, and fries.

"*Bon appétit*," Enrico said, lighting the candle on our table, as I sat there buzzing along with the rest of the bees.

6

Jeff Bridges threw his gorgeous head back, unleashing a sublimely throaty laugh. "Ahhh, Chuck, you gotta write this stuff down," he said, wiping tears from his eyes.

Nodding in agreement way too enthusiastically, I seized upon the distraction to grab a fistful of peanut M&M's. I'd been in a very tense standoff with them for the last three hours. My dad shot me an almost imperceptibly disapproving look. I shot him back the exact same look. We held each other's stare until we both started to giggle. My dad reached into his right shirtsleeve pocket and took out his tiny notepad and black Sharpie. Pretending to cover a yawn, I surreptitiously emptied the fistful of M&M's into my mouth.

"It's all right here, baby." My dad smiled as he scribbled something down on his pad. "I can probably use that on *The Tonight Show*," he said, biting his lower lip, which he always did whenever he was especially pleased with something he'd thought of.

My dad was shooting a remake of *King Kong* with Jeff Bridges and Jessica Lange, and I was beyond ecstatic that I was getting to spend the entire summer with him.

Jeff Bridges, Jeff Bridges, bridging Jeff Bridges danced through my mind as my tongue searched my mouth for the last vestiges of chocolate. I'd never seen eyes as blue as Jeff Bridges's. I mean yes, in nature—a sky or an ocean—but not in someone's head, not *that* blue. Jeff was laughing again at something my dad had just said, and it felt intimate to hear him laugh because, when you thought about it, that laugh came from deep inside Jeff Bridges's body, from right around Jeff Bridges's.... Before I could enjoy the rest of my thought, I was startled out of my daydream by Mister Blue Eyes himself brushing my shoulder as he leaned forward, trying to get a better look out my dad's trailer window.

"Sorry," he said, smiling that smile that caused tingling in an area south of my belly button.

"Oh, that's okay," I said, so excited I instantly gave myself a headache.

"Shit, we're really losing light," my dad said, pulling the little curtain back from his window.

King Kong was played by a guy in an ape suit as well as a mechanical ape. About four hours ago, in midwave, the mechanical ape just stopped moving. The movie was already way over budget, and every minute they couldn't get the ape to move was costing the studio tens of thousands of dollars. I hoped they never got the ape to move so the three of us could just stay holed up in my dad's trailer for the rest of our lives.

Jeff and my dad defeatedly collapsed back into their chairs and Jeff fixed me in his gaze. "So, your dad tells me you just graduated from junior high school." He smiled. Damn. I crossed my legs, trying to subdue the tingling, and nodded my head up and down, blushing so hard I hoped I didn't look like I was having a stroke.

"And she won both the math and science awards," my dad said proudly.

"I'm impressed," Jeff said, running his gorgeous, enormous man hands through his long dirty-blond hair.

"Thank you." I beamed. The tingling crescendoed to the point that I wondered if my dad and Jeff could tell.

My dad leaned over and, squeezing my arm, teased, "Sweetheart, maybe you should take a look at the ape. Seriously, honey, get out there and show us why you won those awards."

Jeff started laughing and joined in. "Yeah, you gotta honor the Grodin name; c'mon, girl, let's put those awards to use!"

We were all laughing pretty hard when suddenly, from behind me, I heard this breathy voice say, "What's so funny?"

It was Jessica Lange. She pulled herself up the two steps into the trailer and, arching her back like a cat, leaned in, placing a hand on either side of the chair between my dad and Jeff. I instantly became hyperaware that my thighs were sweaty and touching and that there was a small flap of stomach flab trying to escape my too-tight waistband.

To say Jessica Lange was beautiful was like saying the most spectacular sunset you'd ever seen was nice. No matter how many times I was lucky enough to lay my eyes on her, I could never really get used to just how beautiful she was. She was an international movie star, and I, I... well, I had just won the math and science awards at I.S. 44. I mean, how was I supposed to compete with *that*?!

"Anything?" asked Jeff. I could have sworn he was blushing.

"They got the middle finger working on his left hand," she answered.

"I bet that's the finger he'd like to give all of us at this point," my dad said.

Everybody laughed except me. I was way too captivated by how rhythmically Jessica Lange's braless, perfectly sculpted, voluptuous breasts were moving up and down. I couldn't get over how, even though they were so full, their weight did not appear to discourage their optimism in the least.

My thighs felt like they were getting sweatier and my culotte waistband was digging into my stomach. I reached for a handful of peanut M&M's, sat back, waited for my dad's "look." But no look came. Hoping for a reaction, I scooped up another handful of M&M's. I waited. Nothing. Nada. Zip. My dad and Jeff were completely and utterly entranced by the sunset who had entered the trailer.

I grabbed another handful of M&M's and pondered the miracle that was Jessica Lange's breasts. About a month before my mom put me on the plane to spend the summer with my dad, I went to bed one night, completely flat-chested, and awoke the next morning to discover that I had breasts! And not like newly arrived, just-got-here, perky breasts. I'm talking very large, fully formed, veiny, saggy, Jewish-grandmother breasts. These breasts had totally bypassed that whole hopeful, nascent, upswooping stage. Breasts that looked like they'd attended more than their fair share of starchy Shabbat dinners and late-night Shiva calls!

It was devastating. I would spend hours in my room, with my arms stretched as high as they could go over my head in what always proved to be a heartbreakingly futile attempt to lift them up, to make them look like they didn't live on the chest of an elderly member of the UJA named Mildred. I would study them as if I had just landed on the moon and was on a crucial fact-finding mission for NASA. When I couldn't stand it for one more second, I would scream for my mother to come in my room. "Mommy, look at these! They're horrible! Big and saggy and veiny. Ewwwwww, I want them off! I'm serious, Mom, offff!" When I'd burst into tears, my poor mom would have no idea what to do with me. No one did. After weeks of this, I'd completely worn her down, and got her to take me to a plastic surgeon's office to discuss getting them "offff." The creepy, morbidly obese doctor looked like *he* could have used a breast reduction. I sat with an enormous binder of "before" and "after" pictures of breasts on my lap. All the "after" breasts had bright-red Frankensteiny scars. We left, and my mom tried to cheer me up with pizza, a hot-fudge sundae, and a trip to see *The Exorcist*. She knew her daughter. Nothing short of a binge and demonic possession could take my mind off my predicament.

I'm not sure who told my grandma Lena, but two weeks later when I arrived in LA to spend the summer with my dad, Grandma and her roommate, Doris, came to pick me up at the airport. Riding the brake, going twenty miles an hour in the fast lane with her left turn signal blinking, my grandmother Lena exploded: "There's nothing wrong with those breasts!"

"Those are perfectly fine breasts," Doris, who had the shrillest voice I'd ever heard, chimed in.

Before I could get a word in, my grandmother shouted, "I know women in our development who would *kill* for those breasts!"

"Rhoda and Debbie Shankman!" Doris cried out in such a piercing voice, I was shocked the car windows didn't shatter.

"Then let them kill! I want them offfff!" I erupted. I had this image of all these flat-chested Jewish women from my grandmother's development chasing me down as I ran toward the tit doc's laboratory, where, by the way, I was sure he kept all these jars of hacked-off breasts.

I was thankful for the knock at the trailer door, rescuing me from my ghoulish fantasy. It was Bobby, the head crew guy.

"Hey, Bobby," everyone said.

Shaking Jeff's hand, Bobby said, "Dino wants to try and shoot the kiss before we run out of light."

I suddenly felt nauseous.

Grinning at Jeff, Jessica leaned toward him, placing both her hands on his shoulders. "You up to it?" she asked flirtatiously.

"Oh, I'm up to it," he flirted back.

Everyone laughed, except me.

"Shall we?" Jessica purred.

Jeff rose out of his chair and placed his hand on the small of her back.

I decided, right then and there, I was done eating for the rest of the summer. I watched Jessica's heart-shaped ass sail down the trailer steps and thought I might actually be done eating for the rest of my life.

As they disappeared into the dusky night, Bobby called back over his shoulder, "Mr. Grodin, you're done for the day."

"Great. Thanks, Bobby," my dad said, handing me the reversible tan cape my mom had made me. "You wanna stop at Moonshadows on the way home and get some dinner?" he asked sweetly, rubbing my back.

I shook my head no, having already embarked on my new way of life. As I descended the steps of the trailer, I felt like I might really throw up. I didn't know if it was the bowl of

M&M's I'd polished off, or Jeff Bridges, or the thought of flying home in six days, but I did know seeing Jeff giving Jessica a neck rub in the distance was not helping one bit.

—

A week later, my dad and I were cruising down the Pacific Coast Highway in his black Cadillac, with the top down, on our way to the airport. We were going to stop at Moonshadows for our last meal together before I had to fly home. My dad was softly singing along with Al Green's "I'm So Tired of Being Alone" on the radio. I placed my right arm out the window, stretching my fingers as far apart as I could, the warm wind blowing through them. My dad glanced over at me, smiling and singing, "So tired of being alone...I'm so tired of being alone..." I laid my head down on my arm, closed my eyes, and began softly humming along with the radio.

"How you doin' over there?" my dad asked. Not lifting my head, I turned my face toward him and opened one eye.

"Okay," I lied.

"Is it about going home?"

With my head still resting on my arm, I shook my head no.

"I should be back in time for your birthday," he reminded me.

"I know," I said, trying to muster a smile.

"We can do anything you want. Anything. Mommy said Al Green is at the Beacon that night." Realizing he wasn't going to get a response, he tried upping the ante. "...maybe the three of us'll go." I did my best to smile. We drove on for another minute, humming in unison to the radio. Then, very delicately, my dad said, "You wanna talk about it?"

Closing my eyes, I shook my head no. I could feel my dad staring at me. After a moment, I turned my head to look at him.

With a big grin on his face, he let loose the word "Moouuth."

"Mouth" was my dad's very affectionate nickname for me. I started talking early, and once I started, I pretty much never stopped. No matter how shitty my mood, my dad calling me "Mouth" was always a surefire way to get me to laugh. But not today. Reaching over and rubbing my arm, he asked, "What have you eaten today?"

"Stop," I replied, utterly annoyed.

"No, I'm just wondering what you've eaten so far today. I think you're in such a shitty mood because you're hungry."

"Omigod!"

After a moment, my dad unleashed another "Mooooouuth."

"It's not about that," I cried.

"Just tell me what you've eaten so far tod—"

"You *don't* get it!" I turned away, my eyes beginning to well up.

"Well, then, help me get it, honey," my dad said, his voice full of compassion.

I continued staring out my window, fighting back tears.

My dad cleared his throat. "I'm just saying you can't go all day without taking something besides Tab or Fresc—"

"I'm *not* hungry!" I shouted, "I'm in love with Jeff Bridges!"

My excruciating admission hung nakedly in the Malibu air for what felt like an eternity before my dad continued, "I just think that if you'd had a bagel or some of grandma's tuna..."

"Omigod, I just told you I'm in love with Jeff Bridges and you wanna talk about *tuna*?!"

We drove on in silence for a horrible minute. Finally, in an almost inaudible, slow, measured voice (as if he were trying to talk a jumper off a ledge), he said, "I hear you. I do." Striving to make his voice even calmer, "... all I'm saying is that if you go all day with no food, everything is going to feel heightened."

"Nothing's heightened, I'm in love with Jeff Bridges," I snapped.

"Honey, Jeff Bridges is a grown man, with a wife and a family," my dad said gently.

"I feel what I feel." My voice cracked, catching as I tried not to cry. "Just please stop talking, you're making everything worse." I felt completely inconsolable.

We pulled into the Moonshadows parking lot and my dad handed the valet his car key. "Thanks, Jimmy."

"Anytime, Mr. Grodin." Jimmy smiled.

As we headed into the restaurant, my dad put his arm around me, pulling me close to him. We walked a couple steps in silence and then, as we stepped inside the restaurant, I mumbled, "Four Frescas... three bites of grandma's tuna."

He kissed the top of my head, squeezing me so tight it hurt in the best way.

7

"Oh, shit. Look who's back!" I heard Roy yell.

"Hey," I shouted, handing the cabdriver a tip as I rolled my big pink suitcase to the bottom of the museum steps. Just then, all the lights in the lampposts lining the block came on. I felt like they were announcing my return. As I ran up the museum steps, I saw Evie and Manny slow dancing to Al Green's "Love and Happiness" as it poured out of Manny's boom box. Cruz was sitting on a ledge, between Shana and Kathy. Roy and Ricky were sitting on a ledge, splitting a pizza. "Oh, *Dios mío*, you so tan; and look how long your hair got. *Bonita!*" Evie screamed as I threw my arms around her.

It was obvious they were all high. "Well, somebody grew titties over the summer." Roy snickered, lowering his blue shades, as he snuck up behind me.

"You don't grow titties! They're not like a crop, you fucking burnout!" Shana blasted, kissing me on the cheek while I wondered if it was possible to die standing up.

"I'm just sayin' she looks good," Roy said.

"She does!" said Ricky, hugging me so hard he lifted me off the ground.

Cruz walked over, flipping open a silver cigarette case. He hopped up on the wall next to me, revealing a dozen different-colored, meticulously rolled joints. They were all just lying there, each hopeful contestant praying they'd be chosen.

"Put it in my mouth," Cruz said. Shana smiled, picked up a fat red joint, and seductively inserted it between Cruz's lips. Cruz took out his lighter, which had a naked girl on the side of it. As he lit the joint, bright-yellow flames shot out of her tits. Inhaling long and deep, he ballooned his cheeks out, like Dizzy Gillespie playing the trumpet. As the smoke belly danced out of his mouth, he held the joint toward me.

"That's okay," I said, passing it to Shana.

"You sure?" Shana said. "This is really good shit."

"Yeah, I should go upstairs; I haven't even seen my mom yet."

"Hang out a little," Evie said as she took the joint from Shana.

I was thinking how much these people really felt like my family. Even with Roy's stupid tit comment. As I stared at my building across the street, I could feel the back of my neck tighten. Then I thought about my dad. I wasn't really sure when I'd see him again. Everything was changing. In a week, I'd be starting high school, and let's face it, Jeff Bridges was a married man. And my breasts, well, they would never, ever look like Jessica Lange's. "Yeah, okay, maybe just a little," I said, getting up to slow dance with Evie.

I was *barely* in the door when Max, my mother's enormous boxer, jumped up and pinned me against the hall closet.

"Get down!" I screamed as Molly and Slippery Eel, two of her other dogs, jumped onto me, mistaking my cry for an invitation.

"Fuck! Mom!" I screamed even louder, struggling to get Max off me, which was virtually impossible since he was so excited and significantly taller than me when he stood on his hind legs with his bright-red pencil dick sticking out. "Max! Molly! Slippery Eel! Get down!"

"Mooooooom!" I screamed again as I wrestled Max down and Angel, my mother's one-eared kitten who never even tried to live up to her name, got so excited she peed on my right shoe. "Angel!" I screamed as I broke free and ran into the living room.

Home had been like this my whole life. But I was still not used to it, and, to be honest, I felt my sanity depended on making sure I never got used to it. Over the years, my brain had become a "What's Wrong with This Picture?" game—something I had learned on a class trip to the museum. We went into this science room where they had all these turtles, frogs, and lizards in glass aquariums. As we filed into the room, we were each given a big red crayon (not to be confused with Max's red pencil dick) and an educational game sheet, at the top of which WHAT'S WRONG WITH THIS PICTURE? was printed in bold letters. The sheet had pictures on it of all the aquariums, and our assignment was to use our big red crayon to circle what was wrong with each picture. For example, there'd be a picture of an aquarium with a frog in some water, near some rocks, next to some plants, with some more rocks in the background. But if you looked really closely, you'd see that on one of those rocks was a sombrero or a boot or a teacup—something that did not belong. I felt like this was my assignment every single day of my life and that my mind had become that big red crayon.

Let's start with the small plaid suitcase lying on the floor of our living room that had just stopped ringing. Why, you may be wondering, was a suitcase ringing? I'll tell you, while I circle it with my big red crayon. Remember Angel? Well, she was a very busy girl, because in addition to peeing pretty much everywhere, she'd also been chewing the telephone cord for months. Finally, one night after I tried to call my dad at a scheduled time and got no dial tone, I had a complete meltdown. My mother assured me she would take care of it, which I foolishly assumed meant she'd find this little chewing/urinating maniac another home. But no. Instead, my mother purchased a small piece of luggage to house the phone.

Next to our ringing luggage was a chair that had once been upholstered in beautiful orange-and-red sun-colored material but was now covered in so much dog and cat hair, it looked like it had an Angora slipcover. On the right side of the room was a wooden table with two wooden chairs, where we were supposed to eat, but the cats spent so much time sitting there, heads held high like supermodels waiting for their close-ups, that large fur balls rolled by during dinner, like tumbleweeds in an episode of *The Wild Wild West*. I hardly ever ate there, opting to hold my plate on my lap in front of the TV. Next to the chair, on a stool, was our record player. *Bridge Over Troubled Water*, our favorite album, was playing.

I poked my head in the bedroom, staring at the unmade bed that I slept in with my mother, that my camp counselor slept in with my mother, and that the dogs slept in with my mother.

"We're in the tub," my mother called out excitedly. The big red crayon in my head went berserk, wondering if "we" could have meant her and my camp counselor. *No*, I thought to myself. *Even she's not* that *nuts*. "Are you coming in?" she yelled.

"Coming," I shouted, walking back through the living room to the kitchen to get a drink of water. Leaning on the doorway to the kitchen as I stepped on the back of my peed-on shoe with my non-peed-on shoe, taking it off, I flipped the light switch. No light. I flipped it quickly up and down another couple times. "Mom, what happened to the light in the kitchen?" I yelled as I stepped back with my shoeless foot and it came down right in a little puddle of pee. I closed my eyes, wishing I were back at my dad's house.

"The bulb blew," she shouted back, which me and my big red crayon knew meant we would now have a dark kitchen. Right before I left for LA I'd noticed that all our clocks seemed to be missing. When I asked my mom what happened to them, she nonchalantly pulled open a drawer in our bedroom bureau. All the clocks were there, faceup, as if they'd been laid to rest in some sort of clock burial ground. When I looked up at her for an explanation, she said, "Too much expectation."

"Seriously?" I said, coming into the bathroom and giving her a kiss.

"What?" my mother said, beaming at me, totally impervious to the "What's Wrong with This Picture?" nature of the situation. She was sitting in a half-full tub alongside Sadie, her small, wiry black-and-white dog—my nemesis and, by far, my mother's most dramatic rescue. Last winter, my mom had rescued Sadie in Central Park from a pack of wild male dogs who, according to my mother, were about to make Sadie the victim of a doggy gang bang.

"Why is Sadie in the tub with you?" I asked, putting the lid down on the toilet so I could sit down and take off my soggy pee sock.

"She rolled around in a dead pigeon in the park," my mother said. "Didn't ya, girl?" She grabbed Sadie's face, kissing her hard on the mouth. A large piece of grout fell from between the wall and the tub into the water. "She's such a pretty girl. You wanna come in with us?" my mom asked, stroking the top of Sadie's head as Sadie lifted her upper lip, snarling loudly while eyeing me menacingly.

"No. That's okay." My mother looked so vulnerable, sitting there naked with Sadie as the grout floated by.

"Take off your cape! I want to hear everything. Did you fall in love with Jeff Bridges? Was Jessica Lange beautiful?" she asked excitedly.

"Yes. Yes," I said, staring at the floating grout.

"So, I bet Daddy took you out to eat all the time," she asked excitedly.

"Not all the time," I answered, not wanting her to feel bad.

"When Daddy took you to all those fancy restaurants, what was the best thing you had?"

"Fettuccine Alfredo," I said.

"Omigod, he probably paid an arm and a leg for that. You know what I could make that for?" she said as Sadie began repeatedly licking my mother's cheek.

"I don't want to know. I just want to enjoy the time I had," I said angrily, noticing goose bumps all over her arms. She'd probably been in that tub forever, and the water wasn't even warm anymore.

"Start from the beginning," she said, like a kid who hadn't gotten to go to the circus.

It was strange, but for the first time in my life I didn't want to start from the beginning. As I watched her capture the grout and lay it on the side of the tub, I wished she had her own circus.

Just as I began to gear up for the story, Molly chased Angel into the bathroom, which sent Sadie flying out of the tub and onto my feet.

"My cape!" I screamed, unintentionally cueing Max, Slippery Eel, and my mother's other two cats, Mona and Roar, to come tearing into the bathroom. Our little bathroom was way too small for this. Angel leapt into my lap as Sadie began snarling at Molly, who, accepting the challenge, got right in Sadie's face and snarled back, even louder. As Sadie and Molly circled each other preparing to rumble they backed Max right into me. Max did not appear to be reading the situation at all. He was wagging his tail so enthusiastically he kept smacking Angel in the face. And his bright-red pencil dick was on full display.

I sat there clutching Angel against my wet cape, doing my best to shield her from Max's relentless tail. I could feel this canine powder keg was about to blow!

Sadie latched on to Molly's face with her teeth. My mother lunged forward, grabbing Sadie around her neck, screaming, "Sadie, let go. Let go! Marion, grab Molly!"

I lunged forward, sending Angel flying into the sink. I struggled to get ahold of Molly's neck.

"Grrrrrrrrrrr... Grrrrrrrrrrr." Sadie and Molly growled furiously at each other as my mother and I tried to tear them apart.

"Jesus!" I shouted as Sadie tightened her grip on Molly's face. "Mom, she's bleeding!" I cried, as my mother and I realized, to our horror, that Sadie was clamping down on Molly's eye. "Omigod, I can't do this!" I yelled angrily, sweating profusely. When had I signed on to be a fucking animal paramedic?

"Pull!" my mom screamed, water dripping from her naked body as she hit Sadie around her face, desperate to make her let go. "Sadie, get off of her!" she yelled. Pulling as hard as she could, she finally managed to yank Sadie off of Molly. "Get her into the bedroom!" she screamed to me.

Adrenaline was shooting through my veins, and I squeezed Molly tightly around her neck and backed us into the bedroom. I kicked the door closed behind us. I pulled Molly over to the bed, sat down, turned her around, and got a better look at her wounded face. "Omigod, you poor thing," I whispered. Molly, completely traumatized, stared up at me with her one good eye. "Mom, I think Sadie ate her eye!" I screamed toward the shut door. I started to cry.

"Bad Sadie. Bad," I heard my mother yelling on the other side of the door. That was no consolation whatsoever to either me or One-Eye. As my mother continued to reprimand Sadie, I stared down at poor Molly, whose pitiful expression seemed to say, *What the fuck did I do to deserve this?*

"You and me both, my friend. You and me both," I said to her. I grabbed a tissue and began wiping the blood from her face. She still had her eye, but she had a horrible bite right next to it. "She's got her eye," I yelled through the door.

"Good," my mom yelled back.

I stared at the closed door separating me and my mother. There weren't enough red crayons.

A minute later, I heard the suitcase ringing in the living room. Grateful for contact from the outside world, I leapt up and raced into the other room. Quickly unzipping the suitcase, I grabbed the phone. "Hello?" I said, noticing blood on the sleeve of my cape.

"I just wanted to make sure you got home okay," my dad said.

"I did," I said, feeling like he was a million miles away.

"Everything okay?" he asked, hearing my distance.

"Uh-huh; I'm just tired," I said, sadly aware that I could not, in fact, make contact with the outside world.

"Okay. I love you."

"Me too," I said, but he'd already hung up. As I bent over, hung up the phone, and zipped up the suitcase, my mom called out from the bathroom: "Honey, why don't you get us some cheeseless cheesecake and come back in. I think this is a really good batch; I just made it!"

"Okay!" I yelled. The lush music at the top of "Bridge Over Troubled Water" accompanied me into the kitchen. For a moment, I stood there in the dark feeling how the bright light of my LA summer with Dad had gone out just as definitively as the light in our kitchen. I opened the refrigerator door and stared at all my mom's macrobiotic dishes—meatless meat loaf, cheeseless cheesecake, creamless cream cheese, all of them missing the very ingredient that made them satisfying, comforting. These dishes felt like a metaphor for my life with her. "When you're weary, feeling small...," Art Garfunkel sang. His voice was staggeringly beautiful. It made me want to cry.

"Bring in a little piece for Sadie. I want to see if she'll eat it," my mother yelled.

Two hours later, after I animatedly recounted the highest and lowest points of my summer with particular attention to Jeff Bridges's face and Jessica Lange's breasts, and my mom and

I polished off our cheeeseless cheesecake (which was actually pretty tasty), my mom went to bed. She'd asked me repeatedly to come to bed with her, but I'd said I was still on California time. I glanced down at the tub. It hadn't totally drained. There was still some pale red bathwater from my mom washing the blood off Sadie and Molly after the smackdown. I dropped my head to the side, looking at my mom sleeping, surrounded by all her animals. Letting out a deep sigh, I reached into my back jean pocket and pulled out the joint Cruz had given me. As I stared at myself in the medicine chest mirror, I put the joint in my mouth, lit it, and inhaled deeply. As I felt the drug begin to take effect, I thought, *I'm going to smoke this till everything looks different.*

8

"I mean, *first* he gives Mia Farrow back to those fucking devils. Then he throws that girl out the window in *Catch-22*. Then, then, he dumps his Jewish wife on their honeymoon for some shiksa goddess—on their fucking honeymoon!" Joel wailed, emphatically gesturing with the joint in his hand.

"Joel, these are movies," I said angrily. I locked eyes with Erin as Joel passed her the joint.

"Let's go," Erin whispered to me and stifled a laugh before she took a quick hit on the joint, turned it around, stuck the lit end in her mouth, and placed her lips on mine.

"...not documentaries," I continued, mumbling, glaring at Joel while inhaling the stream of smoke Erin was blowing into my mouth.

"Look at Joel's teeth," Erin whispered, as she reached over me, passing the joint.

"Uh-huh," I said, overly seriously, as Erin bit her lower lip, trying not to laugh as we trotted up the stairs to the street.

"What? You guys, what?" Joel yelled after us.

"It's not because I'm stoned? They're huge, right?" Erin asked, adjusting her eyes to the light.

"I'm not saying it was recent, but at some point, somebody in his family fucked a horse," I said, completely straight-faced, as Erin almost fell down laughing.

"Sit," I said and pulled her down next to me on the steps of the tenement where we'd just gotten high. For a moment we just sat there, staring at all the people milling about in front of Stuyvesant High School.

"Fuckin' asshole," I said grabbing my pack of Marlboro Lights and my lighter out of the pocket of my jean jacket.

"Mar, let it go. Who gives a shit what he thinks? The guy's mother fucked Mister Ed," Megan said. Our laughter caused us both to fall forward over our knees.

What was so great about Megan Maxwell, along with everything else that was so great about Megan, was she really didn't give a shit what anyone thought or said or did. For a sixteen-year-old, that's amazing. And she was never stuck-up; Megan was just Megan. The day I met her was my first day of high school. Mr. Larson, this very old guy who had this monotonous way of speaking, I swear was designed to induce sleep. He stood at the front of the classroom, droning on about how lucky we all were to have gotten into Stuyvesant and how much harder it would be than junior high, when a tall, stunning girl with short, punky blonde hair flung open the door, apologized for being late, and hurried into the only empty seat, which was right next to me.

When Larson asked for her name, she said, "Megan," in a

deep, throaty voice I was not expecting to come out of a sixteen-year-old's mouth. My head shot around, making sure Brenda Vaccaro hadn't snuck into her seat. I was immediately riveted. The rest of the period, I tried to steal glances at her without her catching me. I couldn't get over how pretty she was, but even more than that, how when she talked she didn't use her beauty or relate through it. She was wearing painter pants (huge in the seventies), a fitted T-shirt (no bra to cover the most amazingly perfect tits!), and black high-top Converse sneakers. She wore a version of this every day. She lived in Brooklyn, and she never said, but I was pretty certain from how she dressed and acted that she was probably from a tough, working-class family. She was vegetarian—had been since she was ten. I thought perhaps because vegetables cost less than meat. And just when I thought she couldn't get any cooler, it turned out she loved to get high just as much as I did. If it sounds like I had a crush on this beautiful tomboy, I did. But not in the I-want-to-stick-my-tongue-down-your-throat way. Just in the I-want-to-spend-every-waking-moment-with-you way. I was thrilled that she felt exactly the same. And that's what we'd been doing for the last three years, since that first day in homeroom. We'd hang out all week and then, when that last bell rang on Friday, we'd jump on the 2 train and spend the whole weekend at her house in Park Slope. Sometimes we'd go to my house, but I always tried to get us to go to her house.

The first time I went home with her, we walked from the subway, down beatific, wide, tree-lined streets, with these magnificent brownstones with little stone steps out front and their wrought-iron gates in front of them. Fresh-faced young couples pushed baby strollers, walked their golden retrievers, or sat on stoops lovingly watching cherub-faced children ride bikes back and forth, staring at their moms and dads for approval. What the fuck was my edgy tomboy best friend, who looked like she could be running a gang on the Lower East Side, doing in this L.L.Bean catalog? I kept waiting for Megan to turn a corner and boom, no more brownstones, golden retrievers, pretty young moms: suddenly it's projects, pit bulls, and crack whores....

"We're here," Megan said, smiling as she jogged up the steps of one of the tallest, most impressive brownstones in the neighborhood. She opened the little gate, walking up another couple steps to the opulent wooden front door. "Forgot my key," she called over her shoulder, and leaned on the doorbell.

As I stood there, staring at my little ruffian juxtaposed with this spectacular home, I thought maybe Megan's mother was this family's maid or cook, and Megan and her family lived in the basement or out back in a shed of some kind. But I wasn't even close. And that is why, to this day, in addition to so many other reasons, Megan is the coolest person I have ever met. She came from everything and never even mentioned it.

She had this fabulous, big Irish Catholic family with six kids, ranging in age from her five-year-old sister, Tara, to her nineteen-year-old sister, Bridget. Megan was the third oldest. All her siblings were smart, funny, warm. Her dad, Ed, was a successful doctor in Manhattan. Her mom, Lynn, was a gentle, sage-like homemaker who definitely got dinner on the table in a very big way! I'm talking casseroles, baby! Meat loaf—with meat. Macaroni and cheese—with cheese. Lasagna—with lasagna! And sides, multiple fucking sides: corn, rice, creamed spinach, homemade mashed potatoes. Are you kidding me? Homemade mashed potatoes! All served in matching floral-patterned dishes with big serving spoons, and sometimes even ladles! Ladles! Lynn would call out, "Dinner's on the table," and the entire family, from wherever they were in the four-story brownstone, would come gather round the long mahogany table in their gorgeous dining room. We'd all sit there eating and laughing and talking for hours.

I could not believe how lucky I was. I had basically fallen into an episode of *Leave it to* Fucking *Beaver*!

One night after listening to everyone debate some weighty political issue for the better part of an hour, I made the most amazing discovery about myself. I discovered I knew the exact right moment to jump in with something so funny that everyone, even Ed and Lynn, would explode into hysterical laughter. Omigod, turned out I was The Beav! Up until then I had only been funny one-on-one, with my mom or dad, or one friend. My first taste of what it felt like to kill as a stand-up comedian was sitting in Megan's dining room.

Sunday nights, when I'd come home, having been in Brooklyn all weekend, I always had a pit in my stomach. No matter how big the smile on my mother's face, or how much she teasingly asked me if I'd missed her or questioned why I hadn't called, I knew my separateness was killing her. It didn't matter how much pot I smoked, I knew.

That night on the steps with our friends, Megan said, "We should go to your house this weekend. I miss your mom."

"Really?" I said, looking up at her.

"Yeah, really, why?" she said, pulling me up by my hands.

"Uhhh, I don't know, because the last time you slept over, you walked into the kitchen naked, and Sadie flew through the air, attaching her teeth to your ass."

"Omigod, I forgot about that," she said.

Across the street, my friend Mary was waving me over.

"I can't believe she still speaks to you," Megan said. I said good-bye to Megan and almost got hit by a car, running across the street. Mary was biracial and, freshman year, whenever I talked about her to Megan, I referred to her as Mary Mulatto. They'd never met, and Megan didn't know Mary was biracial until one day when we were all hanging out in front of school, and I turned to Megan and said, "This is my friend Mary I'm always telling you about."

Megan, a look of recognition washing over her face, said, "Mary Mulatto." She'd thought that was the girl's name.

"What's goin' on?" I said, catching my breath as I went over to Mary.

"Well, I have this friend who goes here, and he really wants to meet you," she said, a mischievous glint in her eye.

"O-kay," I said, looking around for this mystery person. Then, as if someone had yelled, *And, action!* this very handsome boy walked up to me.

"Matthew Siegel, this is Marion Grodin."

"Hi," he said, his voice warm and yummy.

"Hi," I said, instantly loving his face.

"Well, I have go meet...my mom," Mary said, winking at me as she walked away.

"Subtle," I said, pretty sure I was blushing.

"Yeah," he said, blushing right along with me.

We stood there talking through multiple school bells and various groups of kids pouring out of the building. As the final bell rang and the bright-blue sky had begun to soften, he said, "Where do you live?"

"I just moved to Eighty-Fifth and Amsterdam," I said, wishing our time wasn't ending.

He smiled at me, then said, "Come on. I'll walk you."

We walked and talked, and walked and talked, and talked

about everything. He was a year younger, and a grade behind me. I couldn't believe we'd been going to the same school for the last three years, and I'd never seen him before, especially since he made it very clear that he'd seen me for years. He told me how he'd gotten into Stuyvesant because he was great at basketball and that he was the only white guy on the team. I thought that was one of the hottest things I'd ever heard. His parents were divorced too, and he lived with his older sister, his mom, and her husband on Ninety-Fourth Street and Fifth Avenue. He was really happy his mom had found someone who really loved her, who really listened to her. "That's great!" I said, thinking how for my mom, that person was me. "Do you like him?" I asked.

"Yeah, he's a good guy. It's just hard. Y'know, 'cause he's not my father," he said, looking at me.

"Sure. Do you see him, your real dad?" I asked, as we crossed Thirty-Fourth Street.

"I never met him," he said, not trying to disguise how painful that was, which I thought was so brave of him. I mean, I knew he was really sexy right away, but I could not get over how much I liked him. Around Fortieth Street, he said, "I know you said you get to see your dad whenever he's here. What does he do?" he asked sweetly.

I hesitated as I stepped off the curb, knowing we could be coming up on a deal breaker. There were three things he could have done that would potentially end our walk and put me on the C train. He could have gone all Joel on me, accusing my father of being an unfaithful, Devil-worshipping maniac. He could have lost his starstruck mind like some people did when I told them who my dad was. Or, worst of all, he could start auditioning. "He's an actor," I said.

"Really?" he said.

"Really," I said, smiling at him.

After we walked a little, he said, "Would I know who he is?" He said it so sweetly, I felt bad I was the only one who knew we were suddenly on a game show. "Charles Grodin?" I said, studying his face intently.

"I love that guy! He's so funny. Wow. That's great you get to see him," he said.

"Thanks," I said as we walked by the entrance to the C train.

By Forty-Second Street, I'd told him all about my dad and how I really only got to see him on weekends, or in the summer if I went to LA. I loved that Matt was interested but not too impressed. Around Fiftieth Street, I'd developed such a bad blister on my left foot, I was pretty much walking on my heel but having such a great time I didn't even really mind. It's weird, but by Sixty-Fifth Street he was holding my hand, and I felt like I couldn't remember life before him.

By the time we got to my old block, I was so comfortable that when he asked me about living there, I even told him the whole story of how before my mom and I moved to Eighty-Fifth Street so I could have my own room, she'd built a wall out of particleboard, dividing our bedroom right down the middle as a last-ditch effort to not have to move. He was very impressed that she'd done that. I said so was I—thrilled, actually. Until that first night when we were both in our rooms. I was lying on my bed eating some pistachio nuts, basking in the privacy of my new room, when suddenly, through the wall came "Whatcha got in there?" My heart stopped as I stared at my side of the particleboard.

"Mom, I'm in my room," I yelled, crestfallen.

"Sounds like pistachio nuts. Is it pistachio nuts? Boy, I could really go for some pistachio nuts." She persisted until she got her nuts, and I *felt* completely nuts! That next week, I wore my father down and convinced him to pay for us to move into a two-bedroom apartment, something I don't think my mother ever forgave either of us for.

"She sounds great," Matt said, laughing, endearing himself to me even more.

"She is," I said, anxiety creeping in as I realized we were almost at Eighty-Fifth Street. "Can I ask you something?" I said, turning to face him. "How come you never talked to me before?" Our bodies were so close, I felt like we were magnetized.

Looking down, laughing nervously, he said, "I thought you were a lesbian."

"Why?" I said, shocked.

"You're always with that girl Megan, with the really short hair, and you always wear corduroy pants. I just assumed you were both lesbians," he said matter-of-factly.

"Yeah, not a lesbian," I said, laughing and wondering when corduroy pants had become a definitive sign of lesbianism.

"Good," he said as he put his arms around me, pulled me close, and kissed me. We walked the remaining eight blocks slowly, neither of us ready for our time to end. When we got to my corner, I held him tightly around his waist, while he wrapped his arms around me, sheltering me from the growing chill in the air. He could sense the anxiety I was feeling about leaving him. We stood on that corner for over an hour, both of us oblivious to the throngs of New Yorkers pouring out of the subway every few minutes.

"My mom's waiting for me," I said finally. I wondered if she'd *ever* stop waiting for me. "I should probably get going."

"Me too."

Neither of us was able to move. In the last hundred blocks we had fallen completely, undeniably, severely in love.

There was just one really big problem: I was already in a committed relationship with an impish macrobiotic woman. I felt it only fair to let my boyfriend know that his girlfriend, although only seventeen, came with a lot of baggage—like a twelve-piece set of Samsonite, which included a plaid ringing rollaway because Angel was still chewing the phone cord. I tried explaining that, in a nutshell, the key word being "nut," my mother had issues. *I* had issues. Together, we were talking a *lot* of issues.

Matt said, "Issues," along with me as he kissed me softly on my forehead. And then he said the nicest thing anybody could have said. "It's okay," he whispered into my ear, enveloping me in the biggest bear hug as he pulled me inside his coat.

"Yeah?" I said, hating that I'd even had to say any of this.

Kissing me gently as he wrapped his coat tightly around me, holding me against his chest, he whispered, "I get it."

No, ya don't, I said to myself as I turned around in his arms, placing my arms on top of his. We stared out at the park. As he rocked me gently from side to side, the heat from his body warming mine, I decided, even though I was scared out of my mind, I was going to stop trying to talk this beautiful boy out of loving me.

9

Over the next couple months it felt like everything was changing quickly. One night, Megan and I were hanging out at her house watching Anita Bryant spew her insidious homophobia. I glanced at Megan and saw she was crying.

"Meg, you're such an empathic person. You feel so much about something that doesn't even affect you," I said admiringly.

"I'm not empathic. I'm a lesbian. I'm in love with Lily," she said intensely.

"The *nurse*?" I was shocked. Lily was a friend of hers who was a few years older than us, and a nurse.

"Yes."

"Wow," I said, suddenly feeling like my best friend was a total stranger. After a few very awkward moments of silence, I asked: "All those nights we slept in the same bed, were you ever attracted to me?"

"No, never."

I felt both relieved and rejected. After that, everything was just different.

Matt and I couldn't get enough of each other, and we fooled around everywhere: at our apartments when no one was home, in empty cars on the subway, in the stairwells at school, in the art closet, repeatedly, before we were both written up. But we both knew we couldn't go on like this forever. It wasn't just that we wanted each other so badly; the degree of blue balls Matt was suffering had gotten so blue, we were both afraid there might be permanent damage.

So between my best friend now spending most of her time with a nurse, and feeling like I could be ruining my boyfriend's chances of ever having children, it was time for me to lose my virginity. A term, by the way, I'd always hated. It made it sound like my virginity would be missing. There were just two really big problems: my tits and my mother.

My tits we've already covered. Even though I now had my own bedroom, my mom was still trying to get me to sleep with her. I'd prayed that when we moved into this big two-bedroom apartment it could be a new beginning, and that my mom would make a nice home for us. A while ago she'd taken a woodworking class at the Y, and she was amazing. Her specialty was beautiful dollhouses. I used to fantasize that we lived in one of them. But at home, nothing had changed. All the furniture in the living room was from the Salvation Army, including a couch with the springs coming out of it and a very disturbing wooden bookcase she'd started to strip then abandoned, which had all these crazy fucking gargoyles hanging off it.

But the room in our new apartment that just destroyed me was her bedroom. It was an enormous room, especially by New York standards. It had lovely hardwood floors, a very high ceiling, and two sets of very large windows on either side of the room. One set faced Amsterdam Avenue; the other set faced Eighty-Fifth Street. She even had her own bathroom. In the middle of the room was her bed. It was just a box spring and a mattress with a fitted sheet, which was always halfway off the mattress and caked in animal hair. On top of that, in a corner of the bed, was a top sheet that was usually all twisted. On top of that was a blanket with holes, and hair that clearly belonged to her animals. The light-blue bureau just to the right when you entered the room was always covered in dust. The rest of the room was occupied by boxes, which, even though we'd been there for almost four years, still hadn't been unpacked. Below the windows facing Amsterdam Avenue was a radiator with tons of stuff on it: unplugged lamps, telephone books, magazines, vases, etc. Nothing covered or dressed the windows. Hanging from the ceiling, directly over her bed, were huge white paint chips, forever threatening to fall, but they never did.

The bathroom was also dusty and dirty, and there was never a towel or anything in there. There were no lamps, just the ones on the radiator that weren't plugged in. The overhead light fixture didn't work, and she never spoke to the super about it. You could never really see anything if you went in there at night, which I tried to make sure was the only time I did. If, for any reason, I ever had to go in there during the day, to look for something or grab the roll of toilet paper in her bathroom, no matter how many times I'd seen it before, it never ceased to leave me standing there, shell-shocked, wondering why.

My bedroom was right across the hall from hers, and she'd

always ask me to sleep with my door open so she could talk to me at night when we were each in our beds. But no matter where the conversation started, it always ended in the exact same place: her, making her case for why I should come across the hall and climb into bed with her and the Animal Kingdom. Brimming with anxiety, I made my case for why I really didn't want to do that. I felt completely responsible for her feelings. I was never sure which was worse—my pain, if I went across the hall, or her pain and my guilt, if I didn't. The truth is, over the years, we'd grown so intertwined, like the thick, gnarly roots of a tree, I couldn't have told you where she ended and I began. On the nights when she'd wear me down and get me to cross the hall and climb into bed with her and all her animals, I'd just pray that I fell asleep quickly as I fought the animals for at least a piece of blanket to cover myself. Once I was sure she was asleep, I'd usually tiptoe back to my own room. But on those rare occasions when I wouldn't wake up until the next morning, the sight of that fucking room, flooded by morning light, was enough to send me racing back across the hall to get as fucked up as possible before I had to leave for school.

The following Saturday night when Matt's parents went upstate to visit some friends, we'd decided it was time.

"Are you sure no one's gonna be home till late?" I asked anxiously, standing in the middle of Matt's room.

"Yes, sure." He draped his arms around me, kissing me, as he squeezed me tight. "You're shivering."

"Is the window open?" I asked, glancing over at his bed next to the window. He led me by the hand to his bed, sat down, and pulled me onto his lap as he leaned back, closing the window with his free hand. My heart was beating so fast I wondered if he could hear it.

He kissed me deeply. I loved the way he tasted—clean and a little salty, like the ocean. "Omigod, your teeth are chattering."

"I can't stop shivering," I said, throwing my arms around his neck, hoping he could be the buoy in my storm.

"It's okay. Everything's okay," he said as he rubbed my back in a soothing circular motion. We stared at each other as my various forms of shaking escalated.

"I'm a wreck," I said, laughing, as he began gently rocking me back and forth.

"Everybody's nervous their first time," he said in a way that didn't feel at all condescending.

"Were you?" I said.

After a moment, he said, "Not really."

We laughed together, his laughter dying down as mine started picking up steam, seeming to almost take on a life of its own.

"Are you okay?" he said, staring as I convulsed in laughter.

"I ca...n't...stop...," I said, completely overtaken. "I... th...ink...I'm...ju...st...really, really ner...vous."

"Maybe try to drink some water," he said, handing me the open bottle of water next to his bed.

"I'm...o...kay." I struggled to catch my breath as I brought the bottle to my lips. "Ahhh, okay, okay." I breathed slowly, as he stared at me, laughing in a way that put me at ease. "Whew...," I said and leaned back onto him.

Our eyes locked as a seriousness came over us both.

First he kissed me reassuringly, then he reached his left hand over his back, pulling his blue T-shirt over his head. He tossed it on the chair in the corner, next to his basketball. Smiling at him, I raised both my arms into the air as he pulled my black T-shirt over my head, tossing it onto the chair. As I gently let my arms fall around his neck, he reached around, unlatching my bra. I was way too overwhelmed to actually keep my eyes open, but I could feel him looking at my breasts. After a few seconds, my mind started racing. Why isn't he saying anything? Omigod, what if he agrees with me? *You're right, they're hideous. Jesus! Get the surgery. Actually, bring me my mother's meat cleaver! Let's do it right now!*

"They're beautiful" is what he actually said.

"Yeah?" I opened my eyes, glancing over at my bra, which had fallen onto his basketball and was hanging across it, making it look like it was smiling. "Yeah," he said, tenderly kissing each one, as if saying, *Look, I've heard you ladies have some self-esteem issues, but I'm just glad to finally meet you.* Then he twisted around, laying me on the bed as he stood up, unbuttoned his jeans, pulled down his zipper, bent over, and pulled them off. I tried to avert my gaze, but where else was I supposed to look when we'd just been joined by an *anaconda*? No wonder he wasn't nervous his first time. Jesus! I unzipped my jeans, wondering exactly how I was supposed to accommodate the one-eyed reptile peeking at me over the top of his Fruit of the Looms. Matt moved to the bottom of the bed, pulling my pants off one leg at a time. I climbed under the covers as he slid in next to me. For a moment we just lay there, holding hands. Then we each reached under the covers, slipping out of our underwear. I'd never been completely naked with anyone before, and I was thinking even if we stopped now, this was pretty good.

A second later, Matt climbed on top of me, submerging his tongue deep in my mouth while gently moving the hair off my forehead with his right hand. With his other hand, he confidently guided his rock-hard penis inside me.

"Ow!" My entire body tightened in response to this insistent intruder.

"Try to relax," he whispered, as slowly, he began moving himself in and out of me.

Relax, I said to myself as he began to pick up the pace.

It's not that easy, some other part of me said.

But it doesn't even seem like you're trying!

Well, I am; I am fucking trying!

"Mmmmmmm...," he moaned as his head shot back and forth.

He really seems to be enjoying himself. I wish I were, I thought to myself.

It's because you're not relaxed, my mind reprimanded.

Omigod would you just shut the fuck up already? the reprimanded part of me yelled back.

As Matt pumped away, I thought, *Jeez, I can't believe everybody thinks this is so great. I'd much rather get stoned and have a hot-fudge sundae.*

"Oh...oh...oh...," he moaned loudly, placing his hands on the mattress, on either side of me, as he arched his body up. His eyes were closed tight, and his face was so contorted I wondered if he might be having some kind of seizure. Especially when, after one particularly robust thrust, he collapsed on me, his entire body limp. I had no idea what was happening. *Is he dead? Should I call someone?* I thought, *I'll give it a minute and if he still hasn't moved, then I'll go for help.* A minute later, as if back from the dead, he raised his head, smiled at me, kissed me perfunctorily on the lips, and rolled off of me.

"That was amazing," he said, closing his eyes as he wiped the sweat off his brow with the back of his hand.

"Mmmm," I said, feeling left out.

"I'll get you a towel," he said as he swung his legs over the side of the bed, stood up, and strutted out of the room.

"Thanks," I called after him, scooting up in the bed. *Why would I need a towel?* my mind asked, just as the sheet fell off me, exposing what looked like blood. *Blood?* Flinging the covers off, I was looking at a dark-red pool of blood the size of a yarmulke. What the fuck had that *anaconda* done to me? "Matt!" I yelled.

He came tearing into the room.

"I'm bleeding," I cried, sticking my fingers between my legs. "Omigod," I screamed, holding up my red fingers. "You must have hit a vein or something. I think we should go to the emergency room!" I moaned, holding my two red fingers high in the air.

"It's okay. Everything's okay." He put his arm around me. "It's because it's your first time."

"Really?" I said, dropping my fingers to the bed as I stared at the little puddle of blood.

"Yeah," he said, scooping me up in his arms.

"Well, it looks like I was shot in the vagina," I said, laughing as I leaned into him.

"You were," he said sweetly as we both cracked up.

—

Over the next few months, Matt and I spent as much time together as we could. We both knew our time was limited since I was about to graduate from Stuyvesant and I'd just found out I'd gotten into Wesleyan. And after that *CSI* episode devoted to the losing of my virginity, my experience of sex completely turned around. I made sure I was very high during sex. Pot made sex phenomenal! Although pot was a spectacular aphrodisiac, I was using it to turn off the never-ending critical feed scrolling across the bottom of my mind, most of which, sadly, was about Matt. It didn't even make sense. *I hate my tits. I hate* his *tits. I can't stand his new buzz cut. When he's on top of me I feel like I'm getting fucked by a schnauzer. I hate my thighs. How can he not hate my thighs? I hate his shirt. He's not smart enough. He's not cool enough. He's not hip enough.* (Never mind that he turned me on to Richard Pryor, who blew me away so profoundly, confirming what I felt put on this earth to do.) It was nonstop head noise: *He's a fuckin' loser; there must be something wrong with him if he loves me.*

—

My getting high for sex hadn't bothered Matt initially, but ultimately it turned out to be a huge problem. When he asked me to not get high before we had sex, I asked, "Why not?"

"When you're high, you go away," he said, his loneliness suddenly filling the room.

And that was the beginning of our end. Because as much as I loved him, which I did, there was someone I needed to be with even more: the girl I was when I was stoned.

The real me, who had so much noise in her head she thought it might explode, who was shackled by fear and anxiety, who had no idea what to do with all the rage and guilt and love toward her mom—that girl was laid to rest when the stoned Marion stepped in and put that giant fucking red crayon to sleep, once and for all. Or so I thought.

10

"I just love that they let you have animals in the dorms, don't you? They let this girl keep her ferret in her room," my mother said, staring at a picture of a girl cuddling a ferret on her lap.

"Yeah," I said. My mind was a million miles away. I stared out the window as my dad drove us up the long hill onto the Wesleyan campus. Whenever the three of us came together like this, each of us playing our roles, acting as if we were a real family, it made me sad. No matter how committed we were to playing our parts or sticking to our scripts, we weren't a family. My role was pretending I was a normal seventeen-year-old excited about college, who had pretty much decided on English as her major.

The reality was the week before, I was graduating high school, I'd broken up with Matt for the millionth time, Megan was spending all her time with the nurse, and I was smoking more pot than ever.

"Look at this," my dad said, slowing down as we drove alongside a vast bright-green lawn punctuated by enormous oak trees. In the distance was a palatial, pristine white building flanked by enormous pillars with wide steps leading to it. Scattered around it were other buildings—much smaller, very quaint redbrick buildings with black or white trim.

As my mom and dad tried to figure out where to park, I stared out the window. Perched on the edge of my seat, mouth open, I was dumbstruck by all these fresh-faced, hopeful creatures wearing polo shirts, collars upturned, bustling about, clutching books, checking schedules. All of them seemed to be running confidently into futures filled with endless promise. As my parents went on and on about this fucking campus—Yes, we all agree, outstanding campus—I thought, *Let's turn this fuckin' rental around, 'cause there is no way I am ready for any of this!*

"Honey, maybe we should just drop you off. I can't find anywhere to park, and I'm worried about hitting rush hour on the way back," my dad said. He put on his hazard lights and pulled over.

"And I think orientation starts . . . oh, it's now," my mom said, looking up from her brochure. "Chuck, we could drop her here and then take all her stuff over to her dorm room. Whadaya think?" my mother said, twisting around to look at me.

What do I think? I think we should find the girl with the fucking ferret, then hightail it the fuck out of here!

"I wanted to unpack your room with you, but I think given the time . . . ," my mother continued, her sweet smile making me want to go home with her that much more.

"You'll be the first one in the family to graduate college!" my dad yelled, beaming at me in the rearview mirror.

Graduate?! I can't imagine getting out of the car!

The asshole in the car behind us leaned on his fucking horn. As my mother got out of the car, I contemplated throwing myself at her feet and pleading with them to take me home.

"I'll call you tomorrow," my dad said, still beaming. He rubbed my cheek with the back of his hand.

"I wish you guys could stay a little longer," I said, hugging my mom with all my might.

"Me too," she said. The smell of her was so comforting I wished I could just crawl inside it.

"Here," my dad said, passing my mother two crisp one-hundred-dollar bills to hand to me. "Make us proud!"

"Love you," I said, putting the money in my pocket.

"Love you," my mom said.

I felt like they were taking my heart with them as I watched the car drive away slowly. I couldn't move. I stood there, fantasizing that they'd turn around, throw open my door, and scream with laughter: *We're kidding. We're kidding. C'mon, we realize there's nothing we've given you that's remotely prepared you to be on your own out in the world.*

But that didn't happen. What did happen was that I ran after the car as my dad honked the horn three times fast. I could see them laughing, as if I was doing it to be funny. But as I did a little jig in the street, nothing could have been further from the truth.

—

"No. No. I *am* trying. I've given it a chance," I cried quietly into the phone in the dark, hunched over on the edge of Sandy Wilson's bed. "Mom, I'm telling you why," I whispered angrily, trying not to cry harder. "I-I don't understand why I can't just come home," I stammered, standing up to reach for the tissue box on Sandy Wilson's desk.

"Honey, you just got there. It's going to get easier. You'll see. You'll make friends and then you won't even want to talk to your old mom," she reassured, the warmth of her loving, caring voice only intensifying the unbearable ache of homesickness.

"Marion, are you almost done? I really need to get back in my room," Sandy Wilson, my resident advisor, yelled through the door. Her stern tone only deepened my ache.

"Can you please just give me five more minutes?" I called out, doing my best not to sound like I was crying.

"Five," Sandy yelled through the door. Sandy was a senior and the only way to make a phone call. She had been really sweet when I first started asking to use her phone to call my mom, but that was more than five weeks ago, and now that I was asking to call home pretty much every night, well, honestly, Sandy had become a real fuckin' twat.

Look, I understood her frustration, but I really couldn't help myself. Ever since my parents had driven away, I'd felt I was having one long panic attack. For all the endless issues I had with my mother, I missed her with every fiber of my being. I felt completely stranded, abandoned, deserted.

My only comfort was the meals in the commissary, where you could go up as many times as you wanted and, with an old-timey silver ice-cream scooper, take as much ice cream as you wanted from enormous bins that were right next to an enormous hot-fudge dispenser, next to every topping you can imagine: wet walnuts, dry walnuts, sprinkles, whipped cream, cherries! But aside from the food, the whole scene in the commissary shot anxiety straight through my veins. Every table or two was its own little clique. It was all about where you were sitting and who you were in with. It all sent me back to that fucking hot-fudge dispenser until I was so sick, all I could do was go back to my dorm room and unleash the wrath in my ass!

One night, my mom casually announced she'd met somebody and needed to get off the phone so she didn't burn his baked potato. I was sitting in my room, unable to concentrate on a Willa Cather novel about ducks or geese or some farm shit, when I noticed smoke literally slithering along my green linoleum floor. It was pot smoke, and it smelled really good. There was always a party in Margot's room. As I stared down at my book, I could hear the coolest, druggiest people laughing. Margot had just turned up Led Zeppelin really loud. I closed my book, walked over to the mirror, picked up my black eye pencil, ran the dark-black pencil back and forth till I was sufficiently racooned, dabbed some patchouli oil behind each ear, took a deep breath, and went to join them.

As I raised my fist to knock on Margot's door, I thought, *Maybe this is a mistake*. I shut my eyes, took a deep breath, and knocked once. After a minute, when no one answered, I took a step back toward my room just as a voice said, "Where'd ya go?" I turned around and the cutest guy, with long, curly dirty-blond hair, poked his head out of Margot's room. "There you are," he said, as if we were old friends.

"Hi," I said.

"I'm Stuart, but everybody calls me Silver," he said, extending his hand.

"Hi, I'm Marion," I said. I gave him my hand and he pulled me gently into the room.

"Join us." He handed me a large bottle of whiskey from behind his back.

So this is where they all were. I glanced around Margot's packed room. Lying on the bed, sitting on the floor, lounging in a couple of beanbag chairs over by the window were the hippest, coolest, most elite, druggiest kids in the school. I recognized everybody from their big table at the commissary.

"Who goes there?" Margot called out from a beanbag chair, where she was surrounded by a bevy of gorgeous girls passing around an enormous bong.

"Everyone, this is Marilyn," Silver yelled over Jimmy Page's fierce guitar solo.

Just as I started to tell him that wasn't my name, the entire stoned room looked over at me and, in unison, yelled, "Hi, Marilyn."

"Marilyn lives on the other side of the wall," Margot shouted as pot smoke streamed out of her mouth. As if watching a tennis match, they all stared at me, then at the wall, then back at me, as if somehow I had literally come through the wall.

Over the next couple months I was introduced to many new people and many new drugs, but one introduction blew all the others away: my new best friend—alcohol. From the moment we met, I was completely in love. I *was* Marilyn. Where Marion was full of fear, Marilyn had none. Where Marion could never relax, that was all Marilyn knew how to do. Where Marion couldn't get out of her head, Marilyn gave head. Pot had done a lot for me, but with alcohol I was reborn, transformed into this wild, fearless, intensely sexual girl. I went from sitting in my room, passing gas, passing time, all by myself, to being the belle of the ball.

—

It was Halloween and I was following Margot and our friend Daphne onto the enormous wraparound porch of a beautiful off-campus Victorian house.

"Holy shit, who the fuck lives here?" I yelled to Margot's back.

"Older boys."

As she opened the front door, "Psycho Killer" by the Talking Heads ambushed my ears while a pungent combination of pot, cigarette smoke, beer, and sweat attacked my nostrils. As we pushed our way through the sparkly sea of drag, I shouted in Margot's ear: "We should have worn costumes."

Margot grabbed us a couple of beers. A stocky little man/woman with a square-shaped head and slicked-back jet-black hair shot us a devilish grin.

"Ernest Borgnine wants us," I said. I lit a cigarette as Margot handed me a beer. I pulled the tab off, slurping up the foam as I scoped out the room. In the corner was a very tall man/woman in a three-piece suit who was a dead ringer for Frank Langella. Over by a window was a man/woman who bore an uncanny resemblance to Golda Meir, and on the far side of the room, a striking man/woman looked like a combination of James Dean and my aunt Marsha.

He/she was wearing a snug purple summer dress with a black lace shawl, black pumps, and flawless eye makeup. Even dressed as my aunt Marsha, I could tell she/he was hot.

"Who the fuck is that?" Margot asked, throwing her arm around my shoulder.

"Very pretty, right?" Daphne said, leaning into me.

"Uh-huh," I said, wishing they hadn't seen her/him.

"I'm goin' in," Daphne said, licking her lips.

"Me too." Margot squealed, grabbing Daphne's hand as they scurried across the room.

Margot and Daphne both had amazing tits. Perfectly shaped, just the right size, and neither of them ever wore bras. They didn't need to. Their titties were upswooping and optimistic, and just by the sheer perfection of their form seemed to defy not only gravity but any possibility of rejection. Tonight Margot and Daphne were both wearing skintight sleeveless T-shirts that made their tits look particularly enthusiastic. *Fuck my saggers*, I thought, watching Margot and Daphne's Olympians infiltrate the cluster of *ladies* my aunt Marsha was hanging with. *Never mind*, I said to myself in the voice of Gilda Radner's Roseanne Roseannadanna. I decided to scope out the upstairs to see who was getting high. I took a deep drag on my cigarette and poked my head into the last bedroom on the right.

"Do you have another one of those?" a voice asked. I stood there wondering if I was hearing things. "Do you?" the voice repeated.

"Where are you?" I said, giggling at the strangeness of the situation.

"I'm in the closet," the voice said coyly as my aunt Marsha appeared in the doorway of the closet next to the bed.

"Well, come out," I said, trying to muffle how happy I was to see Aunt Marsha.

"I'm sure your family will accept you eventually," I said nervously as he stepped into the light.

"Ya hope," he said, his voice so deep and smooth, it turned me on and put me at ease at the exact same time.

As I took the pack of Marlboro Lights from the pocket of my

jean jacket, I had the most overwhelming sense that I already knew him. I handed him a cigarette and lit it. His iridescent blue eye shadow sparkled in the light. "I love your dress," I said. Cigarette smoke wafted around us, making me feel like we were in our own little nightclub.

"It's my aunt's."

"Well, it looks great on you," I said, losing myself in the dark-green forest of his eyes.

"You don't think it makes my ass look too big?" he said, trying not to laugh.

"I don't," I said, slowly shaking my head from side to side.

"I noticed you downstairs," he said. His breath was an intoxicating blend of whiskey and toothpaste. "What's your name?"

"Marion," I said, thinking how much I loved his face even though his foundation was a little heavy.

"Like Maid Marion," he said, moving just a tiny bit closer to me.

"Not really. What's your name?" I asked, thinking no wonder he smells like toothpaste, his teeth are so white.

"Danny," he said, licking his crimson-red lips.

"Do you live here?" I asked.

"You're standing in my room," he said, in a totally non-dicky way.

"I'm sorry, I..."

Before I could finish apologizing, Danny pulled a joint out of his dress pocket, grabbed the pack of matches lying on the bureau next to us, lit it, took a quick hit, and passed it to me. "I know how you can make it up to me," he said, smiling suggestively.

"How?" I said, passing him back the joint.

"Let me see yours," he whispered, staring at me like the cat that was about to eat my canary.

"What?" I said, concerned Aunt Marsha might be a pervert.

"Your room. It's only fair since you've seen mine." I laughed, grateful that Danny turned out to be more of a tit for tat man than just a straight tit man!

—

In Danny, I had definitely met my match, in every sense of that word. Our chemistry was crazy. We were crazy in love and crazy high all the time. When Danny moved into a fraternity house, I basically moved in with him. It was me and cute, sexy guys who gave me so much attention that it almost became another drug for me. Danny and I did whatever we wanted, whenever we wanted to. When we were eating at the big round table in the Beta House dining room, if we didn't feel like using utensils, we didn't. If we didn't feel like wearing shoes, we didn't. When everyone else went to bed, we stayed up all night getting high. When everybody else was waking up and going about their day, we were going to bed.

I was getting drunk and stoned so constantly that the periods of being straight, of returning to myself, became fewer and fewer until they no longer really existed. I was getting fucked up with everybody, all the time. The jocks, the Dead Heads, the hippies, the wealthy kids—many of whom majored in African drumming because as we all know, the demand for rich, white African drummers is limitless! I could pretty much outdrink and outdrug everyone. This was my arena, where I shined the brightest. I was as much of a celebrity on campus as my father was out there in the real world. My dad kept calling, asking exactly what I was doing with all the money I kept asking him to send me. I'd always make up some bullshit about needing more supplies, new books. Based on the amount of money he was sending, you'd have thought I was building my own fucking library!

I felt untouchable, invincible. I walked around feeling this inviolable sense of freedom. Nobody could tell me shit. Nobody could rope me in. I refused to color in the lines. For me there were no lines. I was way too busy crossing them all and snorting them up, even when it meant breaking Danny's heart by cheating on him with Wesleyan's resident cocaine dealer.

11

When the semester ended, everyone headed home for the summer. Mine was a new home. My mom had decided she wanted to move out of the city. She moved into an old World War II army barracks in Sag Harbor, out in the Hamptons. The plan was my dad would buy it and she'd pay him two hundred dollars a month in rent. Then she and her boyfriend, Mr. Potato Head, who was also Mr. Huge Pothead, would renovate it together. He was supposed to be an electrical genius. I was so excited to see my mom and our new house, I could barely wait for the train doors to open as we pulled into the station. It had been almost six months since we'd seen each other—right before she moved to Sag Harbor. I ran down the stairs toward the red pickup truck my dad had gotten her so that she could transport all the materials for the renovation.

"Omigod, look at your hair! It's so long!" my mother shrieked as we threw our arms around each other.

"Look at *your* hair," I screamed as she practically pulled me through her window.

"Throw your suitcase in the back," she said, laughing as she danced the little side-to-side jig she always did when her joy transcended words. I flung my suitcase in the truck bed, ran around the side, and jumped in.

"I'm so happy to see you," I said, lighting a cigarette as she pulled out of the parking lot. She laughed and shot me the biggest smile. I couldn't stop staring at her. She looked so beautiful. Her hair had gotten really long, and she'd stopped dyeing it; it was a wonderful silver gray. Her face, the freckles on her arms, the red rubber band she always wore on her right wrist, the generous way she laughed, the cozy way she smelled, it was all the inimitable familiarity of my mother. Sitting there next to my mom, laughing, telling our stories, rolling down the back roads of the Hamptons in her little red pickup truck, I realized how much I'd missed her.

"So, how's the house?" I asked, laughing.

For a moment she just stared straight ahead. Then, letting out a deep sigh, she turned her head toward me, smiling a smile I'd seen too many times before. My body instinctively slumped. For the rest of the ride she explained that Ted, a.k.a. Mr. Potato Head, after living in her house, sleeping in her bed, smoking pot every day all day, and eating her perfect baked potatoes, had announced that it was time to move on. I felt terrible for her. This asshole had used her.

"What does that mean in terms of the renovation?" I asked nervously as we pulled up beside a wall of extremely tall reeds.

"We're here," she announced jauntily and hopped out of the truck.

I sat in the truck, staring at the water in front of me and a big yellow sign that said DEAD END. Slowly, I walked around to a narrow opening in the grass wall I'd just seen my mother disappear through. I slipped through the opening, following her several feet, flanked on both sides by insanely tall grass that felt like bodyguard blades, until, on our left, was a break that appeared to be the very early stages of a garden. We walked a couple more feet to a clearing with shorter grass that led to a very weathered, beat-up side porch. The first porch step felt like a hammock as it sagged under my weight. I grasped the banister, which was even wobblier than the steps. I stepped onto the landing as my mother opened the unpainted, shabby-looking door to the old World War II army barracks. *She's got to fucking be kidding*, my head screamed as I stepped inside.

"You have anything to drink?"

"I think there's a bottle of vodka under the sink," she said nonchalantly as she began chopping vegetables.

I was shocked to find a half-empty half gallon of vodka. As far as I knew, my mom didn't drink. I pulled the bottle from under the sink, grabbed a tall glass drying upside down on a paper towel, poured the vodka almost to the top, closed the bottle, and bent down to put it back under the sink.

"Hey, pour me one." I'd never heard my mother utter such a sentence, but she said it casually, as if this was something she'd said a million times. Slowly, I hoisted the bottle back up on the counter and poured her less than half of what I'd just poured myself. "Thanks," she said easily, clinking her glass against mine. As I sat on the upside-down crate in front of the fire, I prayed the effect of the vodka would hit me before any more sadness about my mom did.

We killed that bottle of vodka my first night home. When I got up, or rather came to, the next day, I had no idea if that was a one-time welcome-home situation, or a like-mother-like-daughter one, or maybe the other way around. I got my answer that next evening, when just as the sun went down my mom said, "I could really go for a drink. How 'bout you?"

And so our new way of climbing into bed with each other was born. Every night around the same time, one of us would say, as if this were a completely new idea (all very reminiscent of our we're-wounded-in-the-back-of-a-wagon scene work), "Hey, I could really go for a drink."

Our ritual was to drive into town, get a bottle of Cold Duck. We'd polish it off at the barracks while we took turns making each other laugh. Then one of us would say, "I could go for some more, how 'bout you?" That was my cue to get on my bike, with its flowery basket, and ride the two miles into town for another bottle. Pushing my way through those high reeds, drunk, I always felt like I was on fucking *Gilligan's Island*, and by the time we'd polished off that second bottle, I was. And that horrible sadness that had weighed so heavily on me, well, it had floated out to sea. Around eleven, my mom would signal she was done by turning on the news on her little TV.

But my night was just beginning. With the razor-sharp focus of a soldier preparing for combat, I'd check myself out in the mirror on my bureau, making sure I looked as fuckable as possible from every angle. I'd brush out my long blonde hair, flipping my head over so many times it wasn't unusual for me to pull a muscle in my neck. I'd fortify my already extremely black eyeliner. Then I'd climb onto my bike and ride back into town, searching for other members of my tribe. Usually the sun was on its way up when I'd be on my way home, sometimes so high that I'd swerve off the road into a ditch or ravine of some sort, and get so hot pushing the bike out of whatever I'd crashed into that I'd ride the rest of the way home topless.

After one of my all-nighters, I was so hung over, I could barely lift my head off the pillow when I awoke. I realized I had absolutely no idea where I was and felt way too sick to even try to figure out how to get myself home. I sat down on the side of the bed, holding my head in one hand while I dialed the phone with the other.

"Hello," my mother said with the verve of someone who'd actually had a good night's sleep.

"Hi," I mumbled, barely.

"Where are you? I was just about to start worrying," she said, her voice sounding too loud.

"My head is killing me," I whispered, wishing I could just chop it off.

"Where are you?" she whispered.

"I have no idea. You have to come get me," I said, throwing up a little in my mouth.

"Honey, how can I come get you if you don't know where you are?" she said gently.

Suddenly feeling like I had wandered into some existential vortex, I thought it best to just give her the facts: "I slept at some guy's house." I rummaged through his night table drawer in search of some aspirin.

"Just ask him what the address is there," she said, from her alternate well-rested reality.

"He's not here," I said, slamming the drawer shut.

"Look out the window," she said in full detective mode. "What do you see?"

"A whale," I said, staring across the street.

"Is it possible you're at sea?" she asked matter-of-factly.

"I don't believe so," I said dryly, continuing to squint at the whale. "It's kind of... posing."

"Posing? Is it alive?"

"I don't think so. It's not moving." My eyes closed from the ceaseless pain in my brain.

"Omigod, I know where you are!" My mom burst into laughter.

"Mom, too loud. Where am I?"

"You're across the street from the Whaling Museum on Main Street in Sag Harbor. I'll be right there."

"Hurry," I said, catching a glimpse of my reflection in the full-length mirror on the back of the closet door. My shirt was on backward. Twenty minutes later, my mom and I thanked the whale before driving to a diner, where we had a great time—a lot of french toast, even more laughs, despite the buzz saw in my head—because we were together.

12

Ten days later, I was on a train headed back to Wesleyan. When I got there, I felt like I was in a game of musical chairs where the music had stopped and there was nowhere for me to sit. Everybody else had submitted their housing requests over the summer. Music House was full of musicians and always had music pouring out of it. India House was full of Indians and always had the scent of curry wafting from it. Malcolm X House was full of black students and always had a crackers-not-welcome vibe. Eclectic House was full of pretentious arty people wearing ascots, many of whom were *majoring* in African drumming.

There was nowhere for me to live, until I ran into Margot, who told me about an empty room in her house. Unofficially it was called Drug House, and yes, it was full of druggies. One of my new roommates, Simon Sherman, was convinced he could see the molecular structure of wallpaper after years of consuming tons of acid. He was completely manic, with incredibly long brown hair that he would fling wildly from side to side whenever he'd corner me outside the bathroom or in the kitchen, ranting about the CIA, wheatgrass, or the molecular structure of wallpaper. Another roommate, Sam, also addicted to LSD, was a Dead Head, vegan, and baker. I didn't understand why he was even enrolled in school, since he was literally always on the road with the Grateful Dead. On his layovers between concerts, he'd take over the kitchen, cooking up trays and trays of vegan muffins and brownies, which he'd store in the freezer alongside his numerous sandwich bags of LSD. He'd always make two batches of his yummy treats—one with LSD and one without. On more than one occasion, I was drunk, stoned out of my mind, in the grip of fierce munchies, and I forgot which was which. I spent the rest of those nights hunched over, staring at our wallpaper, pretty sure I too could see its molecular structure.

On Halloween, this guy Zach, the biggest dealer on campus, got a shipment of extremely potent psilocybin mushrooms from Hawaii. Everyone had been buzzing about the arrival of these shrooms for weeks. Zach was the Jerry Garcia of the drug community, and actually bore an uncanny resemblance to Jerry. He was Jewish, crazy cool, and got the most amazing drugs from all over the world. All the girls were praying he'd choose them to do the mushrooms with at his big Halloween bash, but he chose me. I felt like I'd been crowned Miss America!

That night, by the time I walked into the party, I was already pretty buzzed and starving. I hadn't eaten all day in preparation for my big night. The place was packed, wall-to-wall, with people covered in glitter, wearing crazy masks, getting fucked up on all kinds of shit. Behind a small table sat an older white guy with really long dreads, who was painting everyone's faces with Day-Glo paint. He waved me over.

"Hi," I said, taking a seat on the stool in front of his tray of paints.

"Very," he said, laying his paint-stained hands on my face like a blind person. As he started moving his hands around my face, someone behind me stuck a pipe in my mouth.

"Black hash from Morocco," a faceless voice behind me said as I wrapped my mouth around the pipe and inhaled deeply.

As the hash hit me and the mystery man behind me started stroking my hair, I got up and thought I should probably try to find Zach and his mushrooms.

I floated through the crowd, carried by Jerry Garcia singing, "Driving that train, high on cocaine." I found Zach in the kitchen, standing at the stove, stirring a large pot of soup as he bopped his head along with the song.

"There you are," he said, stirring his soup in sync with the music. "Hungry?"

"Starving," I said, taking a seat at the table.

"Good," he said, as he doled out a big bowl of soup, carried it over, and set it down in front of me.

I shoveled the chunky concoction into my mouth. "This is delicious!"

"You want more?" He chuckled.

"Please, sir, I want some more," I said doing my best Oliver impression as I held my bowl up with both hands. He poured some more into my bowl. After practically licking the bowl clean, I looked up at Zach and, not wanting to be too pushy, casually said, "So, when are we gonna do the mushrooms?"

He smiled at me, lit a cigarette, and said, "You just did them…"

"What?" I was instantly anxious.

"They were in the soup," he said nonchalantly as he came over and kissed the top of my head.

"I wish you'd told me," I said, terrified at the thought of how many hallucinogenic mushrooms I had just shoved down my throat.

"Enjoy the ride," he sang, winking at me as he danced out of the kitchen.

Panic engulfed me. I couldn't move. I just sat there staring at the giant pot that he had pretended contained soup. *Okay, okay, let's go into the other room*, I said to myself, pushing back from the table.

I made a mad dash through the crowd, toward an unoccupied far corner of the room, wiggling past a green snake guy in a loincloth. *Just breathe*, I told myself right as I felt a huge hand on the back of my neck.

"You tripping yet?" Zach asked, his face covered in black paint.

He put his hands on my hips and forcefully pulled me into him.

Someone had put on this funky song I loved by the Pointer Sisters, and my body felt so warm and floaty, like I didn't have bones, just flesh. The music was moving from deep inside of me. The top of my head fell forward, and I closed my eyes, dancing backward as Zach ran his hands down the length of my arms, grabbing on to my hands. *You are purple liquid molecules*, I thought to myself.

I'd been dancing like that, my eyes shut, lost in the music, floating far, far away, for what seemed like a long time, when suddenly, this stern voice said, *Where are you?* It scared the shit out of me, shocking my eyes open. The voice had come from inside of me.

"Where are we?" I yelled hysterically, staring at Zach's blackened face.

"What?" he said, continuing to move to the music.

"Where are we?" I demanded angrily.

"Relax. You're tripping," he said, grinding his hips into mine as he locked his hands behind me. "Just go with it," he whispered seductively into my ear before kissing it.

Just breathe, just breathe, just breathe..., I screamed at myself, but I felt like I couldn't... breathe. *Inhale, exhale, inhale, exhale, inhale, exhale*, I told myself, convinced my body had suddenly forgotten how to breathe. I pushed myself back from Zach, staring up at his big blackened fleshy face.

"Cool out." He leered at me; his teeth looked to me like sharp white fangs.

He's the Devil! the voice inside me shouted.

Stroking the side of my face, before cupping his hand around my neck, he said dismissively, "You're just having a bad trip."

He's the Devil! He's the Devil! my mind chanted as I tried to wiggle out from his hold. "Zach... let go of me!" I shrieked, breaking free as I began pushing my way through the psychedelic sea of swaying bodies between me and the front door.

Finally making it to the door, I flung it open, raced down the stairs, and was halfway across the lawn when Zach grabbed my feet and tackled me to the ground. "Get off!" I screamed as he climbed on top of me, pinning me down. "Help... Help!" I screamed, praying someone would hear me.

"Marion, you're not wearing any shoes and it's fucking freezing out here," Zach shouted as he grabbed my face and held it between his massive hands. I turned my face to the side and realized that I was so high I hadn't noticed there was snow on the ground, or that I was barefoot. I couldn't feel my toes, and even though part of me wanted to listen to him, as I stared at his face, a bigger part of me just kept saying, *He's the Devil, and the Devil wants to rape you.*

"Jesus Christ!" he yelled as I continued struggling beneath him. "If I let you up will you just come back in the house and put on your shoes?" he asked, loosening his grip as I slowly nodded my head up and down. As I started to sit up, he shoved his big devil face right next to mine and tried to kiss me.

"Get the fuck off me!" I screamed so loud, a couple guys came out onto the porch.

"What's goin' on out there?" one of them shouted, distracting Zach, while I rolled away from him, got up, and tore ass into the house. I grabbed my shoes and my coat, and was halfway home before I put either of them on.

"What a fuckin' asshole," Margot was saying later as with one hand she took a handful of popcorn from the big bowl in my lap, while with the other she put the needle on the Tom Petty record sitting on the stereo. It had taken a few hours of sobbing and freaking out, along with a lot of pizza, popcorn, and Sam's vegan carrot muffins (with no LSD), but I was finally pretty much down from my trip. It dawned on me that what I really needed was a whole other kind of trip. I decided I would take my junior year abroad in Europe. I'd leave it all behind—that fucking bad trip, that devil. The problem was the devil I couldn't leave behind.

13

I was scouring the room thinking how disappointing the male candidates for my semester in London were when a tall, lanky yet muscular, chestnut-haired, ridiculously sexy guy strutted into the room. "Sorry I'm late," he said, addressing us all in an appealing drawl as he slid into the only empty chair. "My plane just landed."

"That's okay," the middle-aged female teacher said, clearly experiencing the impact of our new arrival along with the rest of the girls. "We were just getting started." She blushed and fumbled with her clipboard. "So, you must be..."

"Cooper." He kicked his long legs out as he folded his arms on his chest and settled back in his chair like a musician in between sets at a blues club at two in the morning.

That first month, every day at lunch, a group of us would go to the pub around the corner. Most would order sodas or maybe one pint of beer. Except me and Cooper. We'd drink beer all through lunch, and then when everyone went back to class we'd start with the hard stuff. One afternoon, after a lot of alcohol, we wound up back in his room near the Hammersmith Odeon, in bed, and that was the start of the relationship. I don't even remember having sex because, by far, the most erotic and intimate thing we did was get high together. So high that we'd find ourselves perched naked outside on his third-floor window ledge, fully visible from the street below, drinking, doing lines of coke, smoking pot or hash, watching the sun come up.

How could a girl so obsessed with body issues and tit-hate perch herself on a windowsill nude? I was so high, it's possible I mistook my skin for a remarkably light summer dress. Plus I was really skinny. Over the years, I'd been feeding myself less and less; I wouldn't eat anything all day except a few delicious chocolate biscuits, which I'd tell myself were healthy since they contained fiber, and chocolate counted as both dairy and protein. The rest of the calories I allowed myself were from scotch—seventy calories a shot. I tried to keep it to no more than twelve hundred a day.

My ferocious drinking, drugging, and starving left me acutely vulnerable to a whole new drug: Cooper. For the first time I felt addicted to a person, and just like my other addictions, Cooper began to have a powerful, unnatural hold over me. Even though I was his girlfriend, I always felt like I was auditioning for the part. It didn't help that he made me promise to never tell anyone we were together, a request he never explained and one I didn't have enough self-esteem to question. We'd been together a couple of months, and I was at his place all the time, so I suggested I give up my place and move in with him. After one of his epic bouts of staring somewhere *I wasn't*, he suggested I rent the room next to his. He might as well have said, *Once we're done fucking and getting high... I don't even want to be in the same room as you!*

Each day I handed over more and more of myself, letting my drugged-out, impenetrably sexy Wizard of Oz pull all my strings from behind his curtain of smug ambivalence. And yes, I know there's an entire section of Barnes & Noble devoted to this shit, with titles like *Women Who Love Too Much*, *Women Who Love Men Who Hate Them*, and *Women Who Hate Men Who Love Them*. But I was nineteen, a full-blown drug addict/alcoholic, and suffice to say, I didn't run in circles where anyone was reading these books; I didn't run in circles where anyone was reading!

It seemed like the minute I moved next door to Cooper, he started spending a lot of time with this very wealthy white South African couple, Tyler and Kitty. One night, he was out with the South Africans very late. When I heard Cooper turn the key in his door, I went over and asked what he'd been doing with them until three in the morning.

"Playing tennis," he said, lying back on his bed as he moved his hand slowly over his face as if it were a washcloth.

"Till three in the morning?" I asked, wishing I sounded as confrontational as I felt.

He smiled at me, superiority oozing from his pores as he grabbed the small mirror off his nightstand, laid out several lines of what I knew was the South Africans' cocaine, cut it up with his credit card, handed me a straw, and watched me forfeit another piece of myself. I never was invited on any of his outings with the South Africans, and it wasn't because I didn't have a racket. With Cooper off with his tennis buddies so much of the time, I was spending too much time on my side of our wall, getting fucked up and feeling like more of a stranger to myself every day.

The semester was coming to an end, and all the other students were buzzing excitedly about where they were applying to graduate school, or medical school, or law school. I felt blank. What the fuck was I supposed to be doing? I watched everybody exchange numbers so they could stay in touch and keep each other posted on what they'd be doing once they got back to the States. I was like a compass whose needle had lost its magnetization and had gone completely haywire. Cooper and I talked about staying in London, but we were both out of money. My father had been wiring money—a *lot* of money—the whole time I'd been there, but I'd spent it all on drugs and alcohol. The first of the month was right around the corner, and neither Cooper nor I could afford rent even if we did move in together. Our solution was to persuade the head teacher to let us live in the school's luggage room, where every day began with some bright-eyed, bushy-tailed student rousing us from our narcotic slumber with a request for their suitcase. "Hello, I don't know if you can hear me. But if you can, would you please send out the four pieces of red luggage with the white trim? The smallest one has butterfly stickers all over it." But even once we were living among the luggage, we still needed money for staples—milk, biscuits, whiskey, coke. Cooper didn't have anyone to call and that credit card of his was just for cutting coke.

After much coaxing from Cooper and not knowing what else to do, I found myself in a red phone booth near Gloucester Road one dark, dank, rainy night, dialing the endless numbers needed to reach my dad.

"Hello?"

"Dad, hi, it's me."

"Hi," he said, chuckling warmly.

After a few minutes of requisite small talk, I launched into my hustle. "Y'know, I've been thinking, and there's really no reason for me to be rushing back to the States. So I thought maybe I'd just stay here through the summer."

"Uh-huh. Did you go and visit my friend at the consulate?" he asked, the warmth suddenly gone from his voice.

"I haven't gotten a chance yet, but I really—"

"What about those historic buildings you told me you'd go see?" he interrupted.

"I-I've just been so busy with school and we just had finals and…" I stammered, looking out at the black night, refusing me any relief. "…But I'm going to…I'm definitely going to. If I stay I'll have more time to do all of it, which is what I wanted to talk to you about—everything's so expensive over here and by the time I pay the rent and buy the food…"

"Mommy told me you dropped the political science part of your major; is that true?" he said, angrily.

Fuck, I whispered to myself, wishing I could just grab a passerby and say, *Excuse me, so sorry to bother you, but could you just see if you can get my father to wire you some money, because I'm pretty sure he's on to me!* But instead, I hung my head and whispered, "Yes," into the phone.

"That was the whole reason we sent you over there. You told both Mom and me that you wanted to study their political system and learn all about their history. I can't even tell you how many calls I've made trying to set up this internship for you in Washington."

At this point I began wishing the phone booth would just explode.

"Don't you want to amount to something? Don't you want to become something that I can be proud of? That *you* can be proud of? I've been sending you all this money... for what? Mommy says you're still drinking all the time and taking drugs. Is that what I'm supporting, Marion?" he yelled into the phone.

My father had never yelled at me. Minutes before, I had been so slick. This would be another conversation where I'd extort thousands of dollars for me and my silent partner. Now I was a daughter, having to hear disappointment in her father's voice. I burst into tears, which were genuine, and also my only hope of getting him to wire me anything. I promised I would find time to go visit Buckingham Palace, or wherever it was someone in a top hat was expecting me, and it went without saying that I would not be heading to Washington for any internship. I hung up the phone, turned up the collar on my leather jacket, and dashed down the wet street, trying to outrun the rain and the creeping sense that something very bad was about to happen.

I stopped off and had several shots, but I was still shaky when I met Cooper at the movie house for a midnight showing of *2001: A Space Odyssey*.

"Hey," I said, walking up behind him in line.

"You get the money?" He barely turned around.

"Yeah," I said, staring at his profile as we moved up in line. I lit a cigarette to keep myself company. Cooper seemed even more remote than usual, if that was possible, but maybe it felt that way because I was in pain about the conversation with my dad. I didn't expect him to ask me anything about the call; he wouldn't. A few minutes later we found our seats, and after waiting for him to materialize, I asked: "Where are you coming from?"

"Tyler and Kitty's," he whispered, staring at the blank screen in the theater.

"What were you guys doing?" I whispered, feeling like I was talking to fumes.

"A little of this, a little of that," he said, chuckling to himself as he closed his eyes and began scratching the side of his face. "Actually, a lot of... that," he said, an enormous grin overtaking his face. Cooper slumped down in his seat and continued scratching his face.

Over the next two hours, I tried to watch the movie, but my focus was drawn to Cooper's head repeatedly and in slow motion almost falling onto his chest just before some mysterious inner cue had him yank it back up.

"A lot of what?" I finally whispered.

"Uh?" he mumbled.

"What did you do a lot of?" I whispered loudly.

Licking his lips and glowing like the sun was inside him, he exhaled the word "heroin" into my ear. He said it with so much reverence, it sounded like he was saying "God." Cooper returned to the warmth of his seclusion. I turned my face back toward the screen. Between my disappointed father and my disappearing boyfriend, I felt like I was levitating in discomfort.

In the movie, the astronaut had lost his connection to the ship, and there was no way for him to get back, ever. As I watched him drift farther and farther away, I thought how unimaginably terrifying that would be, to be out there, floating, lost in space, not connected to anything or anyone, no rescue coming, ever. I sat in that dark theater at three in the morning, next to a ghost, and I realized it was exactly how I felt.

—

I started sniffing heroin with Cooper the night after *2001*. I fell in love with the high immediately. Alcohol and other drugs had helped me feel like I didn't have any worries in the world. But heroin made me feel like I didn't have any world. No boundaries, no constraints; it was the ultimate liberator.

Two months later, Copper and I said good-bye, although I felt we'd left each other long before I got on that plane. Halfway through the flight, I was downing my fifth vodka, unable to get drunk. I felt nothing. *Is it possible I've somehow drunk myself sober?* I wondered, as I set down my book, *Fat Is a Feminist Issue*, and pushed the large chocolate chip cookie that had been taunting me for the last hour to the back of my tray. As I finished that last vodka, I didn't feel the least bit inebriated; I felt wildly awake, like I'd never felt before—supercharged, with an overpowering, unnamable sense of urgency, as if something big was about to happen.

—

"I want to hear everything," my mother said, opening the door to the back porch. "Everything," she cooed, pouring me a glass of Duck before plopping down in the rocking chair across from me. As I watched my mother, sipping her Duck, listening, laughing, savoring every word out of my mouth, I had the most disturbing sense that it wasn't actually *me* talking. I was impersonating myself. The phone rang in the house. "Hold that thought," she said, laughing, as she ran inside to answer it.

I sat there, clutching the sides of my chair, feeling like I was disappearing. Covered in sweat, I stood up, walked slowly into the house, and closed my eyes as dizziness and nausea consumed me. *I'm in terrible danger! I'm sick. You have to help me*, my mind cried.

My mom cupped her hand over the phone. "Two minutes," she said.

I told myself to get to her daybed by the window. *If you get to the bed, you can lie down. What is happening to me?* I made it to the bed, falling onto my back. I closed my eyes, laying my hands across my heart.

"She just got back. Yeah, yeah, she looks great," my mother said.

I lay there, drenched in sweat yet ice-cold, shivering so hard, my teeth were chattering. Nothing I could do could stop whatever was happening to me. I reached up, pulling my grandma Lena's blanket around me, the one with thick black, brown, blue, horizontal, wavy stripes. I lay there in the fetal position, trying to focus on my breathing, and I saw the waves on the blanket move. They undulated like waves in the ocean. I shut my eyes tight, praying that when I opened them, the waves would have stopped moving.

"Okay, okay, I will," my mother was saying from a million miles away.

I opened my eyes; the waves were still moving.

"Whatcha doin' over there?" she called from another universe as she hung up the phone. When I didn't answer, she hurried over to me. "Honey, what's wrong?"

"I don't feel good." I started to cry as a rancid taste began to fill my mouth.

"You're soaking wet," she said, laying her hand on my forehead.

"Mommy, what's happening to me?" I whispered, moving my head into her lap.

"I'm gonna take your temperature and get a cold rag for your head."

I closed my eyes again, begging the waves to stop moving.

"Ah, sweetheart, it's okay, it's okay," she said, laying a damp cloth on my forehead as she cradled me in her arms.

"My saliva tastes so bad," I cried, burying my face in her lap.

"Open your mouth. Let me see." She pulled me up to her chest.

I opened my mouth, and the color left my mother's face.

"What? What?" Panic was exploding in my veins.

"Let's get you into bed," she said, pulling the covers back.

"What...Just tell me," I pleaded as she tucked me in. I put my arms on top of the covers. They were soaking wet, and I could smell alcohol. It was coming out of my pores. "Let me see." I felt delirious.

My mom stared at me for a moment, then leaned over and passed me the small mirror next to her bed.

I held the mirror up to my mouth, opening as wide as I could. The inside of my entire mouth was coated in black soot. I pulled the mirror back so I could see my whole face. I barely recognized myself. My hair was soaked with sweat, and my face was gray. I looked like a girl you see on the news who's been held captive by a sadistic sociopath. As tears streamed down my face, my mother rocked me to sleep.

14

The next day, having no idea what else to do, my mother loaded me into her truck and drove me to my dad's. He was renting a house by the ocean a few towns away. Mercifully, I slept all day.

When I woke up, my dad was on the phone canceling plans to go to some big producer's party in Southampton. I told him not to, that I'd go with him.

At the party, I was feeling more and more uneasy as my dad kept calling me over, proudly introducing his "beautiful and brilliant daughter, who has just returned from taking her junior year abroad." All these showbiz people were fawning over me, asking me what felt like endless questions, and I was answering appropriately. I felt like such a phony. The more complimentary my dad and his friends were, the more I was gripped by self-loathing.

Having no idea what to do with myself, I went over to

peruse the dessert table, this unnamable sense of anxiety escalating by the second. As I poured myself a glass of water, I suddenly heard this voice whisper in my ear, *I'm going to kill you*. I spun around, but no one was standing anywhere near me. My mind was racing, and my heart was beating so fast, I thought it was going to explode out of my chest. Just then, my dad caught my eye and waved to me. I waved back, feeling so far away, wishing with every fiber of my being that he could somehow rescue me. But from *what*? I stared blankly out the large oval window in front of me, my whole body clenched in terror as I waited. *I'm going to kill you*, the voice whispered again. But this time, I knew not to look for where the threat was coming from because, as horrifying and insane as this seemed, I knew it was coming from *me*.

When we got home, I ran upstairs, changed into my nightgown, and got right into bed. I was hoping, *praying*, that I could fall asleep before the voice could "get me." As I drifted off, I placed my hands over my heart and thanked God. My relief felt like a cruel joke when, only minutes later, I was shocked wide awake, my thoughts dragging me down the tracks of my mind with such violent momentum that I shot straight up in bed. On the far wall across from me I watched in horror as flames engulfed that side of the room. I clutched my covers around me and felt my stomach flip so hard I thought I was going to throw up. I sat there, nauseous, transfixed, as a huge reptile slithered its way across the floor, followed by Mickey Mouse riding across the flames on a unicycle, chased by dozens of little mice, some of whom would snicker at me as they ran by.

I stayed up all night, completely powerless to look away from this twisted animated carnival, feeling more and more sick and terrified. Because, while I really was *seeing* all this, I *knew* it wasn't really there, which could mean only one thing: somehow, between the time I had gone to bed and now, I had *lost my mind*. After seven or eight hours, the morning's sunlight began to peek through the little white curtains covered in sailboats. I stared at the clock till the little hand made its way to the nine. I knew my dad would be downstairs by now.

As I took the last step on the stairs, I saw my father sitting in the sun-drenched breakfast nook—reading the paper and sipping coffee. I felt like I was looking at someone in another galaxy, a galaxy I used to belong to. As I walked toward him, he looked up at me with so much love in his eyes I could feel my heart breaking. How was I going to tell my proud, adoring father that even though I was standing right in front of him and *looked* exactly like the girl he'd been showing off all night at that party, that girl was... *gone*?

—

The rest of the summer was a psychotic blur. I remember snapshots: my dad taking me to a doctor, who said, "Based on your daughter's symptoms, I would say she has DTs [delirium tremors] due to alcohol withdrawal." My dad nodded intently.

"Do you drink?" the doctor asked.

I nodded, staring at the floor.

"How much?"

"A quart of whiskey a day," I mumbled.

Without missing a beat, my father said, "She's never known her measurements." How could he possibly even fathom the words that had just come out of my mouth?

At the end of the summer, I went back to Wesleyan. I was in

terrible shape, but neither me, my mom, nor my dad had any idea what to do with me.

One morning, I was lying on my mattress on the floor and staring at the closet from which the demon had tormented me all night. The demon had severed my connection to everyone but him. His voice in my head was my entire and only reality: *Hey, Marion. Sssssss. Marion*, he'd hissed threateningly all night until the sunlight flooded my room.

"Marianne. Your father just called," my roommate, whose name I didn't know, shouted up the stairs.

"Okay," I yelled, my voice flat.

"He said you can reach him for the next thirty minutes, then he's going out." The roommate handed me a piece of paper as I passed him on the stairs.

"Thanks." The thought of my dad "going out" made me feel even more alone.

Walking into the dark kitchen, I decided against turning on the light because the humming from the overhead fluorescent bulb felt like torment by my punisher. I sat down in the hard wooden booth, at the green Formica kitchen table, lifted the phone receiver out of its cradle, and just as I began to dial, I was overtaken by a feeling of sheer futility. I placed the phone back in the cradle and lit a cigarette as I shuffled over to the refrigerator. I took a long drag on my cigarette—my only source of pleasure, before opening the refrigerator door. Bottle of vodka, bottle of scotch, two bottles of champagne, a jar of olives, a jar of pearl onions, a big chocolate cake with pink icing that spelled HAPPY BIRTHDAY, TRISHA. *Nothing you're a part of anymore*, I mumbled quietly to myself, releasing the refrigerator door before shuffling back to the booth. I was not even aware I was sitting in the dark till the phone rang, snapping me back to reality.

"Oh, good, you're there. I wanted to catch you before I had to go out," said the voice that could no longer rescue me. "How you feelin' today?"

"Same," I said, shoving my cigarette in my mouth to stop from crying.

"Mmm. Mmm," my dad said. "Well, I have some news that'll really cheer you up."

Cheer me up, my mind repeated. Those words no longer existed in my galaxy.

"I found a doctor in New Haven who specializes in..." The line went silent. My father was choking back tears, struggling to say out loud words no parent should ever have to utter in reference to their child. "...visual and auditory hallucinations brought on by drugs and alcohol."

"Uh-huh." I was unable to choke back my tears. I pressed my hand over the receiver.

"He can see you tomorrow morning at nine."

"He's treated people... like me?" I asked meekly, wiping my tears with the back of my shirt sleeve.

"That's what he does," he exclaimed with a certainty both of us wished he felt.

"I was out to dinner last night with Jack Warden...," he said, shifting into storytelling mode. Jack Warden had been in *Heaven Can Wait* with my dad, and they'd become great friends. "Well, the other night we were all out to dinner and Jack was telling us about how he'd fought in World War II and what it was like to be in combat..." He continued, his tone now dramatic. "He was actually captured and briefly held behind enemy lines. And, y'know, he just had to hang in there and tough it out until he was rescued. And that's what you have to do. You'll get through this. You're strong, and you'll tough it out. Just like Jack."

I dropped my head into my hand. My father's desperate desire to save me and complete inability to do so was excruciating.

"I mean, we've got to be thankful you're not actually in a war, being held captive behind enemy lines, right?" he said, laughing too hard.

I had no idea what to say. I *was* in a war, being held behind enemy lines. Words like "strong" and "tough it out" had about as much impact as a thimble of water had on a raging fire. "What's his name?" I finally mustered.

"Who?" my dad asked.

"The doctor I'm supposed to go see tomorrow."

"You're gonna think I made this up: Dr. Hedburg! Can you believe it? A guy who does what he does for a living, and that's his name?" Again he laughed too hard.

As I watched two small silver bats fly around the sink, I thought this doctor's name didn't even make the list of what I couldn't believe.

The next morning, after having been up all night again, I caught the 7:42 bus to New Haven and had the first of what would turn out to be, almost word for word, the exact same meeting with Dr. Hedburg every Friday for five months. Dr. Hedburg looked like a detective from the fifties. He was tall, lean, handsome in a completely generic way, and always wore a nondescript gray suit. If I ever had to pick him out of a lineup with five other guys in gray suits, I'm pretty sure I'd fail.

After that initial meeting, where I'd given him my statement of the crime, the conversation always went something like this: "Any change in your state?" he'd ask, staring down at his prescription pad.

"Not really," I'd say, lighting another cigarette off the one I was about to stomp out. "Have you ever seen anyone as sick as me get better?" I'd ask, while he continued to be under the spell of his prescription pad.

"Anything's possible. I mean, there's really no way to predict. Honestly, you've done a lot of damage. The truth is, a lot of people who have used drugs and alcohol the way you have are either dead or in mental hospitals. They don't make it back. But there's really no way to know. Every case is different. I've upped both the Mellaril and the Stelazine. Let's see if that helps at all." He'd hand me a page from his magical prescription pad. We both knew I had destroyed myself. He could do nothing but keep me heavily sedated on a combination of antipsychotics that made me feel like someone had thrown a damp blanket on the cartoonishly violent fantasies my mind was churning out and the visual and auditory hallucinations that were now practically omnipresent.

On the long bus ride back to Wesleyan, I'd often think that crazy people who didn't know they were crazy were lucky. As sedated as I was, I was completely awake to the fact that I was being slaughtered and violated by a mental illness I had brought on myself. When I'd get off the bus on the Wesleyan campus, I'd walk by everybody hangin' out, buzzin' about their big plans for the weekend, and head up the hill to my room, where I'd spend the entire weekend with my captor.

—

"C'mon, it'll be fun," my mother cheered, perched at the bottom of my mattress on the floor. I was lying on my side, looking past her, at the closet—home to the demon that had kept me up until just before she'd arrived. "You always loved to bowl."

Is she out of her mind?! Bowling?! It'd take a fuckin' miracle for me just to sit up, my brain screamed as I kept watch over the closet. "I can't," I said, pulling my sheet up around my face.

"Come on, Little Bo Peep. I'll help ya." She stood up, came around behind me on the mattress, got onto her knees, slid her arms through mine, and hoisted me into a sitting position. My mother's belief that I was salvageable, her conviction that I could be brought back, was unshakable and moved me beyond anything I could ever put into words.

An hour later, at the bowling alley, in the size-seven shoes my mom had rented for me, while the demon called my name, I bowled a strike. Now, if that's not a fuckin' miracle!

—

So that was my semester. My mom would drive up to Wesleyan once a week in her little red pickup truck, take me to the diner for a cheese sandwich and a Diet Coke, and then we'd go bowling. I continued sitting through my classes, seeing and hearing things no one else did.

I spent the summer with my mom in Sag Harbor, mostly sleeping or sitting on the back porch wrapped in my grandma Lena's blanket, praying the stripes held still. At the end of the summer, I tried to go back to school. I got as far as the first hour on campus before calling my mom to tell her to look for a bowling alley closer to home.

Maybe Jack Warden was tougher than me. Maybe he wasn't. War is war. And all I knew was that there was no way I could serve another tour on the Wesleyan campus.

15

The next thing I knew, I'd been deployed to 7M—a furnished studio apartment across from the elevators in the Windermere Hotel. My dad was still stationed in 22K. Down the hall from me was a crazy Chinese woman—a lifer, not a new recruit like me. The first time I heard her screaming, I ran to my door, thinking someone was being stabbed. When I looked out my peephole, all I saw was a ninety-pound woman with long black hair, in a nightgown and slippers that were way too big for her. She was hunched over, pacing frantically back and forth, ranting and raving in Chinese, angrily shaking her fists over her head. In the war she was in, she'd been assigned to patrol the elevators right outside my door, where, unfortunately for me, her invisible tormentors seemed to live.

I ended up enrolled at The New School. It wasn't like Wesleyan, with all its cliques and bustling social scene. No one hung out after class or knew anyone else's name. I fit right in because everybody seemed as adrift as I was.

I went to school at night, taking classes about social media: the effects of social media on the population; the effects of the population on social media; the effects of social media on social media; the effects of the population on the population. During the day, I did the Upper West Side shuffle, wandering between Ninety-Second Street and Seventy-Second Street in my Mellaril/Stelazine semicoma. My eyes glazed over, shoulders hunched up to my ears, tongue resting in my parched mouth like an alligator in a cave with no water. The side effects of all the meds were brutal, and brutally cumulative. They kept me from going completely insane but turned me into the walking dead.

I spent most of my time sitting by my window smoking or watching TV. But the activity that consumed me as much as it eluded me was sleep. Ever since my break, I'd been ravaged by insomnia. I was berserk inside, and so used to being knocked out by drugs and alcohol that even with meds, I could not sleep. Being excruciatingly exhausted all the time was like pouring gasoline on all my other symptoms. After being up all night for nights, the only way I could get through the days, which were all running together, was to constantly drink coffee and smoke cigarettes, which annihilated any chance of getting to sleep that night. I'd be up all night again. My sadistic perpetrator degraded me with depraved, violent, sexual, cartoon-like images. I could never keep anything like a razor or scissors where I could see it; the sight of a potential weapon would arouse the madman in my mind to demand I use it against myself. On those rare occasions when the miracle of sleep did find me, my gratitude was immeasurable. Imagine how disturbing it was to be jolted out of a deep sleep by the crazy Chinese lady doing battle at the top of her lungs right outside my door. But my anger at having been woken was always tempered by how terrible I felt for her. When she got even louder and more agitated than usual, her mother, a small, elderly, infinitely weary-looking woman, would come get her. When I poked my head outside my door, the old woman would stare at me before gently coaxing her daughter, who was still yelling at the carpet, down the long hallway, back to their apartment. It moved me profoundly that even after all these years, she was so tender and patient with her mentally ill daughter.

I'd get to see my own mother once a week, when she'd drive the three hours into the city to teach her woodworking class at the Y on the Upper East Side. She'd stay over on the pullout in her friend Mary's living room, then get up early the next morning and drive back to Sag Harbor. Mary lived in our old building on Eighty-Fifth Street. There were nights when, at four in the morning, ground down to a place of such exhausted desperation, I'd call my mom, throw a coat over my nightgown, jump into a taxi, quietly open the door my mom had left unlocked for me, and climb in bed next to her. The smell of her skin, the warmth of her body, felt like it might just save me. I'd spent my entire life trying to get out of bed with my mother, and now it was the only thing in this whole world that gave me any real comfort.

Usually, I'd fall asleep just as Mary and my mom were getting up. The smell of coffee filled the apartment as they both prepared to greet the day. I would shuffle the eight blocks back to the Windermere, trying not to get knocked over by the dangerously caffeinated nine-to-fivers racing to get to work. As I turned my key in the door to 7M, I always felt like I was returning to the scene of the crime. I'd climb back into bed, pull the covers all the way over my head, and beg God to please, please, please have mercy on my aching mind and body and deliver me, if only briefly, to that magical land of sleep.

A few months into all this sedated shuffling, my parents suggested something that seemed almost as insane as me: I…get…a job! What was I supposed to say my qualifications were? Staring off into space and not attacking myself with my disposable razor?

During a particularly long shuffle I discovered the biggest, densest, most delicious bran muffins in New York City. They lived at a health-food café in midtown. I decided to see if I could get a job there to satisfy my parents and also get closer to the muffins. I asked the very kind young Asian man behind the counter if they were hiring. He smiled sweetly, hired me on the spot, and gave thanks to God. I told my parents, who were both thrilled.

The following day I reported to work at nine a.m. on practically no sleep, and another nice young Asian man handed me a green apron that said HEALTH WORKS. Slipping the apron over my head, I felt a sense of pride I hadn't felt in…I couldn't even tell you how long. The young man explained that I would work behind the counter, which was where the muffins lived.

My job was to label all the little containers of salad dressing. "It's *R* for ranch, *TH* for thousand island, *F* for French, and *HM* for honey mustard," the nice Asian man said, demonstrating with his blue pen. Then he smiled at me, gave thanks to God, and handed me a big red crayon. "This is yours," he said, as if he were handing me a giant gold scepter.

Omigod, I thought, taking the big red crayon from his hand. I was back at the beginning. Back to where it all started. I couldn't believe this. As I stared at my big fucking red crayon, waiting for me to tell it what was wrong with this picture, my mind lost its mind! *What's wrong with this picture? What's wrong with this picture? What* isn't *wrong with this picture? How the fuck did this happen?*

What about your apron? a part of my mind yelled.

The red-crayon part of my mind screamed back: *Fuck the apron! What about the girl with all the promise in the world? The one who got into Stuyvesant, who aced her SATs, who enthralled everyone with hysterical anecdotes, who's been on movie sets with some of the most famous movie stars in the world, and ridden in limousines? I'm Charles Grodin's daughter, for God's sake!*

I noticed other workers staring at me. *Maybe I should start labeling.* I lowered my big red crayon onto a tiny, plastic lid. *HM,* I wrote meticulously, then again and again and again. Every time I completed a label, I'd say, "Honey mustard," under my breath. And then the most unexpected feeling came over me. I felt grateful. Grateful I'd gotten a job where I didn't have to think or feel or *be* anything, just abbreviate "honey mustard"... honey mustard... honey mustard. A tear fell onto my final honey mustard lid, and I heard that little voice that was always getting drowned out by the bully voice whisper, *That's right, honey... you mustered everything inside yourself... just to be here.*

—

I'd been there about three weeks when one afternoon, after I'd finished sneak-eating my second muffin of the day, a heavyset German girl, who was in charge of all the baking, came out of the kitchen and asked if I'd like to join a group of the people who worked there selling little stuffed animals in Times Square to raise money for their church on Saturday morning.

"What church?" I asked, surreptitiously wiping the muffin crumbs off my apron.

"The Church of the Reverend Sun Myung Moon. God's time is now," she said, smiling, as she pulled a little stuffed monkey on a stick from her apron pocket. As she handed me the little monkey, I glanced over her shoulder at everyone working in the kitchen: the tall German guy, staring into his caldron of soup, was married to the fräulein with the monkey; the chubby Asian girl chopping vegetables, staring at her chopping board, was married to the Asian guy who'd hired me; the Norwegian woman, folding and staring at a humongous pile of napkins, was about to marry the Swedish guy stocking the coolers.

"Well, what do you think?" the fräulein said, smiling even wider.

What do I think? I've accidentally joined the Moonies! my head screamed. I smiled back at the fräulein and had to admit to myself that these Moonies were some of the nicest, calmest people I'd ever met. And honestly, I found all their talk of God extremely comforting. Plus, I was just so happy to have a place to go where I felt I belonged, even a little. And it wasn't like I had anything else to do on Saturday besides chain-smoke, stare off into space, and listen to the Chinese lady. "Okay, yes," I said, clutching my monkey in one hand and my big red crayon in the other.

Three days later, at eight a.m., I was standing on the corner of Moonie and Forty-Second Street, right across from Moonie headquarters. It was an aggressively sunny, cold morning and I hadn't sold one monkey. Caitlin, a tall, big-boned Irish girl, with piercing blue eyes and curly blonde hair, had sold six key chains, four monkeys, and two stuffed mice. Caitlin was their top seller, and although she was happy to "train" me, she'd just informed me that she wouldn't be able to meet next Saturday because she was getting married.

"Really?" I said, moving my monkey to my other hand so my right hand could take a break.

"Yes, the Reverend Sun Myung Moon will be marrying us and twelve other couples at our church," she said, smiling, as she stared at something in the distance.

"Well, that's great. And you're in love?" I asked, trying to find what she was looking at.

"Of course, the Reverend picked him," she said, shaking her monkey at a fat family of tourists, all dressed in matching orange tracksuits.

"How long have you been with the church?" I asked, shaking my monkey at the little boy, who stuck his tongue out at me.

"Four years," she said with the same lack of inflection she'd said everything else.

"How did you come to the church?" I wondered how many questions I'd be allowed before Caitlin whispered into her monkey's ear and a van of Moonies pulled up, forced me inside, and took me to meet their leader!

While Caitlin told me, in her no-inflection voice, her long, heartbreaking story of leaving North Dakota as a teenager, having been molested for years by her alcoholic stepfather, getting addicted to drugs, being homeless, and living in the shelter system, I tried to imagine myself as a Moonie. They'd definitely take me. In time, I'd learn how to sell more monkeys, probably get a promotion, surrender my big red crayon, maybe even learn how to make those giant muffins. When the Reverend felt I was ready, he'd handpick a husband for me, and I'd be married alongside my Moonie brothers and sisters from all over the world. I could just hear my grandma Lena: *First she wants to hack off her tits, now she's marrying a Moonie. It's bad enough she's not marrying a Jew, but a Moonie! What did anyone ever do to her that she's gotta join the Moonies?* I handed Caitlin the rest of my monkeys, wished her luck with her upcoming nuptials, and started toward home.

Home. I repeated the word over and over in my mind, until it sounded like a chant echoing up from the bottom of my soul. No matter how strange it seemed to me, that was something all those Moonies had found with each other. I'd found a home too: the House of Drugs and Alcohol, but that home was long gone. They had something else I couldn't quite put my finger on. And as I made my left on Broadway to walk down my street, it hit me. Their faith. That's what had really been so compelling to me. The home inside. That's what I was searching for. I just didn't know it yet.

16

A week later, my dad called, offering me a home. He'd been working out in LA and hated that I was in New York without him. So did I. The endless stimulation of the city and commotion outside my door didn't help the noise in my head. A few days later, my mom was meeting me in the lobby to drive me to JFK. When the elevator doors opened, my mom was standing there next to the crazy Chinese lady and her mother. The Chinese lady appeared to be softly reprimanding someone in the carpet.

I smiled at the elderly woman. She glanced down at my suitcase, then up at me. She looked me right in the eye, nodded twice, then smiled so effusively, clearly wishing me well out there in the world—a world she knew didn't exist for her daughter.

"Ready?" my mom asked, giggling as she looped her arm in mine.

"Not really," I replied, laughing nervously as I walked into my next chapter.

—

Over the next couple months, I lived with my dad and his wife Elissa in a big, beautiful house on a hill, with a pool, overlooking Laurel Canyon. Inside, the whole house was white—white walls, white furniture, white carpet, which I loved. It made me feel like I was living in a really nice mental hospital where I was the only patient. My dad was amazing! He did everything he could to ensure I was having the best time possible during my stay at "the Grodin Psychiatric Center." We took lots of long drives on the Pacific Coast Highway, along the ocean, with the top down, listening to our favorite songs on the radio. My dad loved "Rikki Don't Lose That Number" by Steely Dan. I'd watch him bopping his head, singing along, bracing myself for when the high notes came, because he'd always really go for it, which would reduce me to tears of laughter. A lot of these long drives would end in dinner at a fancy restaurant. We both loved Moonshadows on the ocean. Sometimes it was just the two of us; sometimes we'd meet up with famous friends of his. Watching my dad and Dabney Coleman comedically spar, I always felt like I had the best ticket in town. Watching Jessica Lange do absolutely nothing was riveting. Peter Falk and his wife, Shera, came to the house a lot for dinner. They were an unusual and interesting couple. Shera, who'd played the head hooker in the movie *Risky Business*, was tough, brassy, and street-smart. Peter was as un-self-conscious, earnest, and purely inquisitive as the character that had made him a star.

"Now, Chuck, when you say, 'This is the best chicken you've ever had,' do you mean in your whole life, or would you be referring to more recently?" Sometimes I'd close my eyes and pretend that Columbo had dropped by for dinner.

When I moved to LA, the plan was that I'd live with my dad until I found my own place. Frankly, I was hoping that was off the table, and I thought it was until the day my dad walked into the kitchen and said, "I just got some great news."

Jumping up to sit on the counter, I said, "Great, what?"

"I think I found you an apartment." Excited, he grabbed an apple from the large bowl of fruit next to me. "You want one?" he asked, gesturing toward the fruit bowl.

"No, thanks," I said, stunned.

"Actually, Ria found it." He jumped up on the counter across from me. Ria was one of his best friends, someone I adored.

"Where is it?" I asked nervously.

"Beverly Hills. She says it's really cute, and it's right across from—"

"Wait. Why did you say you *think* you found me an apartment?" I interrupted.

Suddenly somber, he said, "Ah, boy, someone's living there right now—"

"And they might not move out?" I asked hopefully.

"No, she's definitely moving out. It's just not clear exactly when," he said gravely. "The woman living there is very old and in extremely poor health." He choked up slightly.

"I'm waiting for somebody to die?"

"Ria says it'll be any day now. She puts it at a week—max," he said softly. "Of course, they'll have it all cleaned out, y'know, after..." He looked away, unable to finish the sentence.

"After she dies?!" I erupted, staring at him.

Just then the phone rang. "That could be the call," my dad whispered as he pushed himself off the counter.

Over the next week, there were daily calls between my father and Ria, trying to determine, as delicately as possible, what my potential move date might be. Two days in a row, Ria had reported the appearance of paramedic and a van marked SPECIALTY MEDICAL—OXYGEN TANKS. Then one afternoon we got the call. The woman had died the previous morning. I felt sad for both of us. Nine days later, feeling as empty and dark as the narrow, windy, canyon road I was driving down, I had a nagging feeling I'd forgotten something very important at my dad's house. I kept wanting to turn around and drive back up the hill to get it. It was the part of me that had felt so safe, protected, taken care of—rescued—all those months I'd been living under my father's roof.

As I drove farther away from my dad's house, past the Rexall and the supermarket we always went to, I started to feel more and more anxious. I flashed back to that first day at Wesleyan, when I was so scared, I'd chased my mom and dad in the car. By the time I'd parked my car and lugged my big pink suitcase up to the second floor, I was drenched in sweat—a combination of heavy lifting and heavier worrying. Wheeling my suitcase down the length of the outdoor landing, which was carpeted in a tacky bright-green material, desperate to convince everyone it was grass, I could feel the surface below me shaking. *What a piece of shit; y'know what I could have made a sturdy landing for?!* I heard my mother say.

God, I miss my mom, I thought as I turned the key in the door. I'd never lived anywhere we couldn't drive to see each other. I pulled the suitcase into the living room and flicked on the light switch. Not bad. I dragged my suitcase across the light-brown wall-to-wall carpet. A cute little alcove opened into a very cute little kitchen.

I walked through the kitchen, which led to a bathroom and then to a small bedroom. Pretty damn cute and, wow, really quiet. I fell back on the bed delivered that morning, closed my eyes, kicked off my shoes, and placed my hands over my heart. I could feel myself calming down as my breathing started to slow.

"Ahhhhhhhhhhhh..." I exhaled noisily, visualizing all the stress, all the anxiety, leaving my body.

"Ahhhhhhhhh..." I exhaled again.

From the other side of my bedroom wall, came someone else's "Ahhhhhh..."

Adrenaline shot through me again. From a standing position, I stared at the wall, my eyes wide, listening. Nothing. Nothing.

Then, "Ahhhhhhhh...Mohammed...," followed by screaming, then incredibly loud banging, like someone was trying to break through my wall with one of those torpedo-looking things SWAT teams use when they burst through a drug cartel's door. Then a loud, bloodcurdling scream. Then more loud banging. Then silence. I stared at the wall and wondered if Mohammed had fucked some poor woman to death.

I decided to take a long, hot shower to calm myself, and just as I started out of the bedroom, the banging started again. Perhaps he had killed her and was now trying to fuck her corpse through my wall to dispose of the evidence. I grabbed a towel and toiletries from my suitcase and headed into the bathroom. As I stepped into the shower, I dropped my head forward, praying the hot water would pummel the stress right out of my head. I discovered a little window inside the shower and cracked it, grateful for the cool night air drifting in, dancing around my face. Twenty minutes later, I turned the water off, pulled the shower curtain back, and thrust my head as far forward as it would go, listening. No banging. Good. I reached for my towel.

Trying not to get the carpet wet, I tiptoed into the living room and stood over my suitcase. "Too tired, you'll all have to wait till tomorrow," I said to the clothes staring up at me. I tiptoed into the bedroom, slipped my nightgown over my head, made the bed, and was just about to crawl into it when I decided that my favorite purple silk blouse had to be hung. I pulled back the sliding door on the enormous closet next to my bed and saw a giant oxygen tank, replete with dangling hoses and a mask, as if it had all just been ripped from someone's face. I hung my blouse as far away from the tank as possible. I shut the light off, climbed into bed, and had just started my breathing exercises when the banging started up again. Other people fucking and a giant oxygen tank—two of the worst housewarming presents!

Over the next week, I got Mohammed to move his bed off our shared wall. Actually, I moved Mohammed's bed off our wall with his resentful assistance. I got a job waiting tables at Junior's Deli in Los Angeles. The uniform was a brown polyester dress—too tight on top, too loose on the bottom, and hit me below the knee. It always stank of corned beef by the time I got home. The head waitress was a chain-smoking, chubby little troll named Penny, a name whose effervescence completely misrepresented who this evil bitch was. Penny basked in her power as head waitress and took enormous, visible pleasure in waiting till your shift had ended and you were just about to walk out the door to tell you that you had to fill all the ketchup bottles, or fold all the napkins, or clean out some disgusting refrigerator. Penny was a widow. A few years before, her husband had committed suicide, I assumed to get away from Penny.

When I wasn't waiting on customers or executing one of Penny's sadistic chores, I could be found over in Junior's Bakery, sneaking as much sugar-free mandel bread as I could without getting caught. I did eventually get caught and fired by Penny, who looked practically orgasmic when she asked for my brown polyester dress back.

Two days later I got a job waiting tables in a chichi French café in Beverly Hills. Another not-great fit, but it was all I could find. I'd been there about a month when one afternoon, the owner, who'd just flown in from France, was holed up in a corner, smoking, and drinking espresso, just *watching*. At the end of my shift, the manager pointed out that all afternoon the owner had observed me enthusiastically offering customers our special of the day, "crotch paté." How was I supposed to know how to pronounce "Croix"? I'm not fuckin' French. I was pretty certain my days at La Patisserie were numbered.

It was Saturday night, and I was sitting on my bed, having just finished a Lifetime movie marathon. They were all movies with the word "stranger" in the title: *The Stranger Beside Me, The Stranger Inside Me, The Stranger Who Is Me*. Then *It's a Living*, a funny show about waitresses working in a high-class restaurant, was just coming on. Staring at the oxygen tank that still hadn't been picked up, I sang along with the show's theme music: "Life's not the French Riviera.... Life's not a charity ball..."

"Ain't that the truth," I said to the TV.

The phone rang.

"Hey," my dad said.

"Hey." I turned down the volume.

"I have some news I think you're gonna be very happy to hear," he said, barely able to contain his enthusiasm.

"The oxygen people called to tell you we can keep the tank?" I said sarcastically.

"They still haven't come, huh?"

"Not yet."

"Well, I don't think you're gonna be thinking about the oxygen tank when I tell you my news. I spoke to Marlo's brother, Tony Thomas—I'm sure you've met him at Marlo's, at some dinner, or maybe one year at Thanksgiving. Anyway, he read your *Cheers* spec," he said, bursting, "and he wants you to meet with the producers on one of his sitcoms about being a staff writer!"

"But they don't even know me." I walked over to the oxygen tank.

"They flipped for your script!" my dad said, laughing.

"Really? Flipped?" I examined the tags around the neck of the oxygen tank, trying to find a phone number other than the one I'd already called.

"They thought it was excellent. The executive producer's an old friend of mine. And of course, Tony, I've known forever. They want to meet you tomorrow for lunch on the lot. Isn't this great?!"

"It is, but I don't want anyone to hire me just because I'm your daughter," I said softly.

"Honey, nobody gives a fuck who your father is. Trust me. Maybe it gets you in the door, but that's it. This business is way too tough to hire you just because your father is Charles Grodin."

"That's true," I said.

"Hey, whatever happened with that guy on your wall?"

"I helped him move his bed off the wall." I laughed.

"That's my girl. You think I would have shown them your script if I didn't think you could do the job? They'd be crazy not to hire you. And if, for any reason, they don't hire you—which I believe they will—we'll get you a job as a mover." We both laughed. "I'm getting another call. I should take this; it's Marlo. I'll leave all the information on your answering machine. Call me after the meeting."

"I will. Thanks so much. I love you."

"I love you."

Just as I was about to lay the phone back in its cradle, I grabbed it back to my ear. "Dad, you still there?"

"I'm here."

"What's the name of the show?"

"*Earning a Living.... Making a Living,*" he said, trying to remember.

"*It's a Living*?!"

"That's it. Do you know it?"

"I'm watching it," I said in disbelief.

"You're kidding. Let me talk to Marlo, and I'll call you right back!" he said, laughing.

As I hung up the phone, there was a knock at the door. "Unbelievable," I said, laughing, as I hurried toward the door.

"Omigod, you must be here for the tank," I said, smiling at the middle-aged black man wearing a uniform that said SPECIALTY MEDICAL.

"Unless you're not ready to—" he said affably.

"No, no," I said, laughing as I interrupted. "Come in. It's in the bedroom." As I watched him carry out the oxygen tank, I took a deep breath and thought, *I hope I am ready to breathe all on my own.*

—

"Both Marc and myself were very impressed with your spec script," the distinguished-looking older man said, taking a sip of his lemon Perrier.

"Very," said Marc, the attractive, ambitious brown-haired boy wonder of the team. A tiny piece of chicken from his Cobb salad flew out his mouth and landed on my hand.

"Ah, thank you. I really appreciate that," I said, wiping the little piece of chicken off my hand as discreetly as possible before squirming to excavate the pantyhose burrowed deep in my ass.

"You've clearly inherited your dad's phenomenal sense of humor," Bob said, smiling.

"Thank you," I said, reminding myself to breathe as I glanced around the bustling commissary.

"I've known your dad for, God, it must be at least twenty years now," Bob said, waving to Delta Burke at a nearby table.

"Shame she's gotten so heavy," Bob whispered.

My stomach immediately sucked itself in.

"Anyway, Marc and I are both *huge* fans of your dad," Bob said.

"*Huge*," Marc said, a tiny piece of avocado flying onto the saltshaker in front of Bob. "*The Heartbreak Kid*?! That scene at the dinner table where your dad's sitting next to Cybill Shepherd, trying to win over Eddie Albert, and he says, he says, whew, he says..." Overtaken by a laughing fit, which quickly turned into a coughing fit, Marc covered his mouth with his napkin as he tried to compose himself.

"You okay?" Bob said, offering Marc his lemon Perrier.

Nodding as he placed both his hands on the table to steady himself, Marc took a deep breath and said, "'There's no deceit in the cauliflower.' And Eddie Albert's just staring at him. For my taste, it doesn't get any better than that!" Marc continued aggressively. "Bob, am I right?"

"Absolutely!" Bob said so adamantly, a couple waiters turned around.

"He improvised a lot of that," I offered proudly.

For a moment they both just stared at me admiringly as they nodded their heads slowly up and down. Finally, having no idea what else to do, I also began nodding my head slowly up and down.

"One of the all-time greats!" Marc declared, beaming at me.

"Funny you should say that; he actually wrote and starred in a play called *One of the All-Time Greats*," I said.

"The man can do it all!" Bob said, beaming at me.

"He really can," I said, wondering if this staff writer job even existed.

"And don't even get me started on his *Tonight Show* appearances. Genius; I've never seen anyone take on Johnny like your dad. Have you, Marc?"

"Never!" Marc said adamantly.

"Actually, he was under contract to *The Tonight Show* for a long time," I said. I eyed Delta Burke's hot-fudge sundae and contemplated staying after Bob and Marc left and ordering the same thing.

"What was that movie where he played a lawyer?" Marc asked as the pretty blonde waitress arrived at our table. "Julie, can we get this cleared, and we'll take a check."

"Absolutely, Mr. Sotkin," Julie said good-naturedly.

"That's my mom's name," I said as Julie loaded our dishes onto her already full tray.

"Really?" she said, smiling at me, as I passed her my plate.

"Now, does she go by Julie Grodin?" Bob asked intensely.

"She does."

"And what does she do?" Marc asked with such intense curiosity, it took everything I had not to say, *Astronaut; my mom's an astronaut.*

"She makes furniture and works at ARF—Animal Rescue Fund—out in East Hampton, taking care of animals," I said proudly.

"*Seems Like Old Times*!" Marc said, slamming his hand on the table. "I couldn't think of it till you said animals."

"Right, right, where Chuck played a lawyer who was married to Goldie Hawn, and they had all those dogs. Chevy Chase was her ex-husband, and some kind of criminal," he said, chuckling.

"He really is the best," Bob said as both he and Marc pushed their chairs back from the table and stood up.

"One of the all-time greats," I said, forcing a laugh as I stole a glance at Delta's sundae.

"Well, thanks so much for meeting with us," Bob said.

Marc glanced down at his diamond-encrusted watch. "Bob, we've gotta go. I didn't realize how late it was; we've got that conference call at two." Marc shook my hand.

"Right. Right. Be sure to give your dad my regards," Bob said, squeezing my shoulder.

"Definitely," I said, having no idea how to navigate the next moment, praying I didn't look as desperate as I felt. "So should I call you guys or—?"

"That won't be necessary," Mark said perfunctorily.

I felt my stomach flip, hard. I was mortified. I'd thought the lunch went well.

After what felt, to me, like an eternity, Bob cleared his throat and said, “You don’t need to call. Just come in Monday, and we’ll introduce you to everybody.” He squeezed my shoulder again before he and Marc hurried across the commissary.

I stood there for a moment, just soaking it all in. I couldn’t believe it. I’d walked into this place a girl who was about to get fired for offering everybody crotch paté, and I was walking out a *fucking staff writer*! I floated across the commissary.

“Hey, have a great day,” Julie said as I passed her balancing an enormous tray of dirty dishes on her shoulder.

“I’m a staff writer!” I whispered, pulling a twenty-dollar bill out of my pocket.

“Good for you,” she said, laughing as I tucked the twenty in her apron. She wasn’t *my* Julie, but she’d have to do until I got home.

17

I'd been writing for *It's a Living* for about two months. The rest of the writers were all men in their forties, fifties, and sixties. It was a typical Friday night. We were into our tenth hour in the writer's room, trying desperately to finish the episode we'd be shooting Monday morning. For the last hour, we'd all been pitching punch lines to Bob for a setup Marc had come up with for the actress Ann Jillian. I'd been sitting in the same chair, in the same position, for so long that my ass and both my feet were completely asleep. Their message was clear: *You can keep talking, but we've had about as much of this shit as we can take!* There was no doubt that I was physically exhausted, but honestly, I was way more mentally exhausted from the award-worthy performance I'd been giving as the dedicated young sitcom writer ever since I'd gotten the job.

In a sitcom writer's room, even though everyone already

has the job, you never stop feeling like you're auditioning. (An excruciating aspect of all of show business.) So everyone pitches—sells their fucking ass off—because the goal is to get as many of your jokes into that final script as possible.

Remember *The Gong Show*? It's kind of like that. Everyone's just trying their damnedest not to get the gong. And there are many forms the gong can take. It might be as simple as either Bob or Marc looking away in the middle of your pitch, or exchanging a subtle but definite look at the height of your pitch, when you were your sweatiest and most animated—possibly even standing or doing your best French accent. But by far, the worst was when either Bob or Marc would suddenly launch into a discussion of what to order for lunch or dinner. You're jumping around like a fuckin' French monkey, and all of a sudden you hear, "I'd love to order from that new Thai fusion place tonight. . . . Bob, how 'bout you?"

But, for me, far more torturous than pitching was the unspoken expectation that everyone, besides, of course, Bob and Marc, was supposed to laugh at everything that came out of anyone's mouth. Some days I'd fake-laughed so much, I felt like my face was going to seize up and I'd end up in some clinic where there were all these other failed sitcom writers whose faces were also stuck in a big-ass fake laugh.

I felt like a fraud. Everyone else on staff had chosen this and worked very hard, some of these guys for many years, just to be here. I hadn't. Everyone was incredibly nice, and no one ever mentioned it, but I knew that everyone knew. Whenever anyone asked me how I got such an amazing job at such a young age, I'd launch into some bullshit about writing samples, submissions, my *Cheers* spec, but I wanted to say, *Two years ago I had a complete psychotic break from drugs and alcohol, the kind most people don't come back from. It's only fairly recently that I've stopped seeing and hearing shit that wasn't there. I really have no idea what I'm supposed to do with my life. But my father's Charles Grodin, so now I'm a sitcom writer*. No matter how good a writer I may have actually been, I ended up feeling like a fake. Trust me, privilege ain't all it's cracked up to be. Privilege can leave you feeling really underprivileged inside yourself, and that's the only place that truly matters.

We finally came up with that punch line for Ann Jillian. Our meeting broke and we all began walking back to our offices kibitzing about plans for the weekend. I didn't have any. I never had any, other than watching a Lifetime marathon or driving up the hill to my dad's for dinner. I didn't have any friends in LA.

"How'd it go?" Mindy asked. She was the twenty-two-year-old production assistant whose office was across the lot from mine.

"Good," I said, marveling at the height of Mindy's pompadouresque hairstyle.

I had extremely long blonde hair, which I wore pulled back on both sides of my head, secured with barrettes. Throughout the day, I would watch Mindy tug on the front of her hair, locking it into place with an industrial-size can of Aqua Net Extra Hold Hair Spray. She kept the can in her side drawer, along with a pack of Newports, several candy bars, and a makeup case so large it could have been a plumber's kit.

"I just got the schedule for this month; your episode's on it," she continued, beaming at me. "I still can't get over that you're only twenty-three and you're on staff with all these older guys. You must be so talented!"

"Thanks."

"You have any plans for the weekend?" She grabbed a couple of Jolly Ranchers from her drawer, popped a shiny purple candy into her mouth, and held the other candy toward me.

"No, thanks. Uh...not really." Marc and Bob and some of the other writers were all huddled together, laughing outside Mindy's office. She stared at me, hopefully. Mindy had been asking me to hang out since I'd gotten the job.

"It's supposed to be really nice tomorrow. Supposed to get up to eighty. I was thinking about going over to the Santa Monica Pier and just walking around."

"Sure," I said, surprising both of us.

"Really?"

"Yeah, why not. Sounds great...." I reached for the green Jolly Rancher on her desk.

"Wow, great.... Let's meet there at... does three work?"

"Perfect," I said, thrilled to have just made my first friend in LA.

Over the next couple weeks, Mindy and I would meet up every Saturday at the Santa Monica Pier and walk around, taking in the sights. I loved the Pier! It reminded me of Coney Island, but nicer. Everybody was out Rollerblading, riding bikes, playing Frisbee. Plus, there were all these people performing—singing, dancing, playing guitar. One Saturday afternoon, Mindy and I were down at the Pier strolling along, enjoying our frozen yogurt, when we found ourselves moving our heads to an insanely rhythmic technotronic beat, pulsating from somewhere in the distance. We looked at each other and started walking faster in the direction of the beat. As we got closer, we saw an enormous crowd gathered around the action. Mindy and I smiled at each other, tossed our cones in the big garbage can outside the pizza place, and tackled the crowd.

"I can't see, can you?" I called to Mindy as I struggled to stand on my tippy-toes.

"C'mon," she said, taking my hand as she pushed us through the sea of gyrating bodies.

All of a sudden everyone began clapping, loudly and in unison.

"What's happening?" I yelled at the back of Mindy's pompadour as she pushed us through to the very front, where we managed to squeeze in next to a group of hot young Spanish girls dressed in miniskirts and Spandex.

"Go Papi, go Papi," they were chanting as they clapped and seductively moved their bodies to the beat.

Mindy and I looked at each other, giggling, as we started clapping, and chanting, "Go Papi, go Papi..."

In the center of the circle was the biggest boom box I'd ever seen. Next to it was an enormous white bucket. Six feet from the boom box, on both sides of it, were half a dozen muscular young black men in jeans and tight-fitting tank tops, their perfect muscles glistening with sweat. They were also clapping. All of a sudden, a very handsome dark-skinned man, who appeared to be the leader, thrust his right hand high into the air to "count it down" as the other young men nodded their heads energetically, along with his count. The electricity in the air was palpable, the sound of the clapping almost deafening. We could all feel something amazing was about to happen.

Suddenly two young men on opposite sides of the boom box ran as fast as they could toward the middle of the circle, then just as they got there, they each hurled their bodies off the ground. They somersaulted past each other in the air before landing in a split. The crowd went nuts, applauding, fist-pumping, whistling. The Spanish girls exchanged a bunch of high fives as Mindy and I looked at each other, mouthing, *OMIGOD*, at the exact same moment. Then, the leader, on one side, and another very tall, good-looking guy, on the other side, ran into the middle of the circle as the music suddenly got much faster. Interlocking arms and feet, they executed a series of breathtaking gymnastic dance moves.

Half an hour later, Mindy and I were waiting our turn in line to meet our new crushes.

"How you ladies doin'?" the handsome, dark-skinned leader said as his partner lit a cigarette.

"You guys were amazing!" Mindy gushed.

"Thank you. I'm Lawrence," he said with unexpected humility. "And this is Derek."

"Mindy," she said in a voice I'd never heard come out of her mouth before—breathy, Marilyn Monroe-y. I stared at this new version of my friend. Lawrence extended his hand. Mindy shook it for a long time. Finally, feeling the weight of my stare, she said, "Sorry. This is my best friend, Marion."

"You guys are incredible," I squealed.

Suddenly one of the other dancers whistled loudly from down the Pier. "Yo, our ride is leaving."

"Can I get your number?" Lawrence asked grinning at Mindy.

"Definitely." Marilyn Monroe whispered, digging a pen and piece of paper out of her purse. I stood there self-consciously until finally Derek asked for my number.

"I'll call you," Lawrence said to Mindy as he and Derek ran down the Pier.

"Omigod, he's hot," Mindy screamed, looping her arm in mine as we began strolling, leisurely, toward the end of the Pier.

The sun had just gone down, and the lights on all the rides were on. "Wasn't he?" Mindy asked before taking her giant can of Aqua Net out of her purse and giving that front piece a quick spray.

"He was," I said. I unclipped my barrettes and put them in my pants pocket.

We got to the end of the Pier and leaned over the railing.

"Give me that," I said, wiggling two fingers at her cigarette.

"I thought you quit," she said, letting me take the cigarette out of her hand.

"You can always unquit," I said, closing my eyes as I took a long, deep drag on it.

18

"Who needs something to drink?" I called from the kitchen.

"I'll take a soda," Mindy yelled from the living room.

"Water's good," Lawrence yelled.

"Derek?" I asked, handing Mindy and Lawrence their drinks.

Derek just shook his head no as I popped in a mixtape I'd just made.

Mindy was sitting between Lawrence's legs on the floor, her head on his chest, resting between bouts of making out. Every once in a while, she'd lift her head and say something to me while Lawrence rubbed her calves, triggering more making out.

Derek was seated at one end of the couch. I sat down at the other end. We both stared straight ahead, like people waiting to get the results of their colonoscopies. Just when I felt like I could not stand one more second of this, the Pointer Sisters came to the rescue: *"He's so shy…,"* the ladies sang, and Lawrence and Mindy both began giggling.

"Okay, okay, I get it," Derek said, annoyed, as he jumped up.

"He can't help it; he's just like that. Don't take it personally," Lawrence said sweetly as he caressed Mindy's calf.

"I'll take a glass of water," Derek said, and I nodded so enthusiastically, you'd have thought he'd just come out of a coma.

Derek followed me into the kitchen. As I poured him a glass of water from the sink, I could feel the warmth of his breath on the back of my neck. I turned around to hand him the glass of water and our eyes locked. I could feel myself getting excited, just as the Pointer Sisters launched into "I'm So Excited." *Thank you, Sisters, but I believe your work here is done*, I thought to myself as Derek, cupping my buttocks in each of his hands, lifted me into the air, and I wrapped my legs around him. He carried me into the bedroom while we kept kissing.

Derek took his pants and his underwear off. The sight of his erection made me think returning that oxygen tank may have been a little premature.

I took my clothes off, and we climbed under the covers. I hadn't been naked with anybody in such a long time, I'd forgotten how heavenly it felt. We held each other, kissing, our limbs all deliciously intertwined. After a couple minutes, he climbed on top of me. I took a couple deep breaths in preparation, but... Omigod... I needed the tank! I'd never had anything that deep inside me—I felt like I was smuggling a challah bread. "Omigod," I heard myself exhale as suddenly my body just let go, letting him even deeper inside me. As Salt-N-Pepa pounded the air in the next room, "Push it—push it real good..." I shut my eyes, trying not to laugh. Derek slid his hands under me, rocking me gently back and forth as I heard, "Ohhhhh... Derek... Ohhhh, Derek," tumble from my mouth. A second later, drifting in from the living room, I heard, "Oh...Ohhhhh...Lawrence...ohhhhh, Lawrence," followed a couple of seconds later by, "Ohhhhhh, ohhhh, Mohammed...," coming through my wall.

Derek and I cracked up as he pulled himself out of me, and rolled toward the nightstand. I was peripherally aware that Derek was reaching for something. I heard the click of the lighter. *He's smoking a cigarette,* I thought, closing my eyes. Then I smelled it. I couldn't fuckin' believe it. He was smoking a joint. I rolled over to him, laying my head on his chest. Breathing in the pungent pot smoke as it drifted leisurely out of Derek's mouth, I realized I was completely unprepared for this moment. Since my breakdown, I hadn't been around anyone getting high. I braced myself in case I was rendered immediately insane, took the joint from Derek, placed it in my mouth, closed my lips around it, and took a modest hit. I glanced around the room nervously. After a minute, when the Devil hadn't whispered in my ear and no bat had flown out of the closet, I thought maybe this was...okay. As Derek climbed back on top of me, the joint turned around in his mouth, he began giving me a shotgun. I shut my eyes, singing along in my mind with the Al Green song pouring in from the living room.

"Just call on me, baby, and come back home...."

19

The next morning, driving to the lot, I opted not to turn on my usual talk radio station, since the conversation in my head was so loud.

What a night. Omigod. I'm sore. Crazy, but soooooooo fun!

Agreed, but it has to be an isolated incident.

You don't need to tell me that. Seriously.

You cannot let the whole thing start up again.

And I won't! I mean, I know I can't drink.

After spending the last year and a half clawing your way out of Hell, ya think?!

There's no part of me that even associates alcohol with getting high, partying, or having a good time.

So, what's your point?

If I just keep it to pot and only do it every once in a while, maybe...

Before the sane part of me could respond, I switched on the radio.

—

So began my life as a double agent: during the week, I was a hardworking, successful sitcom writer who had just had her first television script produced; on the weekend, I was that other girl again who could be found at the Pier, clad in a miniskirt or Spandex, standing next to my best friend at the front of the circle, cheering on my sexy boyfriend while he blew everyone's minds. My personal mind-blowing came when the sun went down.

Marilyn was back, along with Marianne and Miriam, all of which Derek would call me—everything but my actual name. I joked about it to Mindy, but it was a constant reminder that this guy I was fucking and getting fucked up with had no idea who I really *was*. One Saturday night after the Pier, the four of us were at my apartment, sitting around, eating pizza, listening to music, when Derek stood up and dug deep into his pants pocket, producing a small ball of tinfoil. As if he knew this was his cue, Lawrence stood up. Mindy and I locked eyes, wondering what the fuck was happening. Lawrence began rolling a joint as Derek held a small white rock over it, grinding it between his fingers, sprinkling its flecks into the pot.

I felt my stomach flip. Mindy and I stood up as Derek lit the joint.

Derek took a deep hit, then passed it to Lawrence, who did the same.

Lawrence handed it to Mindy, then me. I was more excited than scared. I loved how chemical it smelled, because I knew that meant I was probably gonna get really high.

20

About a month after I started smoking crack, I began having horrendous mood swings. One minute I was down, the next minute I felt manic. The most disturbing thing was that the swings seemed to come out of nowhere. I decided to see Sharon, a psychiatrist in Santa Monica someone had recommended. I met with her and really liked her, but the only time she had available was Saturday afternoon at five o'clock, right in the middle of my Pier time. I wasn't feeling safe with myself, so even though the time sucked, I agreed. I'd leave the Pier, change out of my shiny unitard with the colorful bandanna tied around my waist into civilian clothing in the car, drive to Santa Monica for my session, then change back into my crackwear and rejoin Mindy, Lawrence, and Derek back at the Pier.

"Are you ever able to trace these mood swings to anything in particular?" Sharon asked, her voice full of concern.

"Not really," I answered, buttoning the last button on my SessionWear! shirt.

"So they don't seem to be triggered by anything going on outside you?" she asked, leaning in.

"They don't," I said, also leaning in.

"Mmmm, so they feel more like they're triggered from within? Would you describe them as ever feeling chemical?" she asked, her eyes full of compassion.

"Yes, yes," I said, excited that we really seemed to be getting somewhere

"More chemical than tied to any particular event?" she continued, mulling over the information.

"Yes, not tied to any particular event," I answered earnestly, neglecting to mention that I was smoking a ton of pot, and now routinely smoking crack. (*How 'bout that particular fucking event?*) I never told her I was smoking crack because it never occurred to my addict brain that it might have something to do with why I was suddenly feeling *so crazy*. What I did tell her was that there was some history of bipolar in my family, and that perhaps I too was suffering from a chemical imbalance. Sharon wrote me a prescription for lithium, told me I'd have to get my kidneys checked at a hospital once a month, and suggested I continue coming to work on my mood swings.

Two weeks later, I started taking lithium. It took a little while, but I noticed I did feel more balanced, despite my crack smoking. What wasn't so balanced was my skin. I'd always had great skin; I had my grandma Lena to thank for that. But about three weeks into taking lithium, I woke up one day, looked in the mirror, and my entire face was covered in severe red acne. I decided it was a sign—not that I needed to stop smoking crack but that I wasn't meant to be on lithium. Crack was in. Lithium was out.

—

Then one night, Derek and I were coming back from the Pier. He was driving; I was in the passenger seat, smoking a cigarette, wearing a silver unitard. We'd just pulled onto my street when we heard "PULL OVER."

"Fuck," we both said, completely panicked. We were high and had more shit on us.

The officers, one black, one white, made us get out of the car, turn around, put our hands on the hood, and then proceeded to pat us down. When they were done, the black officer told us to sit on the curb, while the white officer searched my car. After a few minutes of staring at us, the black officer asked, "What's the relationship between you two?"

"He's my boyfriend. Why?" I said defensively.

"Car's clean," the white officer said.

"This is her *boyfriend*." The black officer sneered.

"What's the issue, Officer?" I asked. Derek glared at me.

"*I* don't have an issue," he said smugly, looking at the other officer.

"You can go," the white officer said.

"What? Because I'm white and he's black, he can't just be my boyfriend?"

"Miriam, shut up," Derek said, pulling me toward the car.

The whole time Derek and I were sitting on that curb, we each had a crack rock tucked in the back of our mouth. We came so close to getting busted, especially with my unhinged this-is-not-my-pimp attitude.

The following week at Sunday night dinner, I was going over to my dad's wife Elissa's brother's house.

"Hi," I said, hugging my dad as he answered the door.

"Hi," he said, hugging me back. "Elissa and Brian are in the kitchen getting dinner ready," he said, walking into the living room.

"Wow, so cute; I love how open it all is," I said as we sat across from each other in floral-print overstuffed armchairs.

"Uh-huh," my dad said, scrutinizing my outfit. "What are you *wearing*?" he said intently.

"What do you mean?" I said, not sure what he was asking.

"What do you call that?" he said, waving his hand in my direction.

"It's a unitard," I answered.

"Isn't that something you'd wear to go dancing?" he continued.

"You could," I answered, suspecting I was about to have to defend the 'tard.

"Are you?" he said.

"Am I what?" I said.

"Going dancing?" he said, his brow furrowing.

"No," I said.

"So...this is what you chose to wear for...Sunday dinner?" he said, holding me in his gaze.

"Uh-huh," I said, laughing uncomfortably as Elissa and Brian's girlfriend walked into the room, each carrying a casserole dish.

"Dinner's on the table," Elissa said.

"Hi, Marion," Elissa and Brian's girlfriend said.

"Hi," I said, checking out what they were wearing. They both had on loose-fitting cloth skirts and billowy blouses. To me, they looked *Amish*. Smiling at my dad as we both rose from our chairs, I said, "I'm a little chilly; I'm gonna go grab a sweater from my car...."

"While you're down there, see if you can find something more like what they're wearing," he said teasingly, waving his hand toward the dining room. We smiled at each other and both laughed before I headed down to my car to try to find something...Amish.

—

Over the months that I'd been seeing my psychiatrist, she'd diagnosed me with obsessive-compulsive disorder. I knew my thinking was obsessive: *What time did my dad say to be at his house for dinner? Seven. He said seven. Or was it six? It's not even dark yet at six. He said seven. He definitely said seven. But what if it's six? Fuck, I knew I should have written it down.*

Lately, a new OCD behavior had surfaced—checking. Lying in bed, trying to get to sleep, I'd get an overpowering impulse to check that the front door was locked or the oven was off, which was really nuts since I'd never actually used the oven. Even though I knew, intellectually, that the front door was locked, and the oven couldn't turn itself on, I'd still have to drag myself out of bed and go check. Repeatedly. If I didn't, the anxiety was more than I could bear. My latest form of checking involved the car. I'd know I'd rolled up all the windows and locked all the doors, but I'd have to get out of bed, go down to the outdoor garage, and check. My psychiatrist was convinced the car represented my mother, and that all the checking was because I was worried about her and felt guilty about being away from her.

One night, I was out by the car in my nightgown and slippers, in bondage to the door handles I couldn't seem to stop pulling/checking, when I heard, "MOVE AWAY FROM THE VEHICLE."

I shot around, blinded by the high beams coming from the cop's car. Shielding my eyes with my hands, I said, "It's my car."

"WE'RE NOT GOING TO TELL YOU AGAIN. MOVE AWAY FROM THE VEHICLE."

"Officers, this is my car!" I yelled, moving away from the vehicle. I couldn't fucking believe it: it was the same two cops who had searched me and Derek.

"Why would you be trying to break into your own car?" the black officer said, while the white officer just stared at me.

"I wasn't."

"Well, then, what were you doing?" the black officer asked.

I contemplated telling him that I was checking on... my mother, the car. (Wasn't that a television show?) But his angry eyes convinced me to try it without the mother part. "It's called checking, where you do something repeatedly as way of discharging anxiety," I said. I knew I'd made a mistake the minute I'd opened my mouth.

The black officer looked at his partner, then back at me. "Like I told you before, I don't have an issue," he said, eyeballing me. "Now, go on, get in the house."

I walked back into my apartment just in time to get the call that would change my life forever.

21

I was on the phone with my mom, and just as we were about to get off the phone, I said, "Love you, Mom."

She said, "Love you..." Just silence. She didn't know my name.

I hung up the phone and called my dad and told him about it, my heart pounding hard, in my chest.

"What do you want to do?" he asked empathically.

"I think I should go check on her," I said, trying not to cry. "I didn't want to worry you, but Nathan called me last week and said she's living out in her house with no heat or hot water, and that she's drinking again."

"Then you should go. Elissa and I fly back to LA tomorrow. I have to start shooting next week. Why don't you and your mommy stay in our Hamptons house? I'll leave a key for you under the mat," he said. "Just call the business office first thing in the morning and get Jane to book your flight."

—

As the town car pulled up to my dad's house, my mom came running out, barefoot, flanked on either side by Sadie and Max. Letting out a big, joyous scream, she practically knocked me over, she hugged me with such force. "There's my girl!"

"Omigod, I've missed you!" I said, kissing her hand before holding it as we made our way toward the house. "Holy shit," I said as she opened the front door and I took in the gorgeous mahogany staircase next to the cozy, spacious sitting room. "This is amazing!"

"Isn't it?" she said, squeezing my hand. "We can walk to the ocean! It's just over that sand dune, out the back door. Are you hungry?"

I followed her into the kitchen. "I could eat something." I studied her face as she reached into the fridge.

"You're in luck! I just made a whole batch of cheeseless cheesecake," she said, handing me a plate and a fork.

"Great, thanks," I said, taking a seat in antique wooden chair as my mother settled into the couch across from me.

"How was the flight?" she asked, beaming at me.

"Fine. This is delicious," I answered with a full mouth of cake. "So, how are you?"

"I'm okay. So happy you're home!" she said, laughing, and gave my knee a little squeeze.

I scooted my chair closer to her. Her hair was long and silver. She'd never looked more beautiful to me.

"Wasn't it nice of your dad to let us stay here?" she said.

"Very," I said, taking her hand.

"I guess he's still in talks abou—" All of a sudden her whole face started convulsing, as if there were an electrical current running through it. I leapt over to the couch, grabbed her hand while I looked on in horror. Whatever it was lasted thirty seconds. Then, just as mysteriously as it had taken hold, it let go.

"What was that?" I cried, staring into her eyes.

"Tremor," she said slowly. "I've been having them for a while," she continued warmly, almost as if she was trying to comfort me.

"What? What's a while?"

"Maybe a month." Shrugging her shoulders, she continued, "I thought they'd go away, and I didn't want to bother you. I was so happy you were working and—"

"Mom, if you're having tremors in your face, you have to tell somebody! Does Nathan know?"

She looked away, angry hurt washing over her face. "We're not together right now."

"Okay, well, we have to get you to a doctor right away."

"You know how I feel about doctors."

"I don't want to hear it. We're going to the doctor. We're not gonna wander out into the yard and treat this with some fuckin' berries from a tree. Don't fight me on this. It's too serious."

"Okay," she said softly, letting herself fall against me as I held her tight, kissing her all over her face and head.

"I'm here now," I said gently as my mother began to softly weep.

The following morning, my mom and I went to one of the top neurologists in East Hampton. I'd called my dad and he'd gotten us in. My mom and I both began to stand up as the doctor entered the room.

"Don't get up. Don't get up," he said affably, walking over to us and shaking each of our hands. "I'm Dr. Ruiz," he said.

"Thank you so much for seeing us on such short notice," I said.

"When your father called me last night, I told him to send your mom right over," Dr. Ruiz said, taking the stethoscope off his neck. "Can I ask you to sit up here for me?" he said as my mom hopped up on the table. Placing the stethoscope on my mom's chest, he said, "Just breathe normally." My mom smiled at me playfully. "Well... her heartbeat's fine," he said, continuing to address only me. My mom and I exchanged a look, both annoyed that he wasn't speaking to her directly. He picked up my mother's right hand, taking her pulse. "Her pulse is perfect.... Y'know, *Seems Like Old Times* has got to be one of my absolute favorite movies."

"It's great," I said perfunctorily.

"What was his character's name? Morris? Stuart?" he said, searching the ceiling for clues as my mother and I stared at each other in disbelief.

"Ira," I said as my mother burned a hole in me with her I-fuckin'-hate-doctors glare.

"Ira Parks, that's it! Remember the scene where Chevy Chase is under the bed and your dad's—"

"I do. I do," I interrupted, placing my hand on my mom's shoulder, attempting to remind him that we weren't here for a round of movie trivia.

"So, what's brought you here today, Ms. Grodin?" he said, finally addressing her directly, as if someone had just yelled, *Action.*

"Call me Julie," my mother said, smiling at him.

"She's having tremors in her face," I said, suddenly wishing we *were* here for movie trivia.

"Really?" he said, as if he'd been told she was coming in for a pap smear. "How often?" he asked, shining his tiny flashlight in each of my mother's eyes.

"It varies," she said with a vulnerable matter-of-factness that made me want to cry.

"Is there anything that might have brought them on?" he said, looking at her.

She smiled, shaking her head no.

"She drinks," I blurted out, knowing not to make eye contact with her.

"How much?" the doctor asked.

"A lot," I said quickly, before my mother could lie to him.

"Over what period of time?" He pulled a small pad from his pocket and began taking notes.

"Most of her adult life," I said, hating that she felt betrayed by my every word.

And just as my mother opened her mouth to tell me how she felt about my full disclosure, her face began to convulse.

"She's having a seizure," the doctor said as we both stood there watching, helpless to help her.

When it was over, my mom said, "That's what they're called?"

"I'd like to schedule an MRI for sometime tomorrow," he said.

"Of what?" I asked.

"Of her head," he said delicately as my mom's eyes darted to me, panicked.

I shot her a reassuring look before forcing myself to ask, "What would you be looking for?"

He smiled sweetly at my mom before uttering, "A brain tumor. I'm sure that's not what this is, but we want to rule that out just to be sure, and to get a baseline MRI, before we start doing other testing."

"Could this be from her drinking?" I asked.

"It's possible. I'll know more once I see the MRI. But don't worry," he said, patting my mother on the back. "Go to a movie; go out to dinner; take your mind off it, okay?"

My mom shimmied to the end of the table, jumped onto her feet, looped her arm in mine, and said, "There's a good new vegetarian place in East Hampton; let's go!"

"Okay," I said, knowing there was no way she had a brain tumor. After the movie, we lingered at dinner, where, between bites of meatless beef stew, and her seizures, we caught up, laughed, and did everything we could not to think about tomorrow's MRI.

—

The day after I'd taken my mom for the MRI, I had just finished having lunch with my good friend Kelly in East Hampton. We'd been walking around, chatting and window shopping, when I remembered I had to call Dr. Ruiz's office to get the results. I was so sure there was no way she had anything like a *brain tumor* that I'd almost forgotten to make the call. I spotted a pay phone at the end of the block, and it was there, on that perfect summer day, that I heard.

"Unfortunately, I have some bad news. Your mother has a brain tumor," Dr. Ruiz said.

"What?" I said as my knees went out from under me. "How is that possible?" I said, grabbing on to the side of the phone booth.

"I'm very sorry," he said genuinely. I stared up the street. Kelly was walking toward me, smiling.

"Is it…big?" I asked, shutting my eyes.

"No, it's about the size of a lemon. She'll need surgery, and then probably chemo and radiation," he said matter-of-factly.

"When?" I asked, falling into the phone booth.

"There's really no rush. The tumor is stable. I can probably set up her surgery for sometime in the next two weeks," he said casually.

"Really? It's okay to *wait* like that?" I asked, feeling like nothing he was saying was making any sense.

"Absolutely," he said, as if we were discussing when to deliver a sofa. "Ms. Grodin, your mother is in no danger whatsoever." He sounded more impatient than reassuring.

I pushed my face as far into the phone booth as it would go. "Can she recover from this?" I whispered, feeling like I was pleading for my mother's life.

"We'll have to wait until we remove it and biopsy it, so we can determine what stage it is."

"So it's absolutely possible she could be okay?"

"Yes, but we'll have to wait for the biopsy. I'm very sorry, but I have to take this other call. My nurse will call you to schedule the surgery," he said, then hung up.

"Everything okay?" Kelly asked cheerfully.

"My mother has a brain tumor," I cried, bursting into tears as Kelly threw her arms around me.

—

"Hey, wait up," I yelled, running down the beach, trying to catch up to my mom and the dogs.

"Hey," she said, smiling as she looped her arm in mine, and we continued walking.

"I can't get over this day," she said, pulling me closer.

"I love you," I said, trying not to cry.

"I love you," she said, laughing her sweet, mellifluous laugh. "Max, drop it! Drop it!" she yelled, running after Max, who had a large squawking seagull hanging out of his mouth. "Bad! Bad Max!" Max dropped the gull and ran down the beach. She loved her animals so much, no matter how bad they were, or how hard she tried, she could never sound angry with them. "He loves birds," she said, catching her breath. "Did you talk to the doctor?" she asked casually, slipping her arm back in mine as we continued strolling.

I looked out at the ocean, then at my mom.

"Tell me."

"I don't want you to get scared."

"I won't. Just tell me what he said," she said, dropping her hand into mine.

I brought her hand up to my face and rested my cheek against it. "You have a brain tumor."

"You're kidding," she said, as if I'd told her I'd just found a bunny in my bed. With pure Nancy Drew–like curiosity, she asked, "So. What do we do?"

"Well, Dr. Ruiz wants to schedule surgery, and then you may have some follow-up treatment," I said, putting my arm around her. There was no reason to talk about chemo and radiation at this point.

"When's my surgery?" she asked, not even a hint of worry in her voice.

"He said within the next two weeks."

"It's okay to wait? I mean, how big is it? What's it look like?" she asked.

"He said it's about the size of a lemon."

"Mmm-mm-mm...fascinating. And that's what's been

causing my seizures?" she asked with the curiosity of a young child.

Nodding my head slowly up and down, I said, "Uh-huh."

"So that's great; they'll take it out, and then I'll be okay," she said, staring down the beach at Max, who was in heated pursuit of a limping gull. "Max! Max!" she shouted, taking off down the beach.

—

"Two weeks? Why would he wait that long?" my dad said, agitated.

"I don't know," I said, perched on the edge of my bed, trying to remember where that guy who sold really strong Thai stick lived.

"I mean, does that seem okay to you?" he asked, as if I'd just finished medical school.

"I-I mean, he's the doctor, and he said it was okay," I stammered.

"Well, I'm going to call Dr. Feldstein in the city and run it by him," he said angrily. "That just doesn't sound right to me. Tell your mommy I'll call her a little later; I want to try and reach Feldstein before it gets too late on the East Coast. You know what to do," he said, as if I were in the military. My whole life, my father had been getting off the phone with me with those five words. The fact of the matter was that I'd never known what to do—about my mom, our life together, my life inside myself—but I so desperately wanted to be the girl he wanted me to be that I'd never been able to tell him I did *not* know what to do.

Grabbing my car keys off the bureau, I ran down the stairs, taking them two at a time. "Nathan just called; he's coming over!" my mom said, looking up from her magazine on the couch.

"Great! I'm gonna go out for a little while; I won't be long," I said, flying out of the house and into my car. As I turned onto the Thai dealer's street, I thought, *I do know what to do.*

—

"Marion, that is not a word!" my mother said, laughing, as she leaned over the Scrabble board, while Nathan stroked her hair. Three days before, my mom and I had taken the Jitney into the city so that we could get a second MRI and meet with the new doctor at Sloan-Kettering.

"I think it might be a word, Jules," Nathan said, kissing her cheek.

"'Solitudinous' is *not* a word. I'm going to look it up," she said, glaring at me playfully as she reached for the small paperback dictionary on the little side table. "Honey, let Max out; I think he has to go," she said to Nathan. "She makes up words, y'know," she mumbled, searching for the right page in the dictionary.

"I heard that!" I yelled, plopping down next to her on the couch and smothering her in sloppy kisses.

"Not a word, but your other words are fine," she said laughing, as I got her in a neck lock.

"Omigod, stop. You're getting me wet," she yelled through her laughter. The phone rang as she pushed me off of her. "Get the phone, Marion, get the phone."

"Hello?" I said, chuckling.

"I need you to talk so you can't be overheard," my dad said urgently.

Doing my best to sound easy, I said, "Mommy, hang up the phone once I pick it up upstairs, okay?"

"Who is it?" she said, glancing up from the word she was assembling.

"It's Daddy," I said, taking the stairs two at a time. "Okay, you can hang up."

As the downstairs phone clicked off, my dad said, "I just got off the phone with Dr. Feldstein. It's larger than we first thought. More like a grapefruit than a lemon. And Feldstein feels Dr. Ruiz's reading of the MRI was inaccurate," he continued, struggling to contain his rage.

"How?" I asked, sliding down the wall.

"Feldstein feels Mommy should be operated on right away. He feels it's a later-stage tumor than Dr. Ruiz told us and that it's aggressive," he said, choking back tears.

"Omigod," I said, starting to cry. "What does this mean?" I asked, terror gripping me.

"According to Feldstein, it means the situation is much worse than we were originally told." We stayed on the line, listening to each other breathe, until my dad cleared his throat and said, "So, you'll decide what you want to say to Mommy, how to handle this, but you have to go right back in. He's scheduled her surgery for a week from Monday at eight a.m. There's a part of the hospital, for families, that you can stay in with Mommy while they run more tests and get her ready for the surgery."

"Okay," I murmured, numb, my whole system shut down in sorrow.

"How's she seem?" he asked.

"Great. Actually, Nathan's staying with us. They've been taking long walks with the dogs, and she's been cooking up a storm. We've been having a great night, playing Scrabble. She just busted me for trying to use 'solitudinous,'" I said, both of us chuckling.

"I told you that wasn't a word," he said affectionately, both of us grateful for the laugh.

I was on the last step off the staircase when my mother glanced up from the Scrabble board. "What did your dad have to say?"

"He said 'solitudinous' is not a word."

"Told you," she said as she pulled me down on the couch, next to her. For a minute, I stared at her pretty little face, unable to even fathom how I was supposed to tell her that what I'd thought was the worst news I'd ever have to tell her... hadn't been

—

"I mean, a lemon and a grapefruit aren't even close in size," she said, staring at me, waiting for some explanation, as we rode the Jitney back to Sloan-Kettering.

"Let's play our game."

"I don't want to," she said, staring out her window.

"Come on, I'll start," I said, laying my head in her lap. "I'm going to Sloan-Kettering and I'm taking... my sleep mask." I looked up at her expectantly.

"I'm going to Sloan-Kettering and I'm taking my... sleep mask, and Max," she said, running her hand over the top of my head.

"I'm going to Sloan-Kettering and I'm taking my sleep mask, Max, and... my black eyeliner," I said.

"Really?" she said disapprovingly, gathering the top of my hair in her hand. "I think you look so much prettier without it."

"Go," I said, laughing.

"Okay, so, I'm going to Sloan-Kettering, and I'm taking my sleep mask, Max, my black eyeliner, and... Debra Winger," she said, both of us chuckling.

"I didn't even know you knew who that was," I said.

"I just saw her in *Terms of Endearment*. I thought she was really excellent," she said, glancing out her window.

"I concur," I said playfully.

"Okay, I'm going to Sloan-Kettering and I'm taking my sleep mask, Max, my black eyeliner, Debra Winger, and... Shirley MacLaine," I said.

"Don't take her," she said abruptly.

"Why not? Didn't you think she was good as Debra Winger's mother?"

"I could see her acting, and I just read an article about her; she seems bossy. I don't want to play anymore." A sadness washed over my mom; she put her hands in her lap and stared out the window. After a minute, still staring out the window, she said, softly, angrily, "I don't get it; a lemon and a grapefruit aren't even close in size."

As my mom and I headed, hand in hand, down the long, carpeted hallway in the building we'd be staying in for the week before her surgery, we passed patients in various states of infirmity, walking with their caretakers. As I walked by other family members, we'd subtly smile or nod, acknowledging that we were members of the same heartbreaking club. As we passed a young black boy with a bandaged head, pushing a pole connected to the IV on the top of his hand, my mother whispered, "Do you think he has a brain tumor like me?"

Putting my arm around her, I said, "Don't know... but I do

know we're in the best place in the world for treating every kind of cancer."

"Be sure to thank Daddy when you talk to him," she said.

By the third day at Sloan, I was so enraged that I needed somebody to blame, somebody to be responsible for what was happening to my mom. "I want to sue this fucking asshole!" I cried into the phone, to my dad. "I mean, really, how could this happen? I want Ruiz's fucking license." I sobbed, unable to catch my breath.

Gently, my dad said, "Dr. Feldstein said he didn't believe it would have made a difference, given what Mommy has."

—

I had always been like my mother's little husband, and now I moved into this role completely—the role I felt I'd been in training for my whole life: I became her caretaker. There was endless blood work, CAT scans, MRIs, stool samples. I submerged myself in every detail, to the point that I could, and did, have lengthy conversations with her doctors using all the same technical terms they used. My mother's arms were covered in bruises from all the blood they were taking.

She never complained, not even once. There was never a shred of self-pity in her demeanor. In my eyes, and I believe, in the eyes of the staff at Sloan, she was a true champion—always asking the nurses about themselves, or just in general, being buoyant, cheerful. Though the circumstances were as dire as it gets, she was thrilled that we were together. And so was I. I loved my mother more than anyone on the planet, and having to watch her go through all this shit, for an outcome that was much worse than she knew, shattered and bludgeoned my heart. But during it all, we had more laughs, more good times, than anyone could imagine.

Six days and what felt like a million tests later, on a rainy Monday morning, I watched as a very large nurse wheeled my heroic, adorable, beautiful mother to the operating room. I knew I was way too full of anxiety to just sit in the waiting room. So, desperate to stop my obsessive mind from trying to visualize every disturbing detail of her four-hour surgery, along with all the things that could go wrong...I decided I'd go to a movie. I'd always loved Grace Jones's music, and she was starring in this movie *Vamp*, playing around the corner from the hospital. I didn't know anything about the movie. I figured Grace Jones played a "vamp" as in "badass femme fatale." Not even fuckin' close. Grace Jones played a "vamp" as in a vampire, who, along with a bunch of other fucking vampires, revel in a gory, violent night of blood sucking...squirting blood everywhere. I might as well have been in the operating room.

After recovering from *Vamp* and killing another hour just walking around, I headed back to the hospital and took the elevator up to the ICU. I spotted my mom in the far corner, her head wrapped in a bandage that was soaked with blood. She had an IV on the back of her hand, a catheter bag half-full with urine under her bed. I was so relieved just to see her. I ran over, took the seat right next to her bed, and squeezed her hand. She squinted at me as a tear fell down my face. A young nurse with a soothing Southern accent came over and placed her hand on my shoulder. "Your mom did real well. She's still pretty sedated. She should be more awake tomorrow." I leaned over my mom, hovering just above her cheek, breathing her in, finding so much comfort in her smell, which no brain tumor, no aggressive cancer, no surgery could ever take away.

—

After a couple days, my mom was more alert. She still wasn't really talking, and the doctors had warned me that because the tumor was resting on the part of her brain that controlled speech, there was a good possibility that her speech would be affected; they just didn't know to what extent.

I went back to my dad's apartment that night, reported to everyone, and passed out, praying that tomorrow she would talk. I didn't even open my eyes till two o'clock the next afternoon. I dragged myself out of bed, into the shower, and back across town to the hospital.

As I entered my mother's room, the sweet nurse with the mellifluous Southern lilt looked up and shot me the warmest smile. "She's talking today," she said, beaming as if it were her mother.

"Oh, thank God," I said, feeling relief wash over me. "What has she said?" I asked excitedly.

"She's very interested in the red Jell-O," she said, chuckling.

Laughing, I said, "She eats very healthfully, so that's probably a big treat for her. Thank you for taking such good care of her." I welled up.

"Hey, if it were my mom, that's what I'd want," she said, reaching over the counter as she put her hand on mine.

I turned and went over to my mom's bedside. "It's so good to see you," she said, pulling my face right up to hers as I leaned in to give her a kiss.

"How do you feel?" I asked, sitting down and holding her hand.

"Not too bad, really," she said. Just listening to her speak, I started crying. "Ah, don't cry; I made it," she said, her humble heroism cracking my heart all the way open.

"Red Jell-O, huh?" I said, squeezing her hand as I wiped my eyes with the back of my sleeve.

"I don't know why it tastes so good to me, but it does," she said with all the joy of a kid. Picking up a spoon, and finishing off one of the many red Jell-O cups on her tray, she said, "I mean, I know it's no good for me, but it's just yummy." She licked her lips animatedly.

—

Two days later, my mom was moved out of ICU into a private room with a roommate. When I walked into her room, she was propped up on a sea of pillows in the bed by the window, chatting away with her roommate. I hurried over to her bed and was so ecstatic to see her head freed from the mummy wrap that I was completely unprepared for the scar on the side of her head.

"Omigod! Your bandages are off!" I exclaimed, throwing my arms around her as I came face-to-face with a scar that was much larger and thicker than anything I'd imagined. It started two inches above her right ear and wound all the way around to the bottom of her skull. It looked like a giant question mark, and I couldn't help but feel it was asking the only question on our minds. We were told we'd get the biopsy results today.

"This is Diane," my mother said, joyfully smiling at the heavyset young Italian woman sitting beside her. "She has the same thing I have," my mom said, as if she'd just found out they'd gone to the same camp.

"Hi," Diane said, her speech noticeably altered.

"Hi, nice to meet you," I said, trying not to stare at the exact same scar my mother had, on the side of Diane's head.

"How 'bout my scar?" my mom said, almost like it was a badge of honor.

"I know. Well, when your hair grows back, you probably won't even be able to see it," I said encouragingly.

"I think it's amazing," my mom said, snatching the mirror off her side table and examining it closely.

"Are you in any pain?" I asked.

Shaking her head no, she said, "I just wanna get out of here. I miss the dogs."

"And Nathan?" I asked, rubbing her arm.

"And Nathan," she said, playfully smirking. "When I get out, the first thing I want to do is go for a walk on the beach with you and the dogs, okay?" She shrugged her shoulders up to her ears and did a little happy dance.

"Definitely. Whatever you want," I said, doing my own little happy dance back before I went to talk with her doctor.

"Hi, Ms. Grodin, come on in," the doctor said, looking up from the file on his desk. "Here, take a seat," he said, indicating the chair in front of his desk. "So, I just got your mom's MRI back, and I wish I had better news for you...."

"Just tell me," I said, clenching my fists.

"Your mom has a very aggressive type of brain cancer. It's a stage-four glioblastoma, and we were able to remove most of her tumor."

"Most? Why not all?"

"Because it would be impossible to remove all the cells of the tumor without removing crucial brain cells; they're commingled. The other difficulty is that this is a very fast-growing strain of cancer. So even if we had gotten all of it, it would most likely just grow back."

"Most likely?" I said, grasping for anything to hold on to.

Nodding his head up and down, he said, "That's what we've seen with similar tumors."

"So... what do we do?"

"Well, I'd like to treat her with a course of a new, very strong chemotherapy and then follow that with radiation," he said. The weight of his words literally pushing my head down, I stared at the floor, feeling as if I couldn't take a breath. "I know this is a lot to take in...," he said softly.

Slowly, I lifted my head, opening my mouth to speak, but nothing came out.

"It's okay; take your time," he said softly.

After a moment, I said, "Is there... any chance... she... could... recover from this?"

And then the doctor did something I will never forget. He stared at me with such compassion then looked away as an expression of anger and defeat overtook his face. He cleared his throat, turned back to me, and forced himself to say, "Not likely. This is a very bad strain. We're working on several experimental chemotherapies that may be able to treat this, at some point, but that won't be for another few years, and..." Sparing me the rest of the sentence, he smiled at me, shaking his head apologetically. "I'm going to set up her chemo schedule, but in the meantime, you can take your mom home in a few days, and then she'll start her chemo within the next couple weeks. I'm very sorry. I can see how much you love your mom. I wish I had more to offer you."

I must have walked to the elevator, because I found myself back on my mom's floor, paralyzed, before waves of grief and panic began rising inside me. I didn't know what was happening. I shot around the corner, praying I'd find a bathroom before this rising tsunami crashed all over my heart. I swung the bathroom door open, the force of my emotion hurling me into the wall. Clinging to the wall, I began crying so hard it knocked me down. I was balled up on the floor, loud sobs convulsing my whole body, as I wedged my head into the corner. After a couple minutes, a nurse came in. She got right down on the floor next to me and took me in her arms. "I know. I know," she said, rocking me back and forth. This nurse helped me clean myself up and walked me to my mother's room. I didn't tell her what I knew.

On the cab ride home, I wanted to drink. As the cab made its way up Third Avenue, I saw only one thing—the gold and red, twinkly, Christmas-colored lights of the many bars, imploring me to step inside, with the promise of... oblivion.

I stared out my taxi window. I wasn't sure if I would drink or not. By the time the cab made a left to go crosstown on Eighty-Sixth Street, I knew my answer: I was not going to drink. It wasn't moral or heroic. I knew that if I could get through that night without drinking, I could get through whatever I had to without a drink. Deep down I understood that if I drank, I could not be strong for my mother. Forget strong—I could not be anything for her.

A few days later, my mom was out of the hospital, and my dad had rented us a phenomenal house in East Hampton—a spacious ranch with an enormous, tree-filled backyard behind it. My mom and I both loved the house, and we settled in easily. She loved that she could open the sliding doors in the living room and let the dogs frolic in their own private forest. We each had our own bedroom at one end of the house, and at the other end of the house was a guest bedroom.

When I'd checked my mom out of the hospital, a nurse had handed me her MRI. What was I supposed to do with this giant X-ray of my mother's brain tumor? I scoured this new house for the best hiding place and decided to put it between the mattress and the box spring of the twin bed in the guest bedroom. I never wanted her to see this terrifying image, ever.

My obsessive-compulsive disorder was in high gear, so, at the end of every night's ritualistic checking—sometimes as many as three times—that all the doors and all the windows were locked, the final "check" of the night would always be that MRI. Just before I went to bed, the last thing I would do every night was make sure that the MRI was where I had left it, that she hadn't somehow found it and taken it into her room. It was a horrible way to end every night, but it must have given me some strange sense of control in a situation where I had none. Or maybe forcing myself to look at her MRI every night was punishment for not being able to save her.

It may sound strange, but these were some of the best times we'd ever had. For the worst reason imaginable, we had been reunited at a time in both our lives when we would never have been living under the same roof talking, laughing, just hanging out. There wasn't anything I could do about what was happening to my mother, but the fact that we were together was *everything*. As the weather got colder, my mother started spending a lot of time in the big kitchen, making her delicious macrobiotic meals, experimenting with yummy soups—squash, parsnip—and macro desserts. I'd hunker down in the living room, spread out on a big blanket on the floor in front of the TV, while my mom cooked. We'd yell back and forth to each other, until she'd proudly walk in with a sensational macrobiotic dish: "Wait till you taste this," she'd say gleefully, handing me a big ceramic bowl. "I'm not sure; but I think this may be my best batch. Let me know what you think."

"Omigod! This is incredible! What's in this?" I'd ask, spoon still in my mouth.

"It's all vegetables, and a little bit of mochi paste, for thickness," she'd say, beaming.

"There's no butter or cream in this?" I'd yell, setting her up to say her favorite sentence.

"No dairy, sugar, or animal products," she'd shout triumphantly.

"Amazing!" I'd say.

My mother's fiercely independent and often defiant spirit was in no way doused by her circumstances. Occasionally, she'd refuse to let me drive her into the city to Sloan-Kettering for her chemo. She'd insist on taking the bus, where, on the trip back home, she'd spend most of her time in the bathroom throwing up. She reported this to me matter-of-factly, with no trace of self-pity or even negativity. She just didn't see it as that big a deal. She truly was my hero.

She lived each day as if she didn't have a brain tumor, as if she weren't in any way sick, even though she was becoming more and more symptomatic. She still went to work at ARF and took care of the animals; she still took her dogs on long walks and cooked us a gourmet macrobiotic dinner every night. But despite all the treatment, the cancer was there, destroying different parts of her brain. She became less sure on her feet. She would get dizzy. We both noticed that she'd forget a word or struggle to remember what it was she was about to tell me, which frustrated her horribly. Then it started getting harder and harder for her to speak.

Another MRI showed the tumor was growing again, pressing on the part of her brain that controls speech. The doctors prescribed very strong steroids to lessen the swelling in her brain that the tumor was causing, but the steroids didn't significantly halt her loss of speech, and they made her heavy and bloated her face.

As winter progressed, there was another symptom that appeared one day that nobody had warned me about. I had just gotten off the phone with my dad, when my mother mumbled, "What were you telling your daddy?"

"What?" I asked, completely caught off guard.

"I heard you talking about me. What were you saying?" she accused.

"I was just updating him on how you're doing." I had no idea where she was coming from.

"Well, I'm recording our conversations from now on," she said, pulling a fairly large tape recorder out from behind her.

Laughing, I asked, "Mom, what are you doing with that?"

Angrily, she replied, "I'm making sure that I'm not misquoted."

"I wouldn't misquote you. I love you."

"Well, I don't love you. I don't like you. I don't want to live with you anymore," she raged at me with her faltering speech.

"Well, I love you, and I don't think you really mean what you're saying," I said, fighting back tears.

"I do," she said. "I hate you."

As much as I knew she couldn't really mean any of what she was saying, she was still breaking my heart. As hard as I tried to stay detached, to tell myself this wasn't her, that she couldn't help it, I felt completely panic-stricken. Not meaning it, but having no idea how to navigate through any of this, I said, "Well, maybe you should go stay with your sister Ellen in Pittsburgh."

"Good, I want to go to Pittsburgh," she said defiantly, staring me down.

The next day, I called her doctor and reported this disturbing incident. He said this was not unusual in patients with her type of tumor. He explained that not only was the tumor affecting her speech, it was also putting pressure on the part of the brain that controls mood, anger, and perception. I hung up the phone, completely numb. Robotically, I started toward the living room, but stopped when I saw my mom sitting on the couch, watching TV, her arms around the tape recorder on her lap. I grabbed my jean jacket and headed out, determined to get as obliterated as possible.

Over the next several weeks, her moods were more and more unpredictable. Her angry, paranoid outbursts were more frequent; she was now carrying the tape recorder in her purse. I was so weary of having to be strong, of having no one to help me, no one to lean on, no one to just "take a shift" so I could have a few hours to myself to sit by the ocean and stare into space.

My dad had just started shooting *Midnight Run* on the West Coast, so I knew he could not come home. But I called him late one night when my mom was asleep. As soon as I heard his voice, my tears erupted with such force, it was as if a dam were breaking.

"Honey, what's wrong?" he said, alarmed.

"I can't do this. I can't do this anymore," I sobbed, my pain pouring through the phone.

"Ah, sweetheart. I'm so sorry," he said, his voice steeped in compassion.

"I'm so tired, Dad. I'm just so tired. And she's..." Choking on my tears, I mumbled, "She's not her.... She's not her.... And I..."

He listened, although I was almost unable to speak through my tears.

"I need help. I can't do this," I cried.

"Should I come home?" he said. "If you tell me you need me to come home, I'll come home," he said firmly.

I shut my eyes momentarily, allowing the fleeting fantasy of rescue to engulf me. "No," I said.

"Is there some support group you could join? Would it help to be around other people going through the same thing?" he asked softly.

I knew as I hung up the phone that I was alone.

Then my mom completely lost the ability to speak. The frustration that comes with being unable to speak is unimaginable. I would sit with her for hours, trying to put into words what I thought she was feeling. One evening after chemo, we were back at the Windermere. She'd been angry and sad all day. Putting my arm around her as she sat in the recliner, I said gently, "Does it feel like you are behind this wall, and you can't get to anybody and no one can get to you?" She stared into my eyes with the deepest hurt.

My mom wasn't in physical pain, but her emotional and psychic pain was torturous. She knew she was not going to get better. Without my ever having said it, she knew.

Yet in the deepest part of herself, who she was remained very much intact. As many times as her doctor had told her she could no longer drive, she would still climb into her little red truck, drive out to ARF, and make sure that every single one of those animals was fed and had enough water to drink. She did this even on the worst winter days, when the roads were their most dangerous. And on those days, she was always the only person there. Some things the cancer could not take from her.

One very cold night in November, we'd just finished dinner and we were sitting in the TV room watching a documentary about dogs in Alaska, when the strangest feeling came over me. When the program ended, my mom went into her room to change into her nightgown. I washed the dishes in the sink and then went to her. She was lying in bed, propped up on pillows. A small candle burned on her nightstand, and shadows flickered across her face. She looked like an angel. I sat down beside her, breathing in the smell of her hair, the warmth of her skin. We looked at each other for a long time. I took both her hands in mine and began to cry. After a minute, I leaned in close, my face pressed against hers, and whispered into her ear: "Mommy, I love you so much, and I know we'll see each other again."

And then she did the most amazing thing. After not having uttered a single word for the last three months, she squeezed my hand and, in a perfectly clear voice, said, "Oh, honey, I love you so much too, and I know we will."

My mother died the next morning. I felt homeless. The world I had lived in was gone.

—

Two days later, after going to the crematorium to make arrangements for my mother's body, my best friend, Greta, and I packed up the house and drove back to the city.

I dropped Greta off at her loft down in the Meatpacking District. I got out of my little brown Toyota Celica and walked around to the passenger side to hug her good-bye. The night was pitch-black and freezing. I could feel the icy wind nipping at the back of my neck. Greta held me long and hard and told me how much she loved me and that she was there for me—whatever I needed. The words struck me as so odd because what I needed had just been ripped from me. The one thing that no one, not even my omnipotent dad, could ever give me was my mother, healed, back the way she'd been before she forgot my name on the phone, before a tumor the size of a grapefruit robbed her of the ability to speak, or think, or ultimately to be who she had been. No one could give me anything I needed.

I drove up the West Side Highway, turned on the radio, and Aretha Franklin was singing "Bridge Over Troubled Water."

By the time I got to Seventy-Ninth Street, I was sobbing so hard that I had to pull off the highway. I got off by the boat basin and just cried with my whole body, rocking back and forth, till I realized I was talking out loud.

"I love you, Mommy. . . . I love you, Mommy. . . . I'm so sorry. . . . I'm so sorry. . . ." I was twenty-eight. My mother had just died at fifty-three. I wanted to die; I wanted to be with her. I felt completely unable to stay here without her. I didn't feel like I had a right to be here without her. I felt that the pain of the loss would kill me. As I grieved, a voice whispered that maybe I deserved to die because I had failed. *I had failed to save my mother's life.*

Back in my dad's apartment, everything looked the same; just nothing felt familiar. I was numb. In a trance I walked into the living room and stared at the recliner where my mother had sat just two weeks before. I placed my hands on each of the chair's arms and bent over to see if I could still smell her there. I closed my eyes and inhaled deeply. I could smell her; it was both reassuring and torturous. After a few minutes, I hoisted myself into a standing position, found my knapsack on the floor, and knelt down, rummaging through it, until I found the rescue I had put all my faith in. I pulled out a plastic bag with a dozen fat joints, a bag of coke, and my lighter. I fired up a joint while laying out the coke on a mirror and cutting it up with a razor. Then, with all the concentrated intensity of a surgeon, I began to operate on myself, praying to God the procedure would take, that I would be lifted so far out of myself that I would not be able to feel that my mother was dead.

22

So there I was, once again, back in the Windermere, with no direction, no prospects, my dad paying all my bills. I agreed to study acting and write a screenplay in return. I only went outside after dark, doing the Upper West Side shuffle, just like eight years before when I had had my psychotic break. I would run into people, tell them I'd lost my mom, and they'd tell me how sorry they were. I could barely hear them, and I really couldn't feel them because I was mummified in narcotics. My week was comprised of acting class and sitting down so high to write my screenplay that the minute I took my pad out to write, I would fall into a nod. My daily intake was now pot, coke, and Demerol. I became more and more vaporous. In the middle of talking to someone, I would black out and come to, having no idea what I was saying. That scared me, but not badly enough to stop me.

My screenplay was called *Thirteen* and was about when I

had just become a teen, on the cusp of everything changing—leaving *the block*, no longer sleeping in my mother's bed, getting high as a way to cope.

One afternoon, I was staring out the window, when my dad—who had just gotten back from shooting *Midnight Run*—called and invited me to Robert De Niro's birthday party. Although I was so stoned I was barely functioning, I couldn't pass up such an amazing invitation. The following night, I found myself on the roof of De Niro's Tribeca loft. High out of my mind on coke, I had just very shakily made my way across what I was sure was a severely tilted floor. I'd been eavesdropping on Madonna, who was sitting on Sean Penn's lap, very animatedly telling an expletive-laden story to Lorraine Bracco and Harvey Keitel. And I think everyone had little white dogs on their laps, but honestly, I was so high, they might have just been sweaters. Anyway, right as I returned to the safety of a flatter part of the floor, I looked up and found myself standing next to De Niro. For a moment, we both just stood there, watching the party. Then he looked at me and said, "Your dad told me you want to be a stand-up comedian."

I smiled and said, "I do."

He nodded and then said, "You should do that." A man of few words, but those four I will never forget.

It was not long after that that my dad called with another invitation I couldn't pass up. It was to a reading in Tribeca at Robert De Niro's theater. My dad had written a comedic screenplay that De Niro, Joe Pesci, he, and some other terrific actors were going to read, and he wanted me to read all the female parts. He felt this could be an amazing opportunity for me. De Niro and Pesci would see how talented I was, and the audience would be full of very important people.

"Wow, thanks!" I said, playing the part of the enthusiast.

The following Saturday, I went down to Tribeca all dressed up—a little black dress and jacket, my hair and makeup fabulous. It was a gorgeous fall day, sunny and brisk. I walked down the cobblestone street to De Niro's place, trying to ignore the chatter starting up in my head.

I want to get high.

It's not even noon. We'll just do this reading, then we can get high.

I walked into the gorgeous, sumptuous theater and over to my dad, who was chatting with De Niro, Pesci, and a couple of other actors.

"There she is," my dad effused, giving me a big hug.

After the introductions, I asked De Niro, "Is there a bathroom I could use?"

"I'm sorry, honey, there's not. Bob's got all this money and the theater, and the restaurant, but he just doesn't believe in bathrooms," my dad teased, as De Niro smiled at me.

"You can use the one in my office. I have to run up there and make a call anyway."

We made a little bit of small talk on the walk to his office. "It's right over there," he said, as he went to the phone on his big mahogany desk.

"Thanks," I said over my shoulder as I shut the bathroom door. I sat on the toilet, staring at the window. I could hear De Niro on the phone.

He won't even be able to smell it. Come on, just do it out the window, my addict coaxed. I pulled my tights up and walked over to the window. I didn't hear him on the phone anymore, so I figured he'd finished his call and gone back downstairs. I lifted the window as wide as it would go, took the joint and my lighter out of my purse, leaned all the way out the window, glancing at the empty street below, lit it, and sucked deeply. I took three long hits, sprayed practically the entire can of Egyptian Musk air freshener, splashed some water on my face, and opened the door.

"You ready to go down?" De Niro said.

I practically leapt into the air. "I didn't realize you were waiting," I said, making sure my mouth was pointed away from him.

"I didn't want you to get lost coming down."

I hoped I'd remembered to leave the window open, as I followed De Niro back to the theater. An hour later, on a stage with a dozen other actors, including De Niro, Pesci, and my father, I stared out at a packed audience, including some very famous people. I stunk. Because I was so stoned, gone were the inflections and nuances that normally made my delivery so funny. I was completely flat. I read every character, every line, the same, like I was reciting a grocery list.

I was terrified of catching my dad's eye and tried not to, but at one point I was reading with him and, momentarily, our eyes locked. What I saw was so painful. It was a look of disorientation, as if he were wondering where the hell his daughter went. As I left that day, I was pretty sure De Niro no longer thought I should be a comic.

Three nights later, still recovering from how ashamed I felt for getting stoned before the reading, I was lying in bed, my shoe box with all my drugs by my side. I snorted a short, fat line, and just as I was about to snort up another, I burst into tears. My pain had finally caught up to me. The grief poured through me for hours, my face drenched in hot, wet tears. At some point much later, I passed out.

When I came to the next day, I stared at my shoe box. I felt as if I were looking at a cemetery plot where my grief had laid to rest the girl who was running. The lines of coke that I hadn't snorted, the buds of marijuana that I hadn't smoked, the blue pills that I hadn't swallowed, all looked powerless to help me. The run was over. I was paralyzed in terror.

Please, please, please, God, tell me: what am I supposed to DO now? Please, God, my brain kept screaming. *Please, please, I need something. I'm begging you.*

I rolled onto my side and stared at the white wall. The wall was blank; I was blank. I thought, *I could lie here like this for the rest of my life, searching the wall's plaster for the only face I ached to see and the only voice I longed to hear tell me not to worry, because we both knew we would see each other again.*

I was about to pull the covers over my head and let the darkness have me, when a voice inside me whispered, . . . *where people like you can go.*

I opened my eyes, trying to figure out what it meant and who was saying, . . . *where people like you can go*. It was the voice of my psychiatrist Sharon from Santa Monica. I'd had a phone session with her a few months before my mom died. I was very high during the call, so I almost missed it when, after getting me to admit that I'd gotten stoned for the fourth time that day, she said gently, "I just want you to know there's a place where people like you can go." *People like me? Funny people? Jewish people? Girls with enormous tits?* Then she said it again. "There's a place where people like you can go." She might as well have said, *There's a flight leaving for the moon, and we're holding a window seat for you.*

I dialed 411 to get the number for the place where people like me can go. I had the strangest feeling that I was being guided by some power that wasn't me to board that flight to the moon.

The meeting was at seven thirty. I told myself I was going—no matter what. Around six thirty, I forced myself into a shower, but while I was rinsing the shampoo out of my hair, a voice whispered, *Maybe you don't need to go to that meeting. You didn't get high all day. Maybe you can control this thing*. I got out of the shower, dried myself off, wrapped the towel around my head, and headed for my shoe box. A perfectly rolled joint welcomed me with the warmth of a long-lost best friend. I sucked in that first deep drag. Some part of me was trying to fight, but a bigger part of me coaxed me back. It was seven. I reached for the remote and tried to get lost in my high and an episode of *Law & Order* I'd seen half a dozen times, but *You have to go* bubbled up from my soul. The high, the show, felt empty. *I* was empty, hollow. If you played me you'd just hear an echo. I took another hit off the joint, trying again to lose myself in the *Law & Order*, but that voice insisted: *You have to go to the meeting*.

"Fuck," I said out loud, turning the TV off as I angrily hurled the remote onto the bed.

It was late September, a new chill in the air. I pulled my collar up and walked, falteringly, down Broadway, embarking on a whole new shuffle. I turned left on Eighty-Second Street and realized the meeting was in the basement of a church I'd walked by for years. I stood at the top of the stairs, staring down at a door. It led to where I was terrified, horrified, didn't believe I could handle. It led to me. I knew *I* was on the other side of that door.

I thought about turning and running home, but that same voice that had whispered, *There's a place where people like you can go*, said, *Just take it a step at a time. You can do this*.

I took a deep breath, feeling like I needed all the oxygen I could find. I walked slowly down the stairs and stopped in front of the door.

It's not too late. You can still just go home, another voice butted in. But that word, "home," struck me as peculiar because I had no sense of how to get home.

I took another deep breath and pulled open the enormous, heavy door. It was a huge room, overly lit for my taste by way too many fluorescent lights. In the distance, about twenty feet in front of me, were at least a hundred foldable chairs, set up ten rows deep on either side of a path in the middle. Every single seat was taken. At the very front of the room, seated at a long table in front of all these people, was a heavyset guy around thirty, wearing a leather jacket. He had a tattoo of a bleeding skull on the right side of his neck. His voice cracked every few words from so much emotion.

The room was as quiet as a library the night before finals. The audience was riveted to every single word coming out of this guy's mouth, which, as I got closer, I saw was pierced in the middle by a small silver hoop. I stood for a moment, and then a woman sitting in the next to last row turned around, smiled at me, and pointed to the empty seat next to her. I hadn't even seen it before she turned around. Her smile felt like the sun.

I skulked toward my seat, feeling painfully self-conscious. A couple of very cute guys turned around and smiled at me. "Sorry, sorry," I whispered as I scooted past five or six people before I sat down next to the nice lady. "Thank you," I said softly as I settled into my seat.

She did something that shocked me: she rubbed my back and whispered, "You're in the right place."

I thought, *How does she know?* But she did seem to know.

"I was just fuckin' sick of it, man. I was just fuckin' sick and tired of being sick and tired. I was alone. I was broke. I'd burned every single bridge in my life. I hated myself. I was just existing to get high. I lived to use and used to live, and you know what? It wasn't fucking workin' anymore. I was using when I didn't even want to use. I wasn't using drugs. The drugs were using me. It wasn't even up to me anymore. I had to use. The really scary thing was they weren't even working. I wasn't getting high anymore; I wasn't even getting straight."

I was so entranced by what he was saying that I barely realized I was rocking back and forth, crying.

"I'd been in worse situations. I'd been shot at. I'd been locked up. I'd been left. None of that did it. I don't know what to tell you. I just knew I was done," he said, taking a sip of water from the cup next to him.

I was rocking faster, crying harder now, a river of sad gushing out of me.

He set the cup down, cleared his throat, and went on. "It was just the way I felt. Or, really, the way I didn't. I didn't feel anything. I saw my best friend get killed in front of me and I felt nothing. My wife took my kids and left me, and I felt, like, *Fuck her*. A year after she took my kids, she called to tell me that my youngest, Luke Jr., had leukemia." He reached for the cup and took another sip of water. "And I'm ashamed to say this, but I felt nothing. One day, I was in a pizza place, and I ran into my wife's sister. She told me that Luke Jr. had died that morning. It must have been a month after he died, I was home, doin' my regular—about to shoot up—and I don't know what happened. It was like all that pain, all of it, my best friend getting killed in front of me, my wife leaving, taking the kids, and then my boy, my son, dying like that—it seemed like all that pain I'd been trying to shoot away just came. And it came hard. It scared me because I hadn't felt anything in so long."

I sobbed, unable to do anything about it, even though people were turning around, looking. A few girls behind me offered me Kleenex, and the woman next to me kept rubbing my back in a circular motion.

Raising his fist in front of his mouth, the speaker began to cry.

"It's okay. We love you, Luke," a couple of guys toward the front of the room called out.

Luke took a Kleenex out of the pocket of his leather jacket and blew his nose. "I know you do, man. I know you do. That night, I came to this meeting. And that was thirteen years, two months, and five days ago, but who's counting? And in that time, I've had a whole bunch of other bad shit happen. I found out I have hepatitis, my twin sister got diagnosed with stage-four breast cancer. But I have not felt it necessary to pick up a drink or a dru—"

Before he could finish saying the word "drug," the entire room burst into applause. Luke stood up and said, "Hold up. Hold up. This is a program of honesty, so let me rephrase that. There were times when I felt it was necessary, but I didn't do it. From the bottom of my heart, man, I have to thank God and all of you for my life."

The entire room burst into louder, thunderous applause, many even standing and whistling. The clapping was so loud, it was as if the weather in the room had shifted, pouring love like rain.

Everyone was hugging and laughing. I just sat, saturated in grief. I was not part of their home and no longer able to find the home inside myself drugs had once given me.

I felt frozen in desperation when a very tall, attractive man came over and said, "You okay?"

I stared at him, my face drenched in tears. It took everything not to blurt out: *My mother's dead, and I don't believe I can survive without getting high, except I can't get high anymore*. Instead I wiped my face with my drenched sleeve and tried to smile, meeting his beautiful light-brown eyes.

"Is this your first meeting?" he asked, his voice full of empathy.

I nodded and tried to straighten up in my chair.

"It'll get easier," he said, smiling in a way that made me believe him.

"Andy," a girl in strategically ripped jeans and a tight blue sweater yelled in the distance. "Come on. We're starving."

Andy smiled at me, turned to walk away, and called, "Keep coming back."

I bent over and grabbed the wad of snotted-up tissues that had fallen on the floor next to my chair.

"Keep coming back," said the nice woman who'd rubbed my back. She was a dead ringer for Linda Evans. She walked to the back of the room and joined a group of women her age.

I opened the giant door I'd entered ninety minutes prior and felt lonelier than when I'd walked in. The temperature had dropped, and the coat I was wearing wasn't warm enough. I buttoned the very top button, shoved my hands all the way down into my pockets, and headed toward Broadway. I watched Andy and, like, twenty really attractive guys and girls head south on Broadway. I walked briskly toward the Windermere. I couldn't fucking wait to get high.

23

You do not need that place, and you definitely do not need any of those people, my shoe box assured me as it welcomed me home.

I could feel my whole body let go as I picked up the lighter from my shoe box and ignited the big fat joint hanging from my mouth.

Absolutely, my brain said. I picked up the remote and channel-surfed until I landed on Al Pacino in *Scarface*. Seated behind a mountain of coke, I settled back to watch and thought, *Now, he has a problem. I'll be okay. I don't have to go to those fucking meetings. Fuck those people. I just won't get high until it's dark out. That's all. I'm not an addict. I'm not fucking "powerless." Such bullshit. I just won't get high until the sun goes down. That's all.* And with my new plan in place, I sucked deeply on my pacifier. I was so happy to be... *home*.

—

It had been fourteen months since my mother had died and my plan was not working. It could be 11 a.m., and if I saw a cloud in the sky, I'd decide it was dark out.

Fuck, fuck, fuck, Marion, can't you just fuckin' control it? my brain screamed as I walked briskly down Broadway. *If you could only wait until it was dark out.*

Well, I can't. I can't. I have no control, I replied, picking up my pace.

Maybe if you just tried a little harder.

No, no, I've been trying. I've been really trying. I don't think it's up to me.

How could that be? God, please, is there any way I don't have to walk back into that fucking room with all those happy fucking people just fucking staring at me?

I stood at the top of those stone steps and searched my soul, but I knew there wasn't.

That night, as I turned the key in the lock of my apartment door, I made a pact with myself that this would be the beginning. Like a soldier who'd just been given her assignment, I walked into the bedroom, picked up my lover, my best friend, my higher power, my mother, my father, my home, carried it into the bathroom, and tilted my shoe box, with all the marijuana living there, into the toilet. For a very long moment, I stared down at the green, brown, and purple buds floating in the toilet. They stared back at me forlornly, questioning the finality of my decision. I flushed the toilet. I remained riveted, watching as the colorful buds spun wildly around in the water, bobbing frantically up and down, as if they were screaming for me to save them. I felt a consummate sense of sadness, a visceral sense of loss as they disappeared.

In the living room, I took a seat in the same chair my mother had sat in when she wordlessly showed me her anguish, and I burst into tears. The chair and I both knew it was my turn. The grief, sadness, despair, animalistic loss I'd been running from had been waiting. It hadn't gone anywhere. I learned, at twenty-nine years old, a profound lesson that night: pain can be postponed, but it cannot be eliminated.

As I sat in that chair, her chair, my tears, her tears streaming down my/her/our face, I knew I was going to need some power beyond myself to get me through this. I felt small and weak, but for the first time since she'd died, I went to sleep without getting high. As I shut my eyes, my mind, my soul begged some power I couldn't name, didn't understand, hadn't talked to in a very long time, *Please, please, please, just help me.*

24

I'd been coming to meetings for three weeks, and the only people I'd spoken to, and the only people who'd spoken to me, were men. Since I'd put down drugs, my new high was male attention. I couldn't bear to talk with the women; it was too close to the bone for me, too naked, too real. With women, there was nothing to "use," and although I'd put down the drugs, I was still running from myself. I continued to go to my meetings, coming out of my coma, but I looked for that feeling in the eyes of men who were looking for the exact same thing in my eyes.

I hooked up with a ridiculously sex forty-year-old Italian named Tony. Our sexual chemistry was amazing, but that was it. He'd ask me, on a regular basis and in complete earnestness, if I felt it would be a good idea for him to join the Mafia. At first, I assumed he was kidding. But he was not. He used to shoot a lot of dope, and now that he was clean, he was exploring all his career options. Tony was also a committed gum chewer, and on more than a few occasions, after we'd had sex, I would find a big wad of green gum stuck in my hair.

Between the Mafia and the chewing gum, I knew our days together were numbered. Then one night after my meeting, I went to meet him at the pool hall on Seventy-Second Street. He was with his good friend Chris. My first thought when I met Chris was that he was so beautiful. He looked almost exactly like the actor Aidan Quinn.

"Hey," I said to Tony as he put his ball in the hole.

"Hey." He smiled lasciviously.

"Marion, this is Chris," he said, looking at Aidan Quinn.

"Hi," we said at the exact same time, laughing nervously. It's funny, but I felt like we both knew right away that there was something sweet between us. I walked home from the pool hall that night with a big smile on my face, thinking, *So that was Chris. God, he was gorgeous*. He had big green melty eyes and the warmest, kindest smile. I tried to put him out of my mind, since I was *shtupping* his friend.

The three of us played pool and hung out a lot over the next few weeks. Then, after yet another conversation with Tony about the pros and cons of joining the Mafia, I realized we had probably reached the end of our road together. I was just about to celebrate my first year clean, and I had gotten really sick with the flu. Alone, home in bed, I had a lot of time to feel. I realized I'd been using men and they'd been using me. I fell into the emptiness that I'd been trying to stave off by sleeping with strangers. I called Linda Evans, that nice woman from my very first meeting, and asked her if she'd work with me in my recovery. She said yes. I was terrified and thrilled.

Two weeks later, I ran into Chris in my neighborhood as I

was about to go into my favorite diner. "This is my diner," I said as he opened the door for me.

"This is *my* diner," he said sweetly, both of us laughing.

"Isn't this delicious?" I soon asked, submerging my big spoon in my bowl of pea soup.

"It's my favorite," he said. We smiled at each other, each taking a bite.

"Is this the best pea soup you've ever had?" I asked, studying the scar over the top of his nose.

"It's close," he said warmly.

"Come on. You've had better pea soup than this?" I said in disbelief.

"My dad makes the best pea soup I've ever had," he said without bragging.

"Really? Your father makes his own pea soup?" I asked.

"He was a fire chief in the Bronx when I was a kid, and he'd make pea soup for, like, fifty guys," he said proudly.

"That's incredible. Wow! Your dad was a fire chief. That's awesome!"

"Yeah," he said, clearly enjoying my enthusiasm. "How 'bout you? What's your dad do?"

I hesitated for a moment. "He's an actor," I said nonchalantly.

"Wow," he said, returning to his soup.

I'd never had anyone respond that way, just content with that information. A minute later, I casually added, "Yeah, Charles Grodin." Staring at his unresponsive face, I continued, "*Midnight Run* with Robert De Niro."

"I don't think I saw that," he said politely.

I shot him a big grin and we both leaned into our bowls, taking our final slurps of our favorite soup.

Over the next few weeks, Chris and I became inseparable. We talked on the phone three, four times a day, and after work he'd come over every night for dinner. Spinach pasta with avocado, olive oil, and tons of vegetables was my specialty and the only thing I made.

"Mar, that was unbelievable!" he'd say, kissing the back of my head as he carried his bowl into my little kitchen.

We loved each other's company, and we never got tired of talking to each other about everything: our families, our issues, our feelings. He was the first person with whom I was able to talk about my mom, and he listened with a loving and patient heart that made me know I could tell him anything.

25

Christopher had already met my father, Elissa, and my grandmother Lena, and everyone loved him. Then it was my turn to meet his large Irish Catholic family. We drove out to Ridgewood, New Jersey, on a gorgeous, sunny Easter Sunday to the house he'd grown up in. "Wow," I said, as we pulled into the driveway of a large gray corner-lot Victorian with a big yard and plenty of trees. As if a director had just yelled, *Action*, three cherub-faced little girls, dressed in pastel-colored dresses, ran out the front door. Deeply immersed in a game of tag, they looked like giant Easter eggs with little legs and Mary Janes.

"Hi, Cacey, Darcy, Calli," Chris called out.

The children all turned around, smiling. "Hi, Uncle Chris," they said in unison before racing across the lawn.

"Hi, Uncle Chris," I said seductively as I slipped my hand in his.

As far as the eye could see were fresh-faced, good-looking Irish Catholic people. The girls all had names like Kathleen, Maureen, Noreen, Doreen, Coreen, Patti-Anne, and Annie-Patti, and the boys, Biblical ones: Matthew, Christopher, Timothy, Patrick, and Patrick Timothy.

And then there was the food. Omigod! I was definitely back in the land of casseroles and sides—crunchy green beans, potatoes with cheese, potato salad. I'd never even seen desserts like this outside of a bakery! Apple pie, strawberry rhubarb pie, blueberry pie, chocolate cake, cheesecake, chocolate cheesecake, Boston cream pie, and something called Snickerdoodles that were like crack. Whenever I didn't think Christopher was looking, I'd snatch another bite with my fingers.

His whole family was great—warm, just like Chris. Just like with Megan's family, they took me in, and I was thrilled to step back into my role as the entertainer at these cake-infested, jovial family functions. I felt like Julie Andrews in *The Sound of Music*—or Jewy Andrews, because they found my Jewish neurotic comedic sensibility exotic and hilarious. The hills were definitely alive with the sound of "Danny Boy." I could have sworn I heard bagpipes. I couldn't have been happier, especially since I was still missing *my* Julie so much. For the first few months that we were together, Christopher and I were very happy. He was the calm to my storm and my big, wild personality was colorful and fascinating to him. Christopher would entertain the guys at his job with tales of my latest calamity, which were so frequent that his coworkers nicknamed me Lucy, as in *I Love Lucy*.

If you're wondering exactly what kind of calamity, let me give you two examples. Christopher and I had been planning to take a week's vacation together down at the Jersey Shore in his family's bungalow, outside of which was a plaque that read IF YOU'RE LUCKY ENOUGH TO BE AT THE BEACH . . . YOU'RE LUCKY ENOUGH. Definitely not written by Jews. Our plaque would say something like, IF YOU'RE LUCKY ENOUGH TO BE AT THE BEACH . . . YOU BETTER PRAY YOU DON'T GET SKIN CANCER.

I was going to pick up Chris downtown, but first I needed to swing by the Chase Bank on Ninetieth Street to get cash for the trip. "Thank you, God," I sang out loud as I pulled into a spot right in front of the bank. I threw a quarter in the meter and ran in. No more than five minutes later, I flung open the door to the bank and stopped dead in my tracks. It was gone. The car was *gone*.

I couldn't fucking believe it! I could never fucking believe it. As many times as this had happened to me—which was a lot—I honestly could never believe it. I knew I had multiple unpaid tickets on my car, yet my first thought was always, *Fuck, somebody stole my car*. "I just parked my car here not more than a few minutes ago, and now it's gone. Did you see anybody?" I frantically asked the two Spanish delivery guys leaning on their bikes.

"The marshal. He take your car," the shorter one said.

"But I was only in the bank, like, five minutes!" I searched their faces for validation.

"But you have tickets?" the taller one said.

That always shut me up *rápido*.

That phone call to Christopher was excruciating, but he was never all that surprised. He handled it with astonishing goodwill and even amusement, later begging me to "tell the story" at a family gathering and beaming at me, laughing harder than anybody as I acted out all the characters and did all the accents.

A second example is *the bags*. "Mar, what's in those? Chris asked, gently pointing to two enormous Hefty bags shoved into the far corner of the living room, almost hidden by the wicker rocker.

"What?"

"Those?" He pointed again.

"Oh, nothing." I sat down across from him.

He nodded his head slowly, biting his lower lip. Then, after a moment, he said, with a just a tad more volume, "No, seriously, Mar... what's in those?" He already knew me well enough to know that even a touch more volume would ruin his chances of ever finding out what was in those bags.

I hung my head, releasing a deep breath. "Mail." I averted my eyes.

"All of it?" he said in disbelief.

Squinching up my face, I said, barely audibly, "Yep."

"From who?"

For a moment I just held his gaze. Then I shrugged my shoulders and softly said, "Not sure. I think it's mostly bills."

The look on his face was as if I had just said, *Mouse droppings, sweetie. Those big bags are full of mouse droppings*. "Why?"

If you don't come from this kind of dysfunction, it just seems insane. I once saw a show on obsession about this girl who, in order to soothe her anxiety, was eating her couch. This was normal to her. To everyone watching, this seemed completely insane. (Well, probably not to everyone; I'm sure a few other couch nibblers felt right at home.) As Christopher stared at me, waiting for some kind of explanation, I took comfort in knowing that I would never, ever eat my couch.

"Mar, I'm not judging"—he said it so kindly it was painful—"just tell me why."

"It makes me tense," I said, thinking maybe I should have

just eaten my mail so I wouldn't have to have this fucking conversation.

"What? Your mail? Your mail makes you tense?" he asked, desperate to understand the ways of the neurotic Jewess.

"Very."

He nodded empathically, then said, "What is it about your mail that makes you tense?" He had no understanding of who he was dealing with.

"I don't want to talk about this right now."

Unfortunately, no safari-clad guide from the Discovery Channel with a bullhorn fell through the ceiling and shouted at Chris: *Run. Run. I know you think you're equipped to deal with the ways of the unresolved, codependent Jewess with lots of daddy issues, but you are not!* Our dynamic was set. Over the next sixteen years Christopher would devote himself to trying to get me to open my mail, pay my bills, be responsible for myself financially and emotionally, grow up, stand on my own two feet.

Chris and I had been together about five months when my dad called to say Barry Kemp, who executive-produced the show *Coach*, had a new show coming called *Princesses*, starring Julie Hagerty, Fran Drescher, and Twiggy. "He's a very smart guy. I've had dinner with him a couple of times with Norman Lear," my dad said. "I told him all about you, and he wants to meet you."

"Really?" I asked. "Based on what?"

"I showed him your *Cheers* spec and the first chapter of your screenplay. He thought they were both excellent."

"Boy, we're really gettin' our money's worth out of that *Cheers* spec," I retorted uncomfortably. "He used the word 'excellent'?"

"Actually, the word Barry used was 'outstanding,'" he said proudly.

"Get out of town!"

"*You* get out of town," he joked. "I set up a meeting for next Tuesday."

"Great. Thanks! Where do I go?" I asked, grabbing a pen and pad.

"California."

The pen fell to the floor. "California? Seriously?"

"That's where they shoot the show."

"So, wait, you want me to fly all the way out to California for a *meeting*?"

"I think he'll hire you," he said confidently.

"What if he doesn't?"

"Then you'll go have a nice visit with Grandma. But I think he'll hire you as a staff writer. He really loved your stuff—thought it was excellent."

"Outstanding," I corrected him.

"I think you should pack a suitcase, take the meeting, plan on getting the job and moving out there to write for the show. It's a phenomenal opportunity!" he said, finishing strong.

"What about Christopher?" I asked.

"What about him?"

"Well, I mean, things are pretty serious between us; we've been talking about maybe even moving in together."

"Could he go with you? Get a job out there?"

"No. He has to work here."

"Then he'll come visit you, and you'll come visit him. Make sure you wear something nice for the meeting."

"Not my unitard?"

"I wouldn't," he said, laughing. "Call me tomorrow. I love you."

"I love you," I said, hanging up the phone. "California." I glanced at my large pink suitcase in the corner of the room.

—

"Really? California? For how long?" Chris asked, leaning on the windowsill across from my bed.

"Well, I'm not really sure. My dad wants me to go out there and take this meeting, and he thinks the guy'll hire me. I guess I would go right to work for however long the show is on." As I sat on the bed, I felt like I was talking about somebody else's life.

"Wow," Chris said, getting his first taste of the Flying Grodins in action.

"What?" I felt we were both on the verge of either laughing or crying.

"I never heard you say this was anything you wanted to do," he said, confused.

For a moment I stared at him. Then, my eyes suddenly moist, I said, "What am I supposed to do? It's a great opportunity. I have to try and make a living, right?"

"Yes, of course."

"The guy said I was an outstanding writer, an excellent writer; the guy said I could really fuckin' write!" I burst into tears.

Putting his arm around me as he sat down, he said gently, "Honey, honey, come on. That's not the issue. We know you're incredibly talented."

"What am I supposed to do—just keep having him wire me

thousands and thousands of dollars, or go back to waitressing? I don't know what I'm supposed to do!" I yelled, so emotionally I spit on Christopher's chin. "Sorry," I said, wiping it off.

"It's okay," Christopher whispered sweetly. After a moment, he said softly, "I'll visit you."

"You better," I said, dropping my head onto his shoulder.

26

I'd been writing for the show for a couple of months, having all the exact same feelings I'd had the last time I did this. Every morning in the writer's room would start with all the writers sitting around, perusing the real estate section in the *Los Angeles Times*, checking out what they might buy with all the money they were making on the show. The air was thick with comments like, *My fiancé and I are going to check out this four-bedroom Cape with a saltwater pool in Laurel Canyon during lunch* or *There's a place in Malibu right on the ocean we just made an offer on.* All of these people, once again, had worked long and hard to be in a position where they could check out a four-bedroom Cape with a saltwater pool on their lunch hour. This was the life they had chosen. They were in their real lives. And, well, we know my story was breakdown, *Cheers* spec, father is Charles Grodin.

At the end of the first season, we found out that the show had been canceled. I was thrilled. It meant I got to go be in my real life in New York with Christopher, my meetings, and Zabar's.

When I told my dad, he said, "I've arranged a meeting for you with this young agent at William Morris. He's just starting out, so he's very motivated. I gave him your—"

"*Cheers* spec!" I finished his sentence and we both chuckled.

"And the first chapter of your screenplay. It'd be good if you could get another job before you fly home," he said matter-of-factly.

"Okay," I said, feeling slightly punished, since, in my mind, I'd just served a long stint in sitcom prison. See, here's the thing. It wasn't that I couldn't work hard and make money, even a lot of money. I'd just never felt umbilically connected to needing to make money in order to live, in order to support myself. It's almost like that wasn't even in my DNA. It wouldn't be until I began serving what would turn out to be, basically, a *lifetime sentence* in therapy that I would even understand that given my issues—where I came from, how I grew up—for me DNA stood more for DO NOT ABANDON. Being supported by my father made me feel safe, secure, taken care of in a way that felt as essential as breathing.

I met with the agent, a nice man, a week later. We really hit it off, and he got me several big meetings almost immediately. I gave great meetings, since that showcased the thing I was best at—schmoozing. By the time I flew home, I'd actually gotten a three-picture deal with Twentieth Century Fox.

I hadn't been home ten minutes when Christopher took me in his arms and said, "Move in with me."

"Yeah?" I said, giggling nervously.

"Mar, I know you have a lot of commitment issues and intimacy issues," he said, cuddling me.

"Food issues, body issues...," I continued, making fun of myself.

"I love your body," he said, squeezing me tight. "I missed you so much. I know this is really hard for you, but it's me, Chris. I'm your guy," he said, kissing me.

"Yes," I said, beaming at him.

"Yes, I'm your guy, or yes, you'll move in?"

"All of the above." I was so happy to be home.

So we moved in together, but something wasn't quite right.

It was Christmas, and we were at Chris's family's house in Ridgewood. It was husbands and wives, babies, small children. The air was filled with *Give me the baby, and I'll take her up for a nap. He needs to have his diaper changed. Can you go help Dad with the turkey?* It was like a Norman Rockwell painting. I was, personally, in my own painting—more like a combination of Edvard Munch's "The Scream" and one of those Renoir paintings, the ones with all those extraordinarily fat women with the very little heads.

As Christopher and I sat there watching all these couples, all the children, all the babies, all these families swirling around us in their happy, domestic chaos, there was no escaping what we both knew: this was not us. We didn't fit the way these people did; we were doing a very different dance, one that might not lead to marriage and babies. A lot of the time it didn't bother us or we tried to avoid dealing with it, but sitting there that Christmas night, when we turned to look at each other, there was a sadness in both our eyes that was undeniable.

—

Over the next few months, I tried to talk to Chris about how "our chemistry" wasn't right, how we didn't fit like the other couples we saw. And he knew it too, but, frankly, there was so much that was good—great—between us that we just pressed ahead.

So much so that the following winter, Christopher proposed. When he presented the ring to me, smiling so jubilantly, although I said yes and promptly began planning my wedding, I knew it wasn't right. My ambivalence was so strong that it felt like another organ in my body. It was a very painful way to walk around.

—

I'd been trying to work on the guest list for the wedding all day, in between working on my screenplay, and I kept having to get up because I had this tightness in my chest. I'd walk around our apartment for a few minutes, it would abate, then I'd go back to working on the list, and it would start again. It almost felt like my heart was trying to talk to me. Then it got in touch with my back, which went into spasm. And by the time I went to bed that night, they both had gotten in touch with my brain. As I lay in bed next to Christopher, I knew I had to tell him what I felt I couldn't. I listened to him breathe all night, until his alarm went off at six the next morning. I told him I couldn't get married. He was devastated; we both were. And then we did what most couples in trauma, living on the Upper West Side, do: we went to an unbelievable amount of therapy. Couples, individual, physical. I could barely stand up at this point. We cried. We talked endlessly, and there were no new revelations. I went to a ton of meetings and even started new ones after eating so much ice cream in the tub, and getting so stoned on sugar, that I fell asleep and almost drowned. There was no new information, but we loved each other deeply. We were family, and like many families, we'd become enmeshed in our own codependent tango. He was the rescuer/caretaker. I was the fabulous disaster. Neither of us was ready to stop dancing, at least not yet.

I was standing in the living room, staring out at the water towers, wishing a SWAT team would land on one of them and come rescue me from my misery, when the phone rang, jolting me out of my stupor.

"Whatcha doin'?" my dad said.

"Staring out the window," I said flatly.

"How'd you like to come work for me on my new talk show as the field correspondent?"

"Seriously?" I said, the warmth of his rescue enveloping me.

"Seriously," my dad said, teasing me affectionately.

"What would I do?"

"You'd be the field correspondent."

"Fantastic!" I exclaimed, still having no idea what that was. "So, I'm in the field," I continue, picturing myself just standing out in the middle of a field.

"Anything outside of the studio, you'd go shoot it. Plus you'll be on-camera with me sometimes. It'll be great."

"Wow! Thanks so much! I really appreciate it!"

"Of course. You're my daughter," he said, warmth pouring through the phone.

As I stared out at the water towers, I couldn't get over how he'd always been able to change my whole life with just one phone call.... My dad, the SWAT team.

27

On my first day as field correspondent, Bill, the very sexy cameraman I wished I wasn't attracted to, and I went out into the field of Columbus Circle, where all the crazed New Yorkers were getting off the subway at rush hour. My assignment was to ask people the "question of the day." This was during the O. J. trial, and I was supposed to ask everybody if they thought O. J. murdered his wife and Ron Goldman.

I spotted an older gentleman in a tweed jacket, so I took a deep breath and walked over to him. "Hi, I'm from *The Charles Grodin Show*," I announced energetically.

"Who?" he said.

"Charles Grodin," I said a little less energetically.

"Who's that?" he said.

"Uh, he's a famous actor.... *Midnight Run*... *The Heartbreak Kid*... *Rosemary's Baby*..." I offered, searching his face for any hint of recognition.

"Never heard of him." He scowled.

"Okay..." I said, smiling uncomfortably as I started to walk away.

"Who was he?" he said, taking a step closer to me.

"In which one?" I asked, trying to catch the eye of Bill, who was flirting with some emaciated nine-to-fiver.

"All of 'em," he said, as if he had paid a fee.

"Well... in *The Heartbreak Kid*, he was the guy who leaves his Jewish wife on their honeymoon for a gorgeous shiksa; in *Midnight Run*, he played an accountant for the Mob; and in *Rosemary's Baby*, he played the doctor who gives Mia Farrow back to the devils...."

Before I could continue my filmography, he snorted and said, "And this guy has his own show?"

I never got to ask him about O. J. He probably would have wanted to know what he'd been in. Not all of my interviews went this badly, but let's just say whatever I thought being a field correspondent would look like was wrong. Actually, not true. I did pretty much feel like I was standing in... a field.

The other half of my job happened every day around three o'clock, when either John or Clay, my dad's close friends who also worked on the show, would yell, "He's going down." That was our cue for the three of us to accompany my dad down to the studio and be his audience during the taping of the show.

One day, after Clay had just yelled, "He's goin' down," I stood up in my cubicle and realized there was a sizable hole in my coat. I would have gone without it, but the studio was always freezing.

Today's guest was Sarah Jessica Parker, and everybody was so excited she was coming. It was all anybody had been talking about all week. *She's so talented.... She's so funny.... She's so sexy*.... had been pouring over my cubicle wall for the last three days, forcing me to ask myself what exactly I was doing with all my talent and all my funny—I mean, besides waiting to ask another bunch of strangers if they thought O. J. did it.

"Honey, remind me to call Grandma. She wasn't feeling well yesterday," my dad shouted, settling into his chair on the brightly lit stage.

"Definitely. I hope she's okay," I said, taking a seat between John and Clay.

"She really is so talented, and smart... and funny," John said, smiling.

"She's got it all," Clay said.

"She really does," I said, examining the hole in my coat.

"There she is," my dad said, pulling off his makeup bib as he stood up, helping Sarah Jessica onto the stage.

"Hello, kind sir," Sarah Jessica said as they embraced. "Charles, you look fantastic!" she exclaimed as they held each other's arms.

"Not as fantastic as you!" he said, laughing.

I saw the camera guys check out her ass. She really did look amazing. She was wearing this dazzling little silk dress with giant purple flowers that clung to her spectacular body in all the right places.

"Chuck, in five," the stage manager said as my dad and Sarah Jessica released each other and settled into their chairs.

"We all know my first guest from her amazing success. The lovely, adorable, and talented movie star, Sarah Jessica Parker. Please give her a warm welcome."

As I sat there, in the dark, clapping, laughing, in all the right places, professionally playing the part of the fan, I couldn't escape the toll that championing other people's bigness while dwarfing my own was taking on me. From as far back as I could remember, I'd flown under my father's wing, staying close, catching all the residual glow that spilled off his shine. As the interview ended, and the lights in the studio came up, I thought, *It has to be better not to ride on anyone else's coattails and just stick with your own... even if there's a hole in them.*

28

The next week I quit my dad's show, told my agent not to submit me for any more writing jobs, and decided to do the only thing I'd dreamt of doing since the first time I heard Richard Pryor. So one steamy August night, bolstered by Chris and our two best friends, I walked the seven blocks down to Stand Up NY, got onstage, and did what I'd been wanting to do my whole life.

The second I got offstage, I called my dad, who was anxiously waiting by the phone. I said, "Well, I've got good news and bad news. The good news is I got *lots* of laughs; the bad news is the *entire* time I was up there, I felt like I might have a heart attack *and* lose control of my bowels." He assured me this feeling would go away. And after about a year, it did, for the most part.

I started getting onstage a lot. I loved it. Christopher was always there to cheer me on, and mostly it went great. Mostly. Occasionally, I'd get heckled, which over time I became a pro at handling. But the first time it happened, it was devastating. I was onstage at a midnight show in the Village at The Duplex. The guy who ran the show, Gus, would bring in these enormous bags of penny candy for the audience. On more than a few occasions, Gus had found it necessary to take me aside and let me know that my candy consumption was unreasonably cutting into the audience's candy allotment. This particular night, I had been on the verge of tears all night due to very bad PMS, when I tried to engage this evil Puerto Rican woman in the front row.

She kept saying, "Why you even *talkin'* to me?! You the one spose to have jokes! Where's your *jokes* at? You mus' have *forgot* to write those jokes, jus' like you *forgot* to iron that shirt!"

I left the stage humiliated, wrinkled, and crying. That experience taught me two very valuable lessons. One, you always have to let the audience know you're in charge, not them. And two, don't ever go onstage without ironing.

I'd just started producing my own show at Gotham Comedy Club. I was feeling pretty good until the day I got a call from my dad telling me my grandmother was very sick. I adored my grandma Lena. After I lost my mom, we became extremely close. Whenever I was in LA, we'd go to our Weight Watchers meetings together, where, without fail, my grandmother would start talking to the thinnest woman in the room—"I know why *we're* here, but what are *you* doing here?" she'd announce, bringing the house down. I wasn't the only stand-up in our family. A few weeks after I arrived in LA, my beautiful grandma Lena passed away.

"Mar, I'm so sorry," Christopher said, throwing his arms around me as I came off the plane from LA. I felt so safe, so secure...like I could live inside those arms forever. It's funny how the landscape of your life, of your heart, can shift in just a moment. With my mom and now my grandmother gone, I felt like my entire sense of "home" was right there, inside Christopher's arms.

—

"Marry me," he said, standing behind me at the kitchen sink.

"What?" I said, laughing nervously.

"Marry me.... Come on... we love each other, and neither of us is going anywhere. I want you to marry me," he said, joining me in the nervous laughter. I let out a deep breath, hoping to diffuse my anxiety.

"I mean it, Mar. I love you, but I want you to marry me. I'm not going to just stick around in limbo with you," he said firmly.

"But that's how I function best... *limbo*," I said playfully, limboing toward him.

"You're not gonna joke me out of this. I'm serious. You marry me or we break up," he said, staring into my eyes.

"Can I have a little time to digest this?" I said, smiling coyly.

"You can have forty-eight hours. Mar, I'm serious this time. I mean what I'm saying."

Having delivered his ultimatum, he grabbed a bottle of water and walked out of the kitchen. A few minutes later, I was eyeballing the pint of chocolate Heath Bar crunch ice cream in the freezer, wondering if it could help me with Christopher's proposal, when the phone rang.

"Mar, it's your dad," Chris called from the living room.

"I'll take it in the bedroom," I yelled, shutting the bedroom door behind me.

"What's going on?" my dad said.

"Christopher wants to get married again," I said quickly.

"I still don't get why you backed out the first time. You better marry him. He's not gonna wait forever. You'll lose him, and then he'll find someone else, and then you'll be walking down Broadway and bump into him and his pregnant wife. How's that gonna feel?" he said matter-of-factly.

"Jesus, don't scare the shit out of me," I said agitatedly.

"I'm not trying to scare you; I'm just being realistic, I mean, you really have to ask yourself how that's gonna feel. He's there with his new wife, a little daughter, a son on the way."

"*A son on the way?!* You just upped the kid thing. Fuck!" I said, anxiety coursing through my veins.

"'Fuck' is right. Life's very short. I don't have to tell you. He's a great guy. Just fuckin' marry him already," he said emotionally. I knew the intensity of his emotion was fueled by his mother's death, both our mothers' deaths.

A few minutes later, I walked into the living room.

"Hey," Christopher said, muting the TV. I walked over to the chair he was sitting in.

"Yes," I whispered, kissing the top of his head.

—

"I want to get married in nature," I said as Christopher and I walked out of the fourth fancy hotel we'd looked at on Fifty-Ninth Street, off the park.

"That would be great," he said, smiling. "What are you thinking?" he continued.

I looked at him then looked across at the park, motioning toward it with my chin.

"Yeah?" he said sweetly.

"Why not?" I said. "I mean, I grew up in Central Park, walking the dogs with my mom, hanging out, and you love the park, running around the reservoir," I said, slipping my hand inside his.

"It's great, but what do you mean? Like, in a *field*?" he said as we both started giggling.

"Yes, Chris, in a *field*... near a hot dog stand. We'll serve hot dogs and Mountain Dew," I said as we entered the park. It was six o'clock. There was a slight chill in the air, and the sky was that wonderful moody blue gray. We strolled among the joggers and baby carriages, and then it hit me.

"The *Boathouse*... omigod... the Boathouse," I said, nodding my head up and down as I turned to face him.

Mirroring my enthusiasm, he said, "Just, like... out on the dock...?"

"Yes, Chris, out on the dock. The caterers can just row by with hors d'oeuvres. I went in the other day to use the bathroom. It's all enclosed, but still outdoors. It's really pretty, honey," I said as he sat down on a bench and pulled me onto his lap. "Whadaya think?"

"I think it's perfect," he said, laughing.

Okay, now, obviously I had no experience planning a wedding. Well, that's not entirely true. I did have those two hours during my *first attempt*, which ended abruptly when I thought I might be having a heart attack. This time it was my *back*. From almost the second we'd set the date and started telling everyone, I was in so much pain, I could barely stand up. But given that I'd already pulled out once, Christopher didn't even want to hear about it. When my back was so bad that all I could do was lie on the living room floor, alternating ice packs and a heating pad, he'd just stare at me and say, "I don't care if I have to wheel you down the aisle on a gurney, we're getting married." Just the words every bride-to-be longs to hear. It wasn't that he didn't feel bad for me, he was just determined to, as he put it—"get me over the finish line."

I couldn't believe how much shit there was to take care of. Who knew. A million and one little and not-so-little decisions, and *nothing* was simple. The flowers, for instance. I couldn't just get some flowers. Oh, no, I had to go some place that fifty people told me was "the best and ONLY place." Then they were so fuckin' expensive, I thought I might have to forgo buying a dress and just appear in some velvet ensemble from Chico's. The food, the music, the guest list, the seating chart... Omigod, it just went on and on and on....

So I literally spent the months preparing for what everyone kept telling me was supposed to be THE HAPPIEST DAY OF MY LIFE lying on the floor, spasming, watching all the Alien movies over and over again. There was something about Sigourney Weaver, lost in space, killing these aliens, that was so comforting to me. I'm sure it was a metaphor for my battle with my own demons. But, whatever the reasons, I could not get enough of those aliens.

So, after meetings with florists, caterers, and the woman making my dress ("Will you be wearing your back brace on your big day?"); extra therapy sessions (individual and couples); massages; chiropractic adjustments; MRIs of my back; recovery meetings (where the leader, when calling on me, would refer to me as "the lady in the back...on the floor"); and conversations with my father, we got married. And you know what? It. Was. Perfect.

29

Two days later, Christopher and I flew to Puerto Rico. I was getting some gum in the airport gift shop when Christopher suggested I get a book for the plane. "Mar, trust me, you're gonna love this," he said, holding up a copy of James Patterson's *Along Came a Spider*.

"Yeah, what's it about?" I asked as we stepped up to the checkout counter.

"A sociopath, living a dual life as a stable family man, while he's running around killing people," he said, handing it to the Indian woman at the checkout.

"I'll take it."

Two hours later, Christopher gently elbowed me. "Mar, look out the window.... Isn't that beautiful? Mar...," he said again.

Barely looking up from my book, I muttered, "Honey, please, my guy's on a killing spree."

On the second day of our honeymoon, I came down with

the flu, and Christopher got a cold sore on his lip that was so big, he couldn't make it to the lobby without at least one hotel maid stopping him and saying, "Ayy, *señor*... what happened to your *lip*?" Yes, the fairy tale continued.

A week and five James Patterson novels later, I arrived back on Eighty-Fifth street a married woman. Christopher's wife. Everyone said I was *glowing*. I mean, I may have still had a touch of the flu, but I was really, really happy. To know that someone sees you with all your shit, all your brokenness, and still says, *You... I want you, forever*. Amazing.

Once you get married, there's an almost automatic momentum that takes over. You're on the newly married express, and after the wedding and the honeymoon, we all know what the next stop is. Babyville!

Remember that "ambivalence" organ I told you about earlier—well, it definitely applied to having a baby. I mean, I definitely wanted one, but I also knew that, in many ways, I still was one. Christopher, on the other hand, was Irish Catholic—I'm fairly certain there's something in all those wafers they give them at church. Seriously, Christopher's little sister, Doreen, was married to a guy who was, like, one of twelve, and that guy's mother was, like, one of nineteen. I'd see her sometimes at family barbecues, and frankly, I never even got how that woman was sitting up! Couple all that with my dad doing everything short of asking for a calendar with my ovulation cycle, and getting pregnant became our primary focus!

That summer we were renting this cozy little red house on the Jersey Shore, high up on a hill, overlooking the water. All the windows were open in our upstairs bedroom, and there was the warmest breeze blowing through the curtains. I was lying at the top of our bed, with my legs up against the wall.

We'd been told this would increase our chances. Christopher would have hung me from the dining room chandelier if he'd thought it would have helped. A little while later, I came downstairs. Christopher was sitting in this comfy chair, playing his guitar. He looked up at me, beaming, as I sat on the couch. I've heard a lot of women say they knew the moment they got pregnant, and I did. Staring at him, as he played, I'd just never felt so much love. I didn't say anything to Chris, just in case I was wrong, and we went about our lives. During the week, I'd do stand-up at the clubs; Chris would work downtown. On the weekends, we'd take the ferry out to our house.

But five days later, my period was supposed to come, and didn't. On my way downtown to host a show at Gotham, I decided to pick up an EPT kit—actually, three EPT kits. I told myself I'd wait till I got home to take a test, but as I sat in the back of the club, waiting to give each comic *the light* (so they know their time's up), it was all I could think about. I brought up the final comic of the night, grabbed my purse, and headed into the bathroom. I took the stick out of the box, peed on it, laid it on the corner of the sink, and waited. I closed my eyes, hoping my slightly distended belly wasn't just all the late-night diner food. I opened my eyes and leaned over. *Omigod!* Two bright-blue lines. I couldn't fucking believe it. I was pregnant!

Suddenly there was a loud, insistent knock at the door. Part of me expected it to be my dad with a bassinet...but it was Brad, the manager of the club and a good friend of mine.

"Mar, he's got the light," he said warmly.

"And I've got the line," I said, waving my stick in the air.

When I got home and told Chris, we were both so blissed out, we couldn't even really *speak*. Our families were over the moon. Everybody was just so happy for us. I had a big show coming up at Caroline's, so I invited *everyone*. It would be a celebration.

I loved being pregnant. I remember one night, going to my narcotics recovery meeting near our apartment. As I sat there, looking around at all the other women I was pretty sure *didn't* have babies growing inside of them, I just felt so womanly, so grateful... so *blessed*.

Summer was almost over, and it was our last weekend in the house. We'd had friends over for dinner, and it had been such a wonderful night. Lots of laughter and stories. I just felt so content, and that was not such a common feeling for me. Everything just felt *right*.

The next day, I rolled out of bed and shuffled down the hall to the bathroom. The house smelled like hazelnut coffee and toast. I could hear Christopher downstairs, playing a Stevie Ray Vaughan song on his guitar. I smiled as I plopped down on the toilet, humming along to the music. I let out a big yawn, as I broke off some toilet paper, wiped, and was about to flush, when I *saw it*. Blood. Bright-red blood. I wiped again. More.

"Chris..." I cried. I could hear him racing up the stairs. As he stepped inside the bathroom, I held up the blood-spotted toilet paper.

"Ah, Mar...," he said, walking into me. "Did it just start?" Compassion poured out of him. Burying my face in his belly, I nodded. "Honey, I'm sure it's nothing," he said unsurely. "We'll go see the doctor first thing Monday morning," he said, squatting down as he held my face in his hands. "Honey, it's gonna be okay; I'm sure this happens all the time." I noticed how hard he was biting his lower lip.

The next day, we sat close, holding hands, my head on his

shoulder, on the top deck of the ferry. Neither of us said anything the whole ride back. As the ferry sped through the dusky night, I couldn't get over how bleak and ominous the sky looked, when just yesterday, it had looked so . . . *hopeful*.

The next morning, I arrived at my gynecologist's office at eight a.m. The waiting room was full of pregnant women and their partners. Everyone looked so *happy*. As Christopher and I sat there, holding hands, I felt like I was looking at a tribe I might not belong to anymore.

"Ms. Grodin," the young, pretty nurse called, opening a door into the waiting area. "The doctor will see you now," she said, so sympathetically I was sure she *knew something*.

"It's going to be okay, Mar. . . . I love you," Chris said as I leaned over to kiss him.

"Love you too," I said, letting go of his hand as I walked toward the door.

"Hi," Dr. Barnett said as I walked into the exam room. Dr. Barnett was in her thirties, had short, light-red hair, and was one of the kindest people I'd ever met.

"Hi," I said, immediately soothed by the sound of her voice.

"So, you said you saw some spotting. . . ."

I nodded.

"Hop up on the table, and let's take a look," she said, squeezing some clear gel on a strobe. "Lay back for me," she said warmly. She rubbed the strobe over my belly. As she pulled the screen closer to her, I stared at her face. *"Mmmm."* She continued to search the screen.

"What?" I said, feeling like all the color had left the room.

For a moment she just continued studying the screen. Then, clearing her throat, she said, "I can't find the heartbeat."

Lying there, I felt like I couldn't find mine either.

"I'm so sorry," she said, with so much sincerity, it almost helped. She reached for some tissues and wiped off my belly.

Emptiness filling me up, I started to cry.

"Ah, I know, it's so disappointing," she said, as I hoisted myself into a sitting position. *Disappointing*, I thought, staring down at my shoes.... What a safe, finite word for such an infinitely disturbing experience.

"Why did it happen?" I heard myself ask meekly.

"We don't know. It's not unusual for a first pregnancy to end in miscarriage," she said.

"Really? How come no one tells you that?" I pleaded, feeling betrayed.

"I don't think most women like to talk about it," she offered gently.

My eyes closing, before I even realized they had, I nodded.

Generously keeping me company in the awful silence, she finally cleared her throat and said, "You're the third patient who's miscarried this week.... I'm wondering if it might not be a virus in the water."

"Really, in the *water*?" I uttered in disbelief.

"It's possible," she said as I contemplated never having another glass of water.

"Well, what do I do now... I mean, with what's still... inside me?" I asked, feeling sick that I was even in this conversation.

"You don't *do* anything. Nature will take its course.... Your body will expel the remaining matter in its own time," she said tenderly as she took my hand.

"You mean... the rest of it's just going to... come out of me?" I asked, horrified.

"Yes... it may come out gradually, or it may come out all at once.... I would suggest you take it easy the next few days and rest as much as you can.... Can you just go to bed?" she asked, getting ready for her next patient, who I hoped was not a big water drinker.

"No, I'm performing at Caroline's tonight," I said, pushing myself off the table.

"Well, can you cancel it? I'm sure they'll understand," she said.

"I can't, and they won't. I have, like, forty people coming. It was going to be... a celebration... of our news," I said, numb.

As we walked to the door, she put her hand on my back. "Marion, I am so sorry, but there's still every reason to believe that you and Chris will be able to conceive. Just wait a little, and you can start trying again," she said as I closed the door behind me.

It was raining lightly when Christopher and I left her office. When we got outside, I told him. We were in shock; we just stood there for the longest time, holding each other in the rain.

After much insistence, I finally persuaded Chris to go back to work. I took a long, deep breath, and headed toward the park. I was in no hurry to get... *anywhere.* The place I thought I was had been taken away, and now I just felt rudderless and so, so, sad.

As I walked in the rain, I kept having this image of me collapsing onstage at Caroline's. But I had so many Jews coming to the show, I thought, *somebody's* gotta be in the medical profession. I had one of the best sets I'd ever had that night. Honestly, having to perform that night probably saved me... at least for the fifteen minutes I was onstage.

—

I'd suffered terrible loss and been savagely heartbroken in my life, but I'd never had my heart break right next to someone else's. Someone I loved more than anyone else on the planet. Everyone kept saying they were so "sorry for our loss." I didn't feel like we'd *lost* this baby. It was more sinister than that. It felt like we'd been tricked into believing we were going to receive the most mind-blowing gift imaginable, and now, with absolutely no warning or reasonable explanation (*water?!*) our gift, our baby, had been taken away.

The grief was surreal. This feeling that my baby who hadn't yet become a baby, and who, now, we would never even get to meet, or hold, or smell, or love, was dead, felt like more than any soul should have to bear. As if this wasn't horrendous enough, my body still thought it was pregnant. I still *felt* like I was pregnant. My breasts and belly were still swollen. My hormones had me bouncing off the walls. I couldn't stop crying. I didn't want to talk to anybody. I didn't want to see anybody. I didn't want to... *be* anybody.

The sadness pouring out of me wasn't just about the miscarriage—although that would have been more than enough. It was as if that grief had woken up all the other grief, which, until the miscarriage, wasn't gone but had been... *sleeping*. Every night, I would lie in the dark, next to Christopher, with my hand over my mouth, trying to stifle my cries. But at some point, inevitably, my pain would run me into the bathroom, where I would sit sobbing about the loss of my baby... and the loss of my mother.

I'd cry most of the night, and be in a haze the next day, hiding behind dark sunglasses, only leaving the apartment to go downstairs to the Häagen-Dazs store, trying desperately to send all the grief back to sleep. It was no different from when I'd gone to the bar, or gone to cop drugs. It was secretive. I didn't want anyone to see me. I felt ashamed. I had no choice.

Sometimes, in order to justify the sheer *volume* of what I was ordering, I would shoot my head around as if someone had just called me from outside. Then I'd look at the person behind the counter, pretend to be annoyed, hold up a finger, and say something like, "Let me just see what they want...." Occasionally, I'd pretend to be ordering for a bar mitzvah.

I went to my recovery meetings, but after the second time someone asked me how far along I was, I stopped going. It wasn't their fault. I was fat, and a lot of people didn't know I'd miscarried. Christopher was completely there for me. But I still felt alone, because no matter what he said or did, I was the one still bleeding a week later, watching what would have been our baby come out of me, one little bloody deposit at a time.

30

One afternoon, when I came to after another brutal binge, there were sprinkles, gummy bears, and chocolate chips encrusted all over my chest. It looked as if I'd bedazzled myself with toppings. As I hoisted myself into a sitting position, I was so hung over (nauseous, stabbing head pains, chest pains) that I just fell back down. Lying there feeling like I was about to be filmed for the Discovery Channel, I knew even if I could manage to get myself dressed and out the door, it wouldn't matter how sick I was—I was going to do it all over again.

I knew I needed to go somewhere so I could get help to stop bingeing, and where no one knew me, and we'd all be fat. If anyone thought I looked pregnant, they'd just assume it was with a roast chicken and not a baby. I went online, and found this not-too-expensive place in Texas that said it provided "a safe and supervised way to fast." The picture on their website was of a group of pleasant-looking fat women sitting under a big ol' oak tree, smiling and sipping cool beverages. I can do *that*. I can sit under a tree with some fellow fatties, sipping a nice cool beverage. Christopher and my father thought I was nuts.

"What happens if you get really hungry?" my dad said emotionally into the phone.

"I'll nibble on one of the other fatties," I said, laughing. That ended my dad's objections. His gratitude that I was laughing again far outweighed whatever fears he had about my starving to death under an oak tree.

A week later, I arrived in Texas, ready to *fast*. A tall man with a red cap and very dirty fingernails met me at the airport. An hour later, I was sitting in Bubba's pickup truck, not sure if I was nauseous because I hadn't eaten since last night or because I was listening to these redneck parodies pouring out of Bubba's cassette player. "All I wanna do is shoot my gun..." set to the music from Sheryl Crow's "All I Wanna Do" was just one of the many atrocities I was forced to endure, in addition to the voluminous clouds of cigarette smoke pouring out of Bubba's mouth.

By the time we pulled up to the psychiatric hospital–looking building, I was fairly certain I had made a terrible mistake, but frankly, I was so weak and sick from not eating and detoxing all the crap I'd been bingeing on that I just wanted to get to my room and lie down.

"Welcome!" an exuberant little man exclaimed as he flung open the porch door. "I'm Joe," he said as Bubba handed him my suitcase. "Thanks," Joe said to Bubba, who spit and walked away.

"Hi," I said, wondering just how Bubba figured into this whole thing.

"How was the flight?" Joe said, leading me up a dusty wooden staircase.

"Good, thanks," I said, wondering where the kitchen was. I was fucking starving. I followed him down a long green linoleum hallway, which looked like every hallway in every movie I'd ever seen that they walk you down right before they strap you to a table and give you electroshock.

"Why don't you get settled, then come on downstairs and meet everybody," Joe said, setting my suitcase down next to the dusty bureau as he closed the door behind him.

"*Omifuckingod,*" I said under my breath, staring up at the high row of windows encased in some kind of sturdy mesh, which I also recognized from every movie I'd ever seen about insane asylums. I sat down on the springy, old twin bed with a gray wool blanket that felt like it'd been made from Brillo pads. As I glanced around my room, with its green linoleum floor, I wondered exactly when the twins from *The Shining* would be showing up.

As I descended the stairs, I heard the sound of a TV. It was coming from a room just outside the kitchen.

"Hey, don't be shy. Come on in," a large woman with large red hair said, peering at me from a couch, where she was squeezed in next to three other very large women. In an old upholstered recliner beside them sat a mean-looking chubby man.

"Hi," I said, taking a step into the room.

"Betty, scoot over," she said to the dark-haired woman next to her. "There's room. I'm Sandy, and this is Betty, Peggy, and that's Dean," the redheaded woman said, smiling.

"Hi, I'm Marion," I said, squeezing in between Sandy and Betty. Everyone smiled, except Dean, who looked enraged. I tried to give him the benefit of the doubt. Lord only knew when he'd last eaten.

"Hi," they all said, immediately turning their attention back to the TV. Realizing that would be the extent of our conversation, I turned my attention to the TV. They were watching *Married with Children.* Sitting there with my ass slammed up against Sandy and Betty's asses as the bad jokes and aggressive sound track assaulted the air, I wondered if there were any crackers in this shithole.

As if reading my mind, Betty said, "Dinner's in ten minutes." ("Dinner," it turned out, was lettuce.) Everybody but Dean nodded their heads excitedly as Sandy let out a big, wet burp.

"'Scuse *me*," she said, as surprised and disgusted as the rest of us. "Joe says it's the detox. Our bodies are letting go of all the poisons," she said, blushing.

"Please, I'm trying to watch this," Dean said angrily.

"Sorry," Sandy whispered as I glanced down at the magazine in front of me. It was called *Texas Weekly* and had a picture of a cow on it. God, I was hungry.

Two nights later, the Academy Awards were on. I was just so grateful not to be watching *Married with Children.* Betty, Peggy, and I were on the couch; Dean was in the recliner. Sandy was MIA, but I was almost positive I could hear her opening containers in the kitchen. Watching Billy Crystal, who was the host, do his opening monologue, I instantly felt better. *My tribe*, I thought as Sandy, who had some crumbs on her chin, squeezed in between me and Peggy. We were all laughing and enjoying the show, when all of a sudden, Dean said, "Billy Crystal. He's Jewish, isn't he?"

"He is," I said, instantly tense. I'd never even heard this guy speak, and now he wanted to know if Billy Crystal was Jewish?

A few minutes later, as cameras panned the audience, Dean

cleared his throat and said, "Now, *he's* definitely Jewish. What's his name?"

"Steven Spielberg," I said as my lower back went into spasm.

"All his movies are about Jews," Sandy piped up, a tiny crumb dangling from her bottom lip.

"All of them," Peggy chimed in. As the camera swung over to Bette Midler, I could feel my left eye start to twitch.

"Oh, she's Jewish," Peggy said, like she was playing a game.

"Why does everyone care so much about *who's Jewish*?" I barked. As they all just stared at me, I felt like Woody Allen in that scene from *Annie Hall* when he sees himself in full rabbinical garb as Annie's Jew-hating grammy glares at him.

"I'm Jewish," I said. They all looked at me as if I'd just said, *My parents are dolphins*.

After a very long silence, Dean said, "You don't *look* Jewish."

"You don't," Sandy said reassuringly.

"I mean, you've got such a cute little nose," Peggy said, smiling.

That's it! I knew I had to get the fuck out of there before I was too weak to fight off these fat anti-Semites! On the flight back to the land of my Jews, I was incapacitated from not having eaten for five days. Which was lucky for the chubby woman sitting next to me, because if I could have, I definitely would have wrestled that chocolate chip cookie out of her hand.

31

I got back from the starving Jew haters, and, of course, put back on all the weight I'd lost, feeling I owed myself a lot of pie. We'd been given the go-ahead from Dr. Barnett to start *trying* again. So we were back on the newlywed express, and the next stop was buying a home. We looked for a two-bedroom apartment in the city, but there was nothing even worth looking at for under half a million dollars. Christopher and I both felt pretty defeated. Then one afternoon, our Realtor showed us an apartment we really liked. Until she opened the door to a closet and asked me how I liked the second bedroom. The next weekend we started looking in Bergen County.

We finally found something we could afford in Paramus. It was a "fixer-upper," which I believe is Realtor slang for "piece of shit." It needed a ton of work, and the plan was that Christopher would renovate it. There were two bedrooms upstairs, which had this depressing maroon wall-to-wall carpeting and a tiny bathroom. Downstairs was a big TV room with this disgusting, old brown shag carpet. Right off that room was the kitchen. It was very outdated. The linoleum floor had a sizable crack in it, where the earth was actually peeking through.

We'd been trying for about a month when I suspected I might be pregnant again. I didn't have a gig, and Chris was in the city, working a double, so I knew he wouldn't be home till late. I went and got a few EPT kits.

As I sat there, staring at the two blue lines, I could not stop smiling. It was almost midnight when I heard Chris's key in the door.

"Hello," he called out.

"Hi," I yelled back. "I'm in the kitchen, with the earth."

"Let me wash up," he called over his shoulder as he headed into the bathroom.

"Okay," I called, trying not to break into song.

"Ah, honey," he said, beaming, as he walked toward me holding the EPT sticks.

"I know," I squealed as he wrapped his arms around me.

—

Once again, everybody was so happy for us. We both tried to relax and trust that this pregnancy would be okay. But I couldn't help but hold my breath every time I went to the bathroom. Chris worked downtown during the week, and on the house on weekends. I did stand-up, mostly in the city, sometimes on the road—pretty much always killing, still not earning a living. Still getting the car towed. It was business as usual. And then, just when I'd started to really trust this pregnancy, I went to the bathroom, and…there they were. Little bloody tears.

A couple days later, I had a D&C. That's where they basically suction whatever's in you *out*. I'm not even sure what "D&C" stands for. For me, it stood for "Depression & Chocolate." What the fuck is *in* chocolate? Seriously. Having to feel all the feelings, having to tell everyone again—it was just brutal.

32

A couple months later we got pregnant and miscarried again.

When you miscarry for the first time, there really are no words for how awful it is, but then you're quickly reassured that it happens to a lot of women and that most women go on to have perfectly healthy babies. Even after your second miscarriage, the wind is, of course, knocked out of your sails, but everyone assures you that you will... sail again.

After your third miscarriage... nobody knows *what* to say. One friend suggested we get a pony. Seriously.

What had started out as an excited, loving wish to start a family had left us completely... wrecked. But you can never underestimate the resilience of the human spirit, especially when it's baby-related. Because just when we, and everybody else, thought we were down for the count, we lifted our heads off the mat and decided we'd embark on the all-consuming process of in vitro fertilization at NYU in the city. I had to give myself these shots that were supposed to send my ovaries into hyperdrive. The goal was to produce and then fertilize as many viable eggs as possible. I kept having this image of myself in the delivery room, with my legs up in the stirrups, and just, like, this assembly line of babies pouring out of my vagina, followed by everything that was missing: my keys, mittens, socks, passport…

After what felt like endless shots and doctor visits, it was time to "fertilize" me. The cost of all of this, emotionally and financially, was so steep. But we were hopeful. The doctor said everything looked great, and I'd produced a lot of eggs, enough for several babies and a light soufflé. We kept our fingers crossed and drove to NYU for the procedure. A few days later, we found out it didn't take. We contemplated somehow finding a way to maybe try to do another round of in vitro, but frankly we were out of money as well as hope.

I don't believe having a baby fixes what's wrong in a relationship, but you know what really doesn't help? Multiple miscarriages and unsuccessful in vitro. We just hadn't had any good news in so long. I still couldn't get over that as good as I was, I couldn't make a living doing stand-up.

And then there was going on "the road," which I *loathed* and Chris always begged me to stop doing. I'd be gone all weekend, but I was trying to support myself by doing stand-up full-time, and the road was something that most comics suffered through. Road audiences could be some of the drunkest, most hostile, homophobic, misogynistic crowds I'd ever dealt with. I'd drive hundreds of miles to these shit clubs, with names like "Bust Ups," "Guffaws," "Cackles," "Chortles," "Haw-Haws," "Ho-Hos," "Snickers," after which I'd often end up *eating* a lot of Snickers or Ho Hos, trying to kill the pain of whatever indignities I'd just endured: "Show us your tits," "Say something funny," "Jew dyke," random requests for blow jobs.... I'd call home, looking for Christopher to cheer me up, which was rough, since he needed someone to cheer *him* up. He'd tell me he'd lie awake, unable to go to sleep because he was having chest pains, knowing I was driving with multiple unpaid tickets on my car, or with a suspended license and that I could, at any point, get towed or even be arrested. Then he'd move on to tell me how worried he was about my bingeing and refusal to open any bills. Those two giant Hefty bags had also made the move to Paramus. He was beyond worn out.

After years of unhappiness, Christopher left his job and was trying to start up his own contracting business. We were both so excited. I even went out and got him these adorable little cards with a man on a roof with a hammer. We'd both thought it would be great, but the reality was that he couldn't afford to hire anyone, so he was working horribly long hours by himself. He'd pull in the driveway while I was pulling out to go do stand-up. I'd promise to come out to wherever he was working and keep him company, but I never did. He'd promise to make it to one of my shows, but he never did. To make matters worse, on the weekends, when his family would frequently have birthdays, graduations, christenings, or baptisms (which, as many times as Chris explained what the difference between the two was, I still couldn't tell you), I was always way too fried from a late night at the club to make these early-morning celebrations of life.

We both felt lonely and isolated, and as much as we tried to somehow meet in the middle of our incongruent lives, it was clear to both of us that the middle was getting smaller and smaller. In addition to all our logistical difficulties, Christopher was desperate to resign from policing my life. He really was trying to stop dancing his part in our codependent tango... but I didn't feel like I even knew any other steps.

It was one of those disgusting, sticky August nights, and I had just gotten home from my gig down on the Jersey Shore. It must have been three a.m., and Christopher had been asleep for hours. All I wanted to do was get in the shower. I started peeling my clothes off as I tiptoed up the stairs.

"Thank you, God," I said out loud as the water washed away the sweat. About fifteen minutes later, I stepped out of the shower onto the little blue bath mat. As I reached for my towel on the back of the bathroom door, my right hand grazed the side of my breast. *What?* my weary mind sputtered as my chest tightened. I drew my hand back, repeating the exact same motion. I felt it again.

It's because you're so tired. You're imagining it, my mind said. Feeling like I was going to throw up, I cradled my right breast with my left hand and slowly ran my right thumb over the *lump*. I have fibrocystic breasts, which basically means they're lumpy, so it wasn't unusual for me to feel lumps in my breasts. But this lump was different. It was harder, more... *insistent*. I looked at myself in the mirror. If I looked closely, I could actually *see* it. I was so tired. Way too tired to deal with whatever this was. I shut my eyes, shaking my head from side to side, as I shuffled into the bedroom. *God, I'm begging you... please, just let me sleep now*, I prayed as I climbed in beside Christopher.

33

The next day, I woke up around one o'clock. I could hear Chris downstairs in the kitchen. I lifted my nightshirt, hoping it had just been a bad dream. It wasn't. I walked into the bathroom, splashed some cold water on my face, and went downstairs. Chris was sitting on the couch in our TV room, staring at the blank television screen.

"Hi," I said, walking slowly toward him.

"Hi, I need to talk to you," he said seriously.

"I need to talk to you too," I said, standing across from him.

"Okay," he said distractedly.

"What?" I said, sitting down in the armchair next to him.

"I'm thinking of moving out," he said.

"*What?*" I said, shocked.

"Thinking about it," he said plainly.

"*Why?*" I asked as my stomach flipped.

"Honey, come on, *seriously*?" he said with a warmth that didn't match the words that had just come out of his mouth.

"Okay, look, can I just ask that we not talk about *that* right this minute.... I found a lump in my breast," I said.

"*What?*" he said, leaning toward me.

"Last night, when I was getting out of the shower...," I continued.

"But you have... fibrocyst..." he interrupted.

"This feels *different*," I said, lifting my shirt. "Give me your hand," I said as we both stood up. "Feel it?" I asked, staring into his eyes.

"No..." he said, trying to find it.

"*There*," I said, placing his index finger on it. "Feel it? Feel it?" I asked, my voice rising.

"I *do*... but you have lumpy breasts, honey," he said, immediately moving into his role as caretaker.

"But this feels *harder*... more... insistent... *different*... no?" I persisted as I guided his fingers around it.

"Have you been eating a lot of dairy?" he asked, staring at me. "Have you? You know you get a lot of inflammation from dairy; you're probably just having an allergic reaction," he said, his tone less comforting than usual.

"I hope so," I said, pulling my shirt down. "I think I should get it looked at right away, just to be sure," I said as the toaster went off in the kitchen.

"It's probably from dairy," he said, grabbing his bagel out of the toaster.

"Ya *think*?" I called out, lifting my shirt up to examine it again.

"I'm sure it's fine," he yelled as he spread cream cheese on his bagel before putting on the lox and onion.

"Ya *think*?" I said again, walking into the kitchen.

"Mar, stop touching it; you're just irritating it," he said as I sidled up next to him, eyeing his food. "No," he said sternly, staring at me, staring at his food. "It's dairy," he said exasperatedly.

"It's Jew food.... You didn't even know about bagels, lox, and cream cheese before you met me," I said flirtatiously.

"I didn't know about a lot of things before I met you," he said as he walked his food into the other room.

—

I'd gone in for a mammogram three days earlier, and we were just waiting for the results. We were watching a movie when my cell phone rang.

"Is this Marion Grodin?" a man asked.

"Yes," I said, my stomach instantly tightening.

"This is Dr. Prado, calling from the hospital," the man said.

"Yes, hi, doctor," I said, my eyes darting toward Christopher as he shut off the TV.

"Okay, so we did see something on your mammogram," he said delicately.

"You *did*?" Anxiety exploded throughout my body. As Christopher took my hand, I shook my head from side to side.

"Yes, but we want you to come in for a needle biopsy and an MRI so we can get a better look...," he continued.

"I don't understand. Couldn't you tell what you were looking at from the mammogram?" I said, trying to control my hysteria.

"Not really.... There is something there; we're just not exactly sure what. An MRI will allow us to get a more accurate picture," he said calmly.

"Is it possible it's just a benign fibrosis?" I asked, closing my eyes. "Because I do have fibrocystic breasts."

"It's *possible*, but we will need to get a better look," he said politely.

"Okay," I said, exhaling deeply. "Well, I don't want to *wait*. What's the soonest you can schedule the MRI?" I asked, rubbing my lower back, which was spasming.

"Let me put you on with Shannon, and she'll get you scheduled. Hold on one moment, please," he said as Queen singing "Another One Bites the Dust" burst on the line.

"What's happening?" Christopher asked, rubbing my back.

"They see something; they're not sure *what*.... I'm waiting for Shannon to schedule my MRI so they can get a better look.... Queen's singing 'Another One Bites the Dust,'" I reported, wishing I could laugh.

"Honey," Christopher said, compassion oozing out of every pore. For a moment, we just stared at each other, in disbelief.

Then I launched into, *"Another one bites the dust.... Another one bites the dust!"* as Christopher bit his lower lip, trying not to laugh.

"Ms. Grodin?" a sweet voice said as Queen went away.

"Yes," I answered as Christopher massaged my back.

"Okay, so we need to get you scheduled for an MRI.... Let me just take a look at the schedule.... Okay, so today is Monday... can you come in on Wednesday?" she asked.

"Yes, this Wednesday?" I asked.

"Uhhh... oh, wait a minute, no, actually the woman who runs the MRI machine is out till... Could you come in a week from Thursday? You could be her first appointment," she said.

"You mean ten days from now... to find out if I have a tumor?" I said, unhinged.

"Jeannie's only in two days a week, and she's all booked up for this week," Shannon said apologetically.

"There's no one else who can operate your MRI machine?" I said, stunned.

"Just Jeannie, and she's only in on—"

"Wednesdays and Thursdays," I said, finishing her sentence. "What is Jeannie *doing* on Monday, Tuesday, and Friday? I mean, is she *around*...?" I asked, imagining myself pulling Jeannie out of a crack house. "...Fine, next Thursday...I'll be Jeannie's first appointment," I said, shaking my head angrily from side to side.

"Okay, we'll see you at 8 a.m. next Thursday, Ms. Grodin. Have a nice evening," Shannon said as she got off the phone.

"Unfuckingbelievable!" I said, hurling the cell phone across the room.

"Honey, *what—what's happening?*" Christopher said, putting his arms on my shoulders.

"They saw *something*....They don't know *what*....I need to get an MRI....*Jeannie's out till next Thursday!*" I said, heading for Christopher's Ben and Jerry's Cherry Garcia in the freezer.

"Who the fuck is Jeannie?!" Christopher said, following me into the kitchen.

"*Exactly!*" I said, pulling the refrigerator door practically off its hinges.

The next day, the moment I opened my eyes, I knew waiting was not an option.

"Hi...it's me," I said quickly into the phone.

"You know anything?" my dad said, his voice taut

"They see something," I said carefully.

"They do?" he said, his voice cracking.

"Yes... but they're not sure *what*.... You know I have fibrocystic breasts... so it's possible that—"

"Is that what *they* said?" he asked, too frightened to let me finish.

"They don't *know*, but they don't *think* that's what it is. But here's the problem: what needs to happen now is that they need to take an MRI of my breast, to get a better look," I continued.

"Uh-huh," he said, holding his breath.

"But the woman who runs the MRI machine can't take me till next Thursday, and I..."

"*Really?*" he said incredulously.

"Really. So I wondered if you knew anybody..."

"Let me call Gene," he erupted, thrilled there was something he could do. Gene was Gene Wilder, who had been one of my dad's best friends for as long as I could remember. They had starred in the wonderful movie *The Woman in Red* together. Gene had successfully battled lymphoma a while back and had not only *survived*, he was *flourishing*... working, playing tennis, everything. So I knew whoever his doctor was, he or she was nothing short of a miracle worker. Out with Jeannie... in with Gene.

About thirty minutes after I got off the phone with my dad, my cell phone rang.

"Hello, is Marion Grodin there?" a warm male voice asked.

"This is... Yes. I am Marion Grodin," I said, laughing nervously.

"My name is Dr. Rifkin. Your dad asked me to call you," he said.

"*Hi,*" I said, shocked at how quickly the call had come.

"Let's get you in for your MRI, Wednesday at nine," he said calmly.

"Really?" I said, about to cry.

"Yes, you'll go to the main entrance at Sloan-Kettering—then I'll take a look, and we'll see what's going on, *sound good?*" he said affably, as if he were inquiring whether or not I'd like to go for a hay ride.

"Oh my God," I gushed, starting to cry. "Yes...yes...thank you so much."

As I hung up the phone, that familiar warmth I always felt the second my father got involved washed over me. I sat there, smiling, thinking how celebrity really *did* feel like it had the power to save your life. And, hey, if this guy was good enough for Willy Wonka...

34

The following afternoon, Christopher and I were sitting in an exam room in what had come to be our usual positions (me on the table, him in the chair), waiting to get the results of the needle biopsy I'd taken yesterday.

"Ms. Grodin?" the stately English doctor asked as he walked into the room, followed by his ruddy-faced nurse.

"Yes," I said as Christopher came over to me.

"I'm Dr. Eldridge. I just got the results of your needle biopsy back," he said as Christopher took my hand.

"Unfortunately, you do have cancer," the doctor said quietly.

"Omigod," I said, gripping Christopher's hand.

"At first we thought it was just what's called DCIS," he said gently.

"What is that?" I asked as Christopher moved closer.

"Ductal carcinoma in situ," the doctor said very slowly.

"W-What is it?" I stammered.

"That's when the cancer is in the milk ducts of your breast. Unfortunately, it's not just in your ducts."

Christopher and I just stared at each other, shell-shocked.

"Am I going to die?" I heard myself ask the doctor.

"We'll need to treat this right away, and aggressively. Once we do that, there's every reason to believe you will recover. My nurse will schedule your next appointment," he said, smiling almost imperceptibly before turning and leaving the room.

"Hi, I'm Maggie," the sweet-faced Irish nurse said. "I know this is shocking," she said, moving toward me, "but I want you to know that my girlfriend had the exact same thing. And she just completed her treatment, and she's fine." Maggie held my free hand.

"She is?" I said, starting to cry.

"She is." Maggie smiled as she and Christopher carried me through to the next moment.

—

As Chris and I walked through the main entrance to Sloan-Kettering, I couldn't help but think about how many times I'd walked through this same lobby with my mom, with her little scarf wrapped around her head. An hour later, I was sitting on the examination table, swinging my legs back and forth, trying, unsuccessfully to defuse my anxiety. Christopher was sitting across from me in a red chair. Every few minutes, we'd smile at each other, almost. We'd been in rooms that looked exactly like this too many times before, held captive, forced to wait for our bad news.

The door opened, and an attractive, kind-faced man in his forties walked over to me.

"Hi, I'm Dr. Rifkin," he said, extending his hand.

"Hi...I'm Marion; this is my husband, Christopher," I said, smiling, as he walked over and shook Christopher's hand.

"Okay, so I just looked at the mammogram from Hackensack, and it looks like there are actually *two* tumors in your right breas—" Before he was even finished, I burst into tears. "I know...it's a lot to hear," he said genuinely. "While I originally thought we'd be able to get it all out with just a lumpectomy, based on what I'm looking at *now*, I'm going to suggest we remove the breast, just to be certain we get it all."

"Omigod," I said, feeling like I was falling into a black abyss.

"Let me give you a few minutes alone, while I go and check the results of your MRI. I'll be back," he said quietly, closing the door behind him.

"Honey," Christopher said, tears in his eyes as he hugged me with all his might. Not even all his love could break my fall. After a while, he went back to his chair. We stared at each other, both too traumatized to even speak.

They're going to cut my breast off. They're going to maim me, my mind was howling, just as Dr. Rifkin walked back into the room. "I just looked at your MRI, and what I thought were two tumors is actually one tumor, in the shape of a barbell...so we won't need to take the whole breast; we can get it with a lumpectomy," he said.

"Thank God," I cried as Christopher ran to me, also crying.

"Thank God, Mar....Thank God," he said as we held each other.

"I'm going to schedule your surgery for next Tuesday morning. Talk to my nurse on the way out, and she'll tell you everything you need to do to prepare," Dr. Rifkin said, smiling compassionately as he turned to leave the room.

Just as he opened the door, I said, "Doctor... is that it? You'll just remove it, and... that's it?" I said, resting my body against Christopher.

He paused for a moment, then said, with the nonchalance of an afterthought, "You may have to have chemo and radiation... but I'll know more once we open you up." He held my gaze, waiting, patiently to see if I had any more questions. After a moment, he said, "But you may not have to do *any* of it."

I smiled at him, cleared my throat, and said, "If I were *your wife*, what would you tell me to do?"

"I'd tell her to do *all of it*," he said instantly.

"Then that's what I'll do," I said determinedly. And with that, Dr. Rifkin smiled and left the room.

—

As Christopher drove over the George Washington Bridge, my head was raging. *How did this happen? I'm sober—I don't drink, smoke, drug... and now... now... after all the shit I've stopped doing... after I've* stopped *killing myself,* now *God is going to fucking give me cancer!* I was furious. I was terrified.

"Whatcha thinkin' over there?" Christopher asked, turning to smile at me.

"I'm just so tired," I said, closing my eyes.

"Omigod, Mar. How *wouldn't* you be," he said, laying his hand on my shoulder. But I didn't tell him the only thought that had been in my head since I'd first heard the word "cancer": *I'm afraid I'm going to die.*

Over the next six days, I did all the things I normally did, but I wasn't *there*. I was in my head, obsessing about this hard, insistent lump jutting out of my right breast. No matter how much I said the serenity prayer, I couldn't turn off all the questions: *Where did this thing come from? How long has it been in me? Could it have come from all those IVF shots I've been giving myself?* A couple people had told me there might be a connection.

"Not likely," Dr. Rifkin said when he called me back.

"Why?" I persisted.

"You've only been giving yourself those injections for the last six months... and this tumor has probably been growing in your body for the last ten years," he said matter-of-factly.

"Really?" I said, regretting I'd even asked.

If I thought my anxiety level was awful *before* this information, I had no idea just how bad it was *about* to get. I knew what it was to be scared of things *outside* me and inside me, but the reality that there was something growing in my body that could very possibly *kill* me left me completely panic-stricken. I kept flashing on that terrifying image in all those Alien movies I'd watched in preparation for my marriage.

I would wait till Christopher had gone up to bed, and then I'd stand in the dimly lit kitchen, poring over all these books that told me my reaction, my feelings, were all perfectly normal and exactly what everyone just diagnosed with cancer experiences. And you know what—I didn't really give a fuck. It was the first time since I'd gotten sober and come into recovery that identifying my feelings and identifying with other people's feelings in the same situation provided me no comfort whatsoever. All I knew was that there was a tumor in my right breast that might *kill* me. Every waking moment, all I felt was fear coursing through my veins, and the only time I could escape it was when I was blessed enough to lose consciousness, which didn't come easily or in big enough doses.

Finally, the day of my surgery arrived. Christopher drove us to Sloan-Kettering at seven o'clock that morning. As we crossed the George Washington Bridge, I thought about my mom.... *Her* tumor was the size of a grapefruit, and it was in her head, and if she was terrified, she never let on.

She never said *anything*.

God, you were brave. You were so fuckin' brave.

As Christopher kissed me good-bye and the nurse turned my wheelchair around, wheeling me down the long, bright white corridor, I kept my mother close. She'd been all the way down this long corridor. The closer we got to the operating room, the colder the air got. That's how you knew you were almost there. Finally, the nurse wheeled me into a white room with medical equipment and a narrow table that had what looked like arms jutting out on either side, just below where your head would go. It looked like a cross. I tried to amuse myself by imagining Madonna being lowered onto the table, singing, *Just like a prayer...*

Thank God for the very large black male nurse, who greeted me with the highest-wattage smile I'd ever seen.

"Hi," he said, grinning from ear to ear. "I'm Hank. I'm gonna take care of you," he said, his voice so deep and warm, I felt like Barry White was in the room.

"Hi... I'm Judy," a sweet-faced little Filipino woman said, taking my hand.

"Can you climb up on this table for me, honey?" she asked, so lovingly I felt like I was being helped into a teacup at Disney World.

"Hi, I'm Sal," a middle-aged Italian man, who looked a lot

like Tony Danza, said, smiling, as he moved the pole with the fluids hanging from it closer to the table.

Boy, I don't know who cast this thing, but they did a helluva job. Everyone was so nice, and just as devoted to putting me at ease as to whatever else it was they were here to do.

"You can just lie back, honey," Judy said, her brown eyes twinkling.

"Just put you arms out at your sides for me. So, what do you do, Marion?" Sal asked so conversationally, I almost forgot he was strapping me to the cross.

"I'm a comedian," I said, aware I was a little short of breath.

"No, really?" His face lit up like Christmas. "I bet you're good at it too," Hank said as a tall, rail-thin, long-haired Germanic-looking guy entered the room and strode right over to the machine next to my face.

"Hi, I'm Kirk," he said, with the slightest hint of a German accent.

"Hi," I said, staring up into his light-blue eyes as Judy inserted a butterfly needle into my hand and started an IV.

"I'm the anesthesiologist."

Of course, I thought to myself. *They would have to cast fucking Riff Raff from* The Rocky Horror Picture Show *in the role of the anesthesiologist*.

"Well, I could tell you some jokes, but you'd be *glad* Kirk'd have you under by then," Hank said, laughing so heartily, I started laughing too.

"Oh, really...you'd be *glad*," Judy said, laughing good-naturedly.

Just as Kirk said, "I want you to just count backward from ten for me," I realized how *genius* this whole team was.

"Okay," I said, and as I heard myself say, "Seven," I thought how Hank's warm face was the sun on the warm beach I was going to.

—

"She's still out," I vaguely heard someone say, from what sounded like very far away. I tried to open my eyes, but I couldn't.

As I floated in and out of my fog, I thought I felt someone holding my hand.

"Marion. Marion," the soothing voice said as I slowly turned my head in its direction. *"We got it all,"* Dr. Rifkin said, squeezing my hand firmly. I smiled through the fog before falling into a deep sleep.

"Hi," my favorite soothing voice said.

"Hi," I whispered, sleep loosening its hold.

"He said they got it all," Chris said, tears in his eyes.

"Thank God," I said, closing my eyes.

"You wanna sleep some more?" he asked gently.

I nodded as sleep pulled me under.

"I'll be right here when you wake up," Chris said, squeezing my hand.

That's all anyone wants: someone to be there when they wake up. I thought as I drifted away.

—

"Yesterday I had cancer, and today—one day later—I *don't*; I can't get *over* that. Had cancer on *Tuesday*, don't have it on *Wednesday*—fucking amazing! Right?!" I shouted into the phone to my best friend, Kath, as Christopher shot me a big thumbs-up from across the room. The sheer sense of relief once they'd removed that thing from my breast was...intoxicating. The calls...the letters...the love...just kept pouring in. And then came the best call of all...from my dad. It consisted of very few words.

And then came the *other* call.

35

Christopher and I were just about to head out to the diner when the phone rang. "Hello?" I said as Christopher grabbed my jacket off a chair.

"*Marion?*" the familiar voice said.

"Hi, Dr. Rifkin... everything okay?"

"Absolutely... So, now we just need to wait for the results of the biopsy," he said.

"Of what? I thought you said you got 'clear margins,' that you got it all," I said frantically, staring at Christopher.

"We did," he said evenly. "But we just need to make certain none of the cells got into your lymph system, so we're testing what we call the sentinel node. If that comes back clean..."

Feeling like I might pass out, I said, "You mean even with the clear margins... there's a chance that some of the cancer cells got into my... my..." Struggling to catch my breath, I softly said, "... lymph system?"

"Right. We'll get the results of the biopsy in about four days.... I'll call you as soon as I know. Listen, try to relax," he said, well aware of the effect of his call.

"Yeah, that's not gonna happen.... Ughhh... thanks... thanks for calling.... Please, please, call me the second you know!" I said as Christopher put his arms around me.

"You can count on it," Dr. Rifkin said, hanging up.

"Mar, what?" Christopher cried.

"I'm not in the clear..."

"B-but I thought they got clear margins," Christopher stammered.

"They have to check the sentinel node to make sure no cancer cells got into... my lymph system," I whispered as Christopher tried to hug me hard enough to squeeze the fear out of us both.

—

I was at the Korean market on West Eighty-First Street, waiting to pay for my Diet Coke, when I overheard the heavyset woman in front of me turn to her girlfriend and say, "*The Sentinel*, with Michael Douglas—we just rented it. I loved it.... But then, I love Michael Douglas! It drives Harvey crazy, but I say, hey, maybe if *you* looked like that, I'd love *you*!"

Michael Douglas as "the sentinel node," I thought, smiling. Just the image of Michael Douglas, standing watch over all my lymph nodes, making sure no cancer cells—played by Mickey Rourke, Ray Liotta, Eric Roberts, etc.—slipped by, had me smiling for the first time since I'd heard about the sentinel node.

As I sat in my meeting, the same meeting I'd sat in feeling so blessed because a baby was growing inside me, I now felt sick as I waited to find out if cancer was growing inside me.

After the meeting, I crossed the street, climbed in my car, and was just about to turn the key in the ignition when I fell back against my seat. It had been four days, and I still hadn't heard if Michael Douglas had kept Ray Liotta and the rest of the lot out of my lymph system. I closed my eyes. I could feel the anxiety coursing through my body.

You can't drink or drug. Bingeing just makes it worse. There's nothing you can use to numb your terror. You just have to wait.

As I sat back up, I remembered that I had turned my cell phone off in the meeting. I quickly turned it back on. I had one message.

"Hi, this is Dr. Rifkin. Please call me as soon as you get this. I'll be reachable at this number up until seven thirty; if it's after seven thirty, call me in the office tomorrow..."

"*Fuck!*" I screamed, staring at the time on my phone. It was 7:33. "Fuck. Fuck... Fuck!" I yelled into the phone, hitting SEND. "Please be there, please be there, please be there," I chanted as I closed my eyes, listening to the eternity between rings.

"Hello," Dr. Rifkin said.

"Oh, thank God, you're still there." I exhaled frantically into the phone. "I just got your message and was so scared I wouldn't be able to reach you till tomorrow," I said, panicked.

He didn't need me to explain. "The sentinel node was negative," he said.

"Oh, thank God... thank God," I said, slumping over as relief washed over me. "So that means I'm in the clear... right? No cancer... right?" I said, my head on the steering wheel.

"Yes" is what he said, but I heard something that felt more like "maybe."

"*What?*" I said.

"I think to be a hundred percent sure, you should still do the chemo and radiation," he said slowly.

"Really?" I said, stunned. "I thought since you got clear margins, and now that the sentinel node was negative . . . I wouldn't have to . . ." I said quietly as the searing sense of doom that had just left me returned with a vengeance.

36

I'd seen enough people go through chemo—including my mom—to know that it was brutal on a level I couldn't even fathom. After my surgery, I'd joined a support group at Sloan, which quickly became like family. Almost everybody in the group had gone through or was going through chemo, and I knew that everybody responded differently. There were several women who weren't having such bad side effects and a couple who were even still going to work. Maybe I'd be lucky. Maybe I'd dodge the chemo bullet.

A few weeks later, Christopher and I were at Sloan, sitting in a very nice private room, waiting for the affable Irish nurse to come back in and get me started.

"So, have you gotten to go to Ireland?" she said as she started the chemo pumping into me through the IV in my arm.

"I have. My father's brother has a farm over there," Christopher said as a cold burning sensation shot through my vein.

"Really?" the nurse said, laying her hand over mine as she took a seat next to me.

"I went once," I chimed in as Christopher laid his hand on mine. "There were a lot of goats," I said, and we all laughed. *Maybe this won't be so bad*, I thought as once again, Christopher and a lovely Irish woman carried me through to the next moment.

I couldn't get over how good I felt. My next treatment wasn't for another couple weeks, and in the meantime, I pretty much just went about my life. I went to my meetings, to therapy. Christopher and I would go out to eat. I even did a little stand-up, so long as it was in the city.

I had just gotten home from Gotham. I was hosting, and the crowd had been amazing all night. Plus, at the very end, Jerry Seinfeld had come in and done thirty minutes. I was in a great mood as I stepped into the shower. I was singing Madonna's "Lucky Star," which they'd been playing at the club, as I soaped up my hair. "You must be my lucky star…'Cause you shine on me wherever…" As I took my hand out of my hair, I felt something in my hand. Staring at the long strands of hair hanging through my fingers, I felt sick. I glanced down and saw even more hair sitting in the drain. I ran my hand through my hair again. Another big clump came out. I opened my hand, stretched my fingers apart, and watched as my hair disappeared down the drain, along with whatever illusions I'd had about dodging the "chemo bullet."

That night, I decided rather than be tortured by watching my hair fall out a clump at a time, I'd just get my head shaved and start wearing a wig. One of the women in my support group had told me about a place a lot of the women in our group had gone to. The next day, Christopher and I climbed the three flights of stairs up to this high-end wig shop, whose clientele, it turned out, was predominantly made up of cancer patients and soap opera stars. Needless to say, this made for a unique ambience.

I sat in the chair. Christopher stood beside me, holding my hand as the last bit of my hair hit the floor. We just stared, transfixed by the reflection of my bald head.

"Mar, you look beautiful," Christopher said while the pretty young Spanish girl with long black hair swept up what we no longer had in common.

I listened to the two surgically enhanced soap actresses behind me go back and forth about whether or not to get bangs on their new wigs, as I thought about what I'd said when Dr. Rifkin told me I might lose my hair: *I don't care about that…it's just hair.* How insanely naive those words seemed now, I thought, staring into the mirror as Yul Brynner stared back at me.

I came home with a very pretty shoulder-length, dirty-blonde, highlighted wig that actually looked exactly like my own hair. And initially, I was very excited about my wig. But here's the problem: I am an extremely claustrophobic person and having my head incarcerated in this tight meshed hot itchy skullcap was torture. I was always scratching and tugging on it.

There were several evenings where I would leave the house with my wig looking superb. Hours later I'd pull back into the driveway and Chris would come to greet me laughing so hard, I'd have to say, "What…what?"

"Ah…honey," he'd say lovingly in between laughs. "Your *wig*…"

"What *about* my wig?" I'd say defensively, grabbing my rearview mirror to get a look.

"I think it's on...backward," he'd say, trying to stifle his laughter as he adjusted the wig.

"I hate this fuckin' wig!" I'd shout, snatching it off my head.

"Honey, I love your head; you have a perfectly shaped head," Chris would say, as I got out of the car.

"I got it from my mother," I'd say proudly, clutching my wig as we walked into the house.

"Mar, why don't you just go bald?"

"Because, honey...I'm not a Nazi skinhead lesbian wrestler."

"No one's gonna think...," Chris said as we walked into the TV room.

"When a man's bald, nobody thinks shit, nobody *says* shit. When a woman's bald...The other day at the pool, this guy came up to me and asked me if I had cancer. *Why is that okay?* You'd never ask a bald *man* if he had cancer," I said, falling into the recliner.

"Whadya say?" Chris said delicately.

"I said I was a Nazi skinhead lesbian wrestler and I knew where he lived," I said sarcastically as I leaned over to turn on the light. "Shit, I meant to get a lower-wattage bulb—I feel like the chemo's making me more light sensitive."

"You want me to go and get a softer bulb...I will," Chris said, kissing my nose.

"Not necessary," I said, plopping the wig over the lamp.

For my second treatment, my dad and his best friend, Phil Donahue, along with a very loud comedian friend of mine, joined me and Chris at Sloan in the chemo room.

You know how rappers will say, *No sex in the champagne room*? Well, we were so loud, and having so much fun, that the nurse, after several complaints, had to come in and ask for...*fewer laughs in the chemo room!* I think it's safe to say that wasn't a request she got every day.

And those were pretty much the last big laughs I would have for a very long time. The effects of the chemo are cumulative, and the side effects of all the drugs they had me on to better handle the chemo were *horrific*. A few days after all those big laughs in the chemo room, I stopped being able to take a shit. And when I was able to squeeze out something so tiny, it looked like it had come from a gerbil's ass, it was so painful, I'd instantly burst into tears.

I now understand old people who can do a solid twenty on their bowel movements. Because when you can't shit, day after day, after day...it's all you think about. There's no "Isn't it a beautiful day?" "Isn't this pizza yummy?" "Wasn't that an amazing *Criminal Minds*..." I was so uncomfortable, I couldn't even pay attention to my favorite crime shows. That is, unless someone was killed in a bathroom, and then all I could think was *Hope he took a nice shit before someone hacked off his head*. If it wasn't about shit, *it wasn't shit*.

And it wasn't only my bowels. I was nauseous from the moment I woke up to the moment I lost consciousness. If I'd wake up in the middle of the night to go pee, my first awareness would be how severely nauseous I was. And this wasn't just stomach nausea; my entire body felt nauseous. Chemo is poison, and that's exactly what it felt like—like I was being murdered from inside.

Nothing felt the same....The liquid in my eyes...the saliva in my mouth—which tasted like I'd been sucking on pennies all day—my mind. I'd heard women in my support group talk about it—"chemo brain," they called it. It felt like I was moving through this awful haze all the time. I felt completely out of focus, and depressed—so depressed—in a way I'd never experienced before. My hair, my eyes, my skin felt depressed. My soul felt depressed. I just felt completely foreign to myself. And then, when I'd look in the mirror, looking for the reassurance of something familiar, the image of my bald head, which I never got used to, only made me feel like more of a stranger. It was so unwaveringly stark. I looked like someone in Auschwitz. And, if, for a fleeting moment, I was fortunate enough to not be thinking about cancer, my reflection in the mirror was always there to remind me. I prayed. I talked to God all the time; I wasn't well enough to get to meetings, so once a week, a friend from the city would drive a few people out to my house, and we'd have a meeting in the TV room. And for those minutes, I did get some comfort; but the truth was, as my treatments wore on, I couldn't find any real relief—any real sanctuary. Not outside of me, and nowhere in either my mind or my body.

By the fourth treatment, I was so sick and so exhausted, I wasn't even coming downstairs anymore. I had never experienced this kind of fatigue. It took every bit of strength I had just to brush my teeth. By my fifth treatment, I was just in bed... logging time... counting the days till my final treatment, which I didn't believe I'd make it to. Despair had zipped itself around me like a tight sleeping bag. I cried all the time, yearning, aching to just feel like myself again. I felt *unrecognizable*—even my tears were different... like chemo tears. I would tell Christopher every day that I didn't feel like I could handle any more of it. And as always, he was my greatest champion—cheering me on every step of the way as I crawled over the finish line, miraculously making it through that final dose of chemo. I felt like I'd just won the top title in the WWE—like

I'd wrestled the biggest, baddest opponent...and I kind of *looked* like that—I was still bald.

They gave me a few weeks off, and then told me I had to start radiation. Every day away from my last chemo, I felt better—like I was re-inhabiting myself. My stomach was still wrecked, but my nurse practitioner told me to start taking Probiotic Acidophilus, and that was like a fucking *miracle*. It started to heal my stomach, and the next week I started radiation. I'd heard it might make me tired, and I was, like, *Tired? Please, after the nightmarish experience of chemo, radiation can kiss my able-to-have-a-bowel-movement ass!* Every day I'd drive myself to a facility near our house, climb up on the table, and two extraordinarily tan young women would radiate my right breast in the hopes of killing any remaining rogue cancer cells. As I lay there on the table, I could never get over how tan these girls were—to the point that I had to wonder if, when no one was around, they were climbing up on that table and taking turns radiating each other.

37

When my hair first started growing back, I had this wispy baby peach fuzz sprouting all over my head.

"Mar, it's so soft; I mean, it's really starting to come in," Chris would say, rubbing my head, which was so cute of him, because you could barely even see it. He'd gotten me this gorgeous blue tie-dyed scarf at the Sloan-Kettering gift shop, for my reentry into the world. I was chomping at the bit to go to a meeting. So one Tuesday night, I decided I was going to drive into the city for my favorite overeater's meeting, on the Upper West Side. It was winter, and freezing out, so Christopher made sure to wrap my beautiful tie-dyed *shmata* tightly around my head. I felt like I was heading out for my first day of kindergarten. Omigod, the feeling of freedom as I drove—I felt as lit up as the twinkly bright lights on the bridge. I was so ecstatically grateful just to be back in my life, I could not stop giggling.

As I turned off the West Side Highway onto Ninety-Sixth Street, I screamed, "I'm back, bitches.... Baldie is baaaaaack!" Driving down Broadway, everything looked so shiny... all the Korean markets, the newsstands, even the homeless guy peeing behind the parked Mercedes.

Let it flow, bitch.... We're free, mothafucker my head railed as I turned onto Eighty-Sixth Street. I didn't even care that it took me forever to find a parking space. I finally found a spot around the corner from where my mom and I used to live on Eighty-Fifth Street, next to the basketball courts, across the street from Brandeis High School. I locked up the car and ran to the meeting.

As I walked up the stairs into the meeting space, I went to turn off my cell phone and noticed that I only had one bar left, and it was blinking. When I opened the door to the meeting, everyone turned around. All these loving faces, mouthing, *You look so beautiful.... We love you.... Welcome home.* I did feel like I was home. This community was *family* to me. They'd been there for me through all the greatest and worst shit, over the years—my struggle to get married, to get pregnant, to earn a living, to grow up. This was the room I came to to get the help I needed to get onstage for the first time, to get married, to get through my miscarriages, to deal with my cancer diagnosis.

Being in this room, I felt so cared for, so seen. And just when I thought I couldn't feel any more *embraced*, the chairperson, a woman who had twenty-five years free of bingeing, asked me if I'd speak. Such a great homecoming.

I walked to the front of the room, took off my scarf, and told my story, and for the first time, in a long time... I felt like me. Afterward, still buzzing from the amazing energy in the meeting, I pulled my scarf tightly around my head, braving the frigid wind whipping around my face as I sped down the two blocks back to my car.

I turned left on Amsterdam, running down the street, till I got to the middle of the block. I got to the lamppost where I thought I'd parked, but there was a maroon BMW there. *Wait...did I park closer to Columbus? No, I was definitely across from Brandeis...next to the basketball courts.* My mind fumbled frantically as I walked quickly down the street. *Is that it?* I wondered, coming up on a small, dark car. "No, shit....Is it the other side of the street?" I mumbled, dashing cross the street. *Is it possible I parked between Columbus and Central Park? Could I have parked on the next...?* My mind gave up before finishing the thought as I stood in the middle of the cold, dark street, knowing exactly what had happened. I felt sick.

"God, help me," I said, the air so cold, I could see my breath. I dug in the pocket of my coat, pulling out my phone. I turned it back on, and now there wasn't even a blinking bar....It was just a blinking box.

38

"Please be awake, please be awake, please be awake," I chanted, dialing Christopher's number as the empty box blinked at me threateningly.

"Hello?" Chris mumbled sleepily.

"Oh, thank God," I cried, relief washing over me.

"You okay?" he said, waking up.

Closing my eyes, I said softly, "The car got tow—" Before I could finish saying the word "towed," my phone made that xylophone sound it makes right before it powers down.

"*Uhhhhh!*" I screamed at the top of my lungs. "This is not fucking happening... Dammit!" I screamed, holding down the END button on the phone, *praying* it would come back on.

"Thank you, God," I said out loud as the phone turned back on. I quickly hit SEND.

"Mar, where are—" Chris said quickly, just before the xylophone sound. "Fuck, fuck... motherfuck!" I screamed as a young black couple walking toward me hurried across the street, steering clear of the crazy, bald woman shouting obscenities to no one.

"Thank you, God," I mumbled, spotting a pay phone up the street. I ran to it, grabbed the receiver, put it to my ear... and, "Seriously? Seriously?!" I yelled, listening to... *no dial tone*. Suddenly remembering there was a pay phone in front of the supermarket on Columbus, I raced around the corner, tightening the scarf around my head as the icy wind assaulted me. I grabbed the receiver, practically pulling it off the cord. I pressed it against my frozen ear and felt my whole body exhale when I heard the reassuring hum of the dial tone.

"Thank you. Thank you, dial tone," I whispered, as I cupped my stiff, frozen hands together, blowing into them, hoping I wasn't getting frostbite. That was all I needed after my lumpectomy—a fuckin' pinkyectomy!

As I dialed Chris's number, I looked around at all the people walking by... *not* in crisis, no panic in their eyes, not having just gotten their car towed while still being radiated for breast cancer. As I stood there, bald, freezing, waiting for Chris to come rescue me once again, I just felt so sad that I was the way I was, and that I didn't seem to be able to change.

"Two dollars and fifty-five cents," the female operator said with such disdain, I was certain she knew all about me.

"Two dollars and fifty-five cents," I repeated, stalling as I dug into my coat pocket.

"That's *what I said,*" Cuntypants said.

"Okay... just let me...," I mumbled, pulling out a fistful of singles and buttons. "Fuck!" I cried, slamming down the phone.

Running over to a well-dressed older man coming out of the

supermarket, I said, "Excuse me, would you happen to have change for a dollar...actually, for three dollars?"

"I'm afraid I don't," he said, not even breaking his stride.

"Excuse me, would you happen to have change for...," I said, walking behind a heavyset woman, who sped up. *"Bitch,"* I mumbled under my breath, hurrying back to the phone. *Collect...call collect*, my brain shouted as I grabbed the phone.

"How may I assist you?" a warm, Southern male voice asked.

You can start by coming to get me! my head roared.

"I need to call my home, collect, can you do that for me?" I asked, giving him the number and then crossing the fingers on both my hands. For a moment there was just silence.

"Hello...*Hello?*" I said, staring at the phone. Suddenly the phone rang—once.

"Hello?" Christopher said anxiously.

"Will you accept a collect call from..." The nice man paused.

"Marion! Marion!" I yelled into the phone.

"...from Marilyn?" he said confidently.

"Yes," Christopher said flatly.

"Thank fucking God! Uhhh...my phone died, and I ran to this pay phone—but it was broken, and then I found this other pay phone, but I didn't have any change, and then I couldn't get anybody to *give* me change, and...Chris...are you there?" I said.

"Uh-huh," he said, his voice tight.

"What?' I said, confused.

"I was in bed when you called," he said matter-of-factly.

"Oh...I'm sorry.... Well, can you come get me?" I asked, assuming this was a given.

"Honey, I'm in my pajamas, and I have to get up at six to go to work," he said wearily. For a moment, I just stared off into space as an assortment of unafflicted couples entered my field of vision.

"Well, what am I supposed to *do*, Christopher? I mean, I don't have any money on me, and I have to get my car back..." Shaking my head, I exhaled noisily. "...but I don't even know if they'll *give it to me*.... I'm not sure, but I think my license might be suspended," I reported with the matter-of-franticness that was all too familiar to both of us.

After a pause so long, I didn't know if he was still on the line, I whispered, "Chris?"

"Yeah," he said, sounding much farther away than Paramus. "Where are you?" he asked, his voice saturated in angry resignation.

"I'm in front of the supermarket on Columbus, between Eighty-Fourth and Eighty-Fifth Streets.... Also, can you bring some money? I'm probably gonna have to pay the tickets and a towing fee.... They always really stick it to ya with that fucking towing fee."

"Let me get dressed, and then I'll come get you," he said robotically.

"Okay...hurry, though.... It's freezing out here," I said, quickly returning the phone to its cradle before running into the supermarket.

39

Forty minutes later, Christopher pulled up in front of the supermarket. I ran outside, jumping in the passenger side of his truck. "Hi," I said, wishing some of the warmth in the truck would make its way into the expression on Christopher's face.

"Are you okay?" he asked, glancing over at me.

"Yeah, I just can't believe they took my car. I mean, I was only gone, like... an hour," I said, in full victim mode.

"Uh-huh," he mumbled, staring straight ahead as he drove down Broadway. "You probably had *tickets*...." He seemed beleaguered.

"I *guess*...but it just happened so fast," I said, aware my plight wasn't having any effect on Christopher's expression. The rest of the drive down to the tow pound, I tried massaging his ire with my usual arsenal—humor, charm, affection—but it was no use. Christopher's anger felt just as frozen as the ice on the ground.

Christopher and I walked into the room, which smelled of cigarette smoke and french fries. We went over to the window at the counter. "Hi, I think I got my car towed a couple hours ago," I said easily, as if I were handing a coat check girl my ticket. See, as fucked up as this was, and for whatever myriad reasons (all of which I'd been exploring in therapy for so many years, I'm sure I've paid for at least one pair of my therapist's Ferragamos), this all felt normal to me: crisis/rescue, rinse/repeat. But not to Christopher—he was just trapped in my spin cycle.

"What's the plate number?" the zaftig black woman with the duplex of braids and three-inch zebra-striped nails said as she cracked her gum loudly.

I told her, and I added that it was parked on Eighty-Fourth Street, between Columbus and Amsterdam.

Looking down at the book in front of her, she cracked her gum five times fast, then said, "Yeah, we got it."

I smiled at Christopher, who did *not*.

"Seven-hundred and forty-two dollars," she said, patting her braids.

"*What?*" I said as Christopher just stared at me, seething.

"That's what you gotta pay, in tickets, plus the tow fee, if you want it back," she said, tapping the braids on the side of her head.

"Omigod," I mumbled, closing my eyes, wishing there could be any other words than the ones that were about to come out of my mouth. "Do you... have your card?" I asked quietly, looking down. "I'll pay you back," I said, both of us knowing that would *never* happen. As he took his wallet out of his coat pocket and handed me his credit card, the look on his face made my breath catch in my throat.

"And I'm gonna need a driver's license and the registration," the woman said as I handed her Christopher's card and my license. Then, hoping not to enrage Christopher any further, I leaned over the counter and, practically whispering, said, "The registration is in the glove compartment.... I have to get it."

"You're gonna have to wait till Corey gets back from his break; I can't let you back there by yourself," she said, glancing at her zebra-striped watch. "Just take a seat.... He'll be back," she said, waving the drunk couple behind us up to the counter.

"How many times do I have to tell you?!" the woman said angrily.

"I didn't see the sign," the man said defensively.

"No, you saw it... You just didn't *see* it," she said, plopping her purse on the counter.

"I guess we'll just have to wait for *Corey* to come back," I said over my shoulder, walking toward the seats on the other side of the room. I was about to sit down when I realized Christopher hadn't moved. I walked over to him. He had a look on his face I'd never seen before.

"Honey," I said, staring into his eyes. He just stared back at me. "Christopher, please.... What's happening?" I pleaded.

"I need to move out."

"*What?*" I whispered, anxiety seizing my chest. "What are you talking about?" I said, shocked.

"If you want to go get your registration, Corey's back there now," the woman called across the room as I stood there staring into my husband's eyes, which were filled with so much pain.

"Can we please talk about this later?" I said, walking toward the back door as Christopher said nothing.

—

"Hi," I said tentatively, walking up behind Chris washing a dish in the sink.

"Hi," he said, smiling.

"Honey, I'm so sorry about last night—you know I am. I really *get* how not-okay it is. You know I do... I really do and I promise I will make sure I know what's going on with my car from now on, and that I *won't* get myself into a situation where I get towed again. Really, Chris, I know I can do better... really... and you know I'm sorry, honey.... I am really, really sorry," I said.

For a moment he didn't say anything, which I assumed meant my apology had been accepted. "Yeah, no... I know you are.... I really do. It's just that the minute you were up and running again... It's just all the same stuff, y'know, Mar." His tone was so normal, so understanding, I was sure his whole I've-got-to-move-out thing was off the table.

"I know. I know. It's not good; I really do get it," I said as the strangest feeling came over me that even though he was just inches from me—he *wasn't*.

"Yeah...," he said, lowering his head, staring at the floor.

Taking a small step toward him, I said, "So... what you said last night.... I mean... You're not gonna move out, right?"

For a second he didn't say anything, then he looked up, smiling so lovingly as his eyes filled with tears. "I have to, honey. I can't do this anymore. I'm sorry," he said, then hung his head and very slowly walked out of the room.

I just stood there in shock. I had no idea what to do... or say... or even *think*. No idea how to even live through the next moment. He was the sweetest, fairest, most generous, loving person I had ever met. And I knew—I mean, really knew—how deeply he loved me. He loved me with everything he had... with *more* than he had, I would come to find out over the next few agonizing, torturous weeks.

Go in there and tell him that he's a bastard! Tell him he cannot leave. Talk him out of it, my head raged. But I couldn't. Because as unbelievable, as excruciating, as traumatizing as this was, if he was saying he had to move out, I believed him.

I was in so much pain, and it was different from anything I'd experienced before. Although I had lost my mom, it was because she had *died*. But Christopher was right here, lying beside me, talking, grieving, weeping, laughing. And although he was, yes, moving to a depressing one-bedroom in Cliffside Park, New Jersey, he wasn't actually *dying*.

I had just finished my hellish year of treatment for breast cancer. My follow-up MRI, mammogram, blood work, etc., all showed that I was cancer-free. It really should have been the most glorious, celebratory time, but it wasn't. I don't know what the devastation of Christopher leaving would have felt like if I *weren't* just coming out of a year of breast cancer treatment, and I don't know what coming out of that year of breast cancer treatment without Christopher leaving would have felt like.... What I do know is that the combination was well beyond anything I felt I could handle. My terror of the cancer coming back covered me like a second skin. *Everything* was cancer. At one point, I had this mysterious swelling on my right ankle, and I was sure it was "ankle cancer—I've got cankle!"

Here's what I know about pain. You have to go through it. It takes time. I screamed, I cried. Every day, for hours, for months. Like a wounded animal in the wild. Howling. There were no shortcuts. No cold cuts. With the deepest, worst pain, there's not enough drugs, booze, food, sex, or shopping to "fix" it. It's just time—that distance between the wound and the healing. And love. There's a wonderful saying: "Go where it's warm." And they don't mean the Bahamas, although if you get a good deal... It means go where the love is, where people care about you and love you, until you can make your way back to finding it in yourself.

40

"Fifty. Fifty? This is bullshit," I mumble, staring at my naked body as I tug on the inner tube of fat encasing my stomach. "Happy Birthday," I announce with way more zest than I feel.

Hey, at least you made it to fifty.

You're right, I think as I lift my gaze up to my pink lumpectomy scar.

"Wait... what...," I whisper, taking a step closer to the mirror as I notice a small, pink lump right in the middle of my scar that definitely was *not* there yesterday.

"What the fuck is that?!" I say, the weight of my terror forcing my head to drop, as I stand there, frozen, feeling like I'm going to throw up. Trying to breathe in as much oxygen as possible, I slowly lift my right hand, which feels paralyzed, up to my breast, gently cupping it as I speak to God very, very quietly.

God... honestly, that would be a really shitty birthday present.

Please, I can't go through this again, I plead, just before lowering my finger delicately onto the intruder.

"What?" I hear myself say, realizing *something* has fallen into my hand. I look down, and see that the lump appears to have just... fallen off. Very carefully, as if I'm holding a bomb, I bring my hand up to my face. *Are those... SPRINKLES?!* I wonder, as a sweet aroma fills my nose. *Omigod.* I start laughing as I realize my "lump" is actually a small piece of a strawberry Munchkin from the Dunkin' Donuts box sitting on my nightstand.

Popping my "lump" into my mouth, alternately chewing and laughing as Eddie and Snuggles, my cats, hurl themselves against the door, flying into the room, I slip my nightgown over my head, escorted out of my cocoon by my two feline bodyguards.

As Eddie trots toward the kitchen, Snuggles turns around, plants herself right at my feet, places her right paw on my calf, and looks up at me with so much emotion, I could have *sworn* she was saying, *Look, no one saying it's easy.... Fifty, single, broke, fat... I get it. I really do. But hiding out in that cocoon, bingeing on sugar, waiting for Christopher Meloni, William Petersen, Thomas Gibson, or any of the leading men in any of your* Law & Order, CSI, *or* Criminal Minds *reruns to come visit you in a dream... You can do better than this. I mean, shit, you were on* The View*—twice! And not to make this about me, but it's two o'clock in the afternoon, and even though Eddie and I are, yes, remarkably resourceful, we still have not figured out how to actually open those little cans of Friskies.... I don't need to go on.... You get it.* Confident she'd made her point, she turned and continued escorting me toward the kitchen.

Okay, before we go any further, it's *crucial* that you understand who Eddie and Snuggles are. While they're both "rescues," they came to me in very different ways. One night, about two years ago, the week that I lost my lucrative day job fundraising for a nonprofit in Harlem, I was lying on my red velvet Pottery Barn couch, having just polished off the last chocolate chip cookie in the Mrs. Fields bag, well into my fifth or sixth episode of *Law & Order: SVU*, wondering how the *fuck* I was ever going to be able to pay the blanket of bills covering my torso, when the phone rang.

As I grabbed my cell phone from under the notice of cancellation from my car insurance company, I said, "Who the fuck is calling me this late?!"

"Marion?" a high-pitched voice said.

"Uh-huh," I said, not recognizing the voice.

"I hope I'm not disturbing you," she said, *immediately* revealing that she was a comic, since no one *but* a comic could even utter that sentence at 2:40 a.m.

"*Who is this?*" I asked, wanting to get back to my show, as myself and the rest of the SVU team were about to bust a major sex-trafficking ring.

"Ohhhhh, sorry, sorry. It's Shecky... Shecky Beagleman," she said, as if I needed that last name in order to distinguish her from all the other... *Sheckys*.

"I don't mean to be rude, but it's late, and I've got a lot going on," I said, farting a little.

Her voice suddenly speeding up, she said, "Of course.... My husband, Ken, has been out of town, playing Felix in a production of *The Odd Couple*...." Shecky went on to explain that the first night, everybody was leaving the theater through the back door that spilled into the alley, when out of the darkness walked this funny-faced, adorable little girl cat. She said the cat approached them with so much sweetness and affection, instantly winning them all over to the point that, that same night, they moved her into where they were all staying, named her Snuggles, and basically made her their mascot. Problem was, now that the show was over, they had no choice but to leave Snuggles back in the alley where'd they'd found her. Plus, at some point, some fucking idiot must have taken her in, declawed her, then tossed her back into the street, so not only would she be homeless, but she'd also be completely unable to defend herself.... Dabbing at the tears in my eyes with my notice of cancellation, I shouted, "I'll take her!"

The next night, Snuggles Grodin moved in and, frankly, changed my life. From the second I laid eyes on her, she reminded me of the actress Rachel McAdams. Something about her spunk and how unstoppably optimistic she was—to the point that even when she was very bad (e.g., finishing off my *entire* dinner from the frying pan on the stove) and I was really yelling at her, grabbing her, even spanking her, she was still purring—loudly! Rachel McAdams.

Her pretty little heart-shaped face was dark gray, except for a fairly thick, lopsided white line over her lip, which made her look like she had an uneven mustache. Her body was also dark gray, except for a large swath of white running from her shoulders down to her stomach, making her appear to be wearing an ascot; she also had white running halfway up her back legs, making her look like she was wearing knee socks. And last, there were her front paws, which were *so* white, they made her look like she was wearing laboratory gloves. All these things combined made her look like a fashionably sporty lesbian forensics expert.

Now, the way Eddie came to me was a whole different story. Late one night, about two months after Snuggles moved in, and into the third hour of our swatting the new glow-in-the-dark, blinking, squawking ferret across the room to each other, it became clear to both of us that no matter how much I adored her, and no matter how enthusiastically or energetically I swatted our new glowing ferret, mouse, rat, etc., back to her, I was *not* in fact, a *cat*. A fact I believe we'd both been in some denial about since she'd moved in. My task was clear. My girl needed the real thing.

So, the next day, a Saturday, I drove over to the Petco on Route 4 in Paramus. I knew this was their big day for adoption, where the FOCAS animal rescue people set up, trying to find forever homes for all their animals. I felt certain I'd be able to find the perfect little playmate for my Snuggles. As I walked into the Petco, I was instantly overwhelmed by the sheer volume of people crowded around all the cages in the middle of the floor, and even *more* overwhelmed by the insane cacophony of sounds emanating from all these people. The crowd looked to me to be a nightmarish fusion of the casts of *Toddlers and Tiaras*, *The Real Housewives of New Jersey*, and *Dance Moms*. Everywhere I looked, there were deranged, unhinged, sugared-up, screaming children, begging, pleading, conniving, like miniature crackheads; saying whatever they had to, to get their exhausted, frazzled, beaten-down parents to adopt little *Snowflake*, *Pop-Tart*, *Fluffernutter*, *Waffle*, or *Cupcake*.

Honestly, more than a few of these parents looked like they might just have a full-on nervous breakdown right there at Petco. I actually heard one of these little devil children say to her mother, whom she had pinned up against a giant bag of kitty litter, "Mommy, I am *begging* you to pleeeease let me take Snowflake home with us *today*! And if you do, I *promise*, cross my heart and hope to die"—the demon dramatically drew a cross over the place she pretended contained her heart—"if you do, I will not only take one hundred percent responsibility for Snowflake, I also promise that I will never, ever tell *any* of your boyfriends, ever again, that you sometimes drink in the morning."

I watched as the poor woman's face collapsed into an expression of such defeat, it took everything I had not to intervene. Thinking it best not to take on one of the Children of the Corn, I turned around, making my way through the crowd.

Let me get a look at this fuckin' Snowflake, I said to myself, remembering my mission. As I got closer to the action, I saw that there were about eight cages on the floor, then two more levels of eight stacked on top of those. As I searched for my replacement, my eyes darted from cage to cage. In order to get a better look, I had to push past a little curly-haired girl who had just hurled herself to the ground, screaming, "I want Fluffernutter!" as she went down. As I got right up to the cages, I saw that each cage had a three-by-five laminated index card attached to the side of it. The cards contained the occupant's name, age, where it had come from, physical description, and whatever attributes or *talents* the cat might possess. I found *Snowflake* two cages down on the top row. I leaned in closer. The card said: SNOWFLAKE. ONE YEAR OLD. BORN IN CROTON-ON-HUDSON, NY. PERSIAN, WHITE. EXCEPTIONALLY WELL BEHAVED. ADORES CHILDREN. HIGHLY ATHLETIC. HAS AN OUTSTANDING SENSE OF HUMOR.

Wait, did I read that right? An outstanding sense of humor? I leaned in, staring this little blue-eyed Aryan goddess right in the face. *Please, this bitch ain't got jokes!* I thought, amusing myself as I made my way down the line of cages.

The cat next to Snowflake was a cute little brown fella; there were a lot of people gathered around his cage, wildly clapping, and one particularly large gentleman was jumping up and down. The more attention this cat got, the more frenetically he would leap through the little hoop hanging from the ceiling of his cage. His card, fittingly, read JUMPER. Next to Jumper was Fluffernutter, the cat that had triggered the exorcism in the little girl behind me. Next to Fluffernutter was Fluffernutter 2, who, I assumed, was Fluffernutter's twin. The Fluffernutter sisters were white, regal-looking cats with jet-black eyes, and came as a pair. Their card said they hailed from Upper Saddle River, New Jersey, had just turned three, had been brought up in a yoga studio and were extremely "harmonious creatures, bringing peace and balance to anyone fortunate enough to adopt them." *Jesus.* Then there was a jet-black cat with ice-blue eyes named Gemini, whose card alleged he could "stand on his front paws and dance . . . backward."

Holy Fuck, this place is like The X Factor *for cats.*

But even with all their *credits*, none of these stars of tomorrow felt like the right fit for my down-to-earth Snuggles. Just as I was thinking maybe I'd head out, I noticed a young man on the other side of the cages demonstrating a large beeping, flashing rat. I was rounding the cages, heading for the rat, when, suddenly, in a cage all the way in the back . . . *I saw him*. Smack-dab in the middle of this parade of preciousness, with their sugary-snack names and their mind-blowing attributes, there he *was*—this enormous, menacing, black, gray, and gold tabby, staring at me with such . . . anger . . . such hurt, such *resentment*, with a look on his face like he couldn't even *believe* the hand he'd been dealt and all the *shit* he'd had to go through just to find himself trapped in a cage that was clearly too small for him, surrounded by all these pretty young posers at fucking *Petco*! I knew it immediately. I'd found my replacement. Because, and I know this may sound weird, but . . . I saw . . . *myself.*

I leaned in to read his card. It didn't have a lot on it, like the other cats'. It just said EDMOND. OLDER. THE BRONX. NEEDS A VERY SPECIAL PERSON. And then, in very tiny print, under NEEDS A VERY SPECIAL PERSON, it said, HISTORY OF BOWEL DIFFICULTY. Wow, no attributes, no talents, no nothin'. This guy's never going to get adopted, especially with that *bowel difficulty*. I stared at him, realizing that who he *really* reminded me of, even more than myself, was that psychotic killer Javier Bardem played in *No Country for Old Men*. Something about the way he held his head—kind of back, and slightly cocked to the side, like a cobra about to strike—and the crazy look in his eyes. Eyes that were cold and dark, like Javier's in that movie. Plus, in the outer corner of his right eye, he had these tiny, gold pear-shaped drops that looked like those tear-shaped tattoos that only the *most* violent prison inmates have. You know, the ones who are serving multiple life sentences, who always sit on top of those picnic-looking tables in the prison yard, surrounded by all their fellow gang members, who deify them because of how many people they've killed. In fact, I'm pretty sure the number of teardrops *signifies* the number of people they've killed. According to his teardrops, so far, Edmond had killed four people.

I stood up, looking around for anyone wearing a FOCAS T-shirt. In the distance, on the other side of the cages, I spotted a chubby, middle-aged woman wearing one. She was seated behind a table with a stack of "Adopt a Pet" forms in front of her. In front of the stack of forms stood a cardboard picture of a gorgeous, exuberant, happy-faced cat, leaping into the air, with a bubble coming out of its mouth that said, "Ask meow!"

"Excuse me," I said, lowering my eyes to her name tag. "Sally, what's Edmond's story?" I asked, feeling ridiculous calling him this.

"Oh, our Edmond," Sally said, letting out a deep sigh as she bit her lower lip. "Where to begin...," she said woefully, revealing a slight Southern accent, as she motioned for me to sit down in the chair next to her behind the table. "Well, we were *finally* able to place Edmond with a lovely young family, and everything was going *okay* for about a year," she said in a very measured tone. "But then they had a baby, and Edmond..." She paused, averting her gaze, as she lowered her head. "Well, Edmond... Poor thing just really couldn't *handle* it."

"Uh-huh," I said, assuming specifics would follow. After a moment, it was clear that no specifics were coming. I glanced back over at Edmond, his giant, rabbitlike feet pressed up against the side of his cage. Turning back toward Sally, I said, "I'm interested in Edmond, Sally, I am; but before I could adopt him, I'd really have to know what you mean when you say, *He couldn't handle it.*"

Looking around, making certain no one was listening, Sally leaned in, as close to my face as she could get without kissing me, and whispered: "He became... *violent*!"

I fucking *knew* it! I *knew* this motherfucker was Javier Bardem in *No Country for Old Men*. I shot around in my chair, scrutinizing Edmond's face. From this angle, and with the way the light was hitting him, the chunky black streaks on his forehead even looked like those crazy bangs Javier had!

Turning back toward Sally, leaning in very close, I said, "What do you mean, exactly, when you say *violent*?" Biting her lower lip so hard a tiny spot of blood appeared, she said, *very* softly, and with the *greatest* reluctance, and *only* because she knew, in order to get him a home, she had to, "He began swatting the baby, *hard*, and, of course, he was bigger than the baby, so it was very... frightening."

"Of course," I said, glancing over at Edmond, who, was eyeballing the little devil girl who had pinned her mother against the kitty litter. She was standing next to his cage and seemed to be contemplating petting him.

"This couple would always have their baby in one of those seats, y'know, with the wheels, and the tray attached, so the baby can eat and push themselves around the floor. I think they're called Get Arounds."

"Right. Right," I said.

"Well, there were *several* occasions where the wife found the baby *standing up* in the Get Around, trying to *defend* the food on his tray from Edmond, who apparently was *also* standing up, hissing wildly, swatting at the baby repeatedly with one paw, while trying to grab its food with the other. The mother said it was almost like they were *sparring*. And I just think this whole *sparring* thing was where she felt she had to draw the line. I don't think she felt her child should have to be some type of gladiator, just to enjoy his meal."

"Of course," I said, glancing over at Edmond, thinking, *That's what they should have put on his card: baby fighter!*

"I just feel so badly for him," Sally continued, her eyes moist. "Bless his heart. Poor thing just can't help himself; underneath all his tough-guy machismo, I think he really feels very abandoned and scared; nobody even stops at his cage. I mean, he *knows* he can't compete with all these adorab—"

"I'll take him," I heard myself say.

"Really?" Sally said, tears filling her eyes.

"He needs a home. I can give him that," I said definitively.

"You can always bring him back if it doesn't work out," Sally said, wiping a tear from her eye.

"He won't be back; we'll just make it work. I have faith in

him," I said confidently as I turned around just in time to see Edmond bite the little girl.

—

"Meoooooooooow," Eddie cries, jolting me back to the kitchen, which is *such* a fucking disaster, it looks like it should have crime-scene tape around it. Especially when I glance down at Snuggles and Eddie, who, when they stand side by side, like they are now, look like one of those crazy buddy teams from one of those awful movies or TV shows. Y'know, the ones where the most unlikely characters are thrown together, through the most unlikely circumstances, to fight crime? Snuggles would be the brilliant lesbian forensics expert. Eddie, the sociopath out on parole, with deep ties to the criminal world that he's *only* willing to share with Snuggles, because he'd rather *fuckin' die* than ever go back to prison!

"Okay, okay," I say, emptying a can of Mariner's Catch onto their plate, as the lesbian forensics expert slams herself into my leg. Turning my attention to the high-rise of dirty dishes teetering precariously in my sink, I spot something that forces me to say out loud, "Fuck, did I... *bake*?" I have no memory of baking, but I did just start taking Ambien. And I remember, a while back, seeing all those stories on the news about people who had taken Ambien getting up in the middle of the night, going into their kitchens, and whipping up, like, an entire lasagna or tuna casserole, all while sound asleep. I close my eyes, trying to remember.... *Wait a minute, it's all coming back to me.*

—

I'd performed at an Elks Lodge the night before in Pennsylvania, where, while I was on*stage* (i.e., two, small, thin, *very wobbly* wooden platforms that *someone* had left a *space* between when they pushed them together), at the very *beginning* of my act, I got my foot stuck between the two platforms and had to do my entire show with my foot dangling between these two fucking platforms. When I finally hobbled out of there after being heckled by a very angry little woman (Me: "I used to be fat." Her: "You still are."), I went out to the parking lot, clutching my envelope with my two hundred bucks, and just as I got to my car, I encountered one of the head Elks, who was sponging down the rear of my car after getting very drunk during the show, wandering outside, and *urinating on it*. Not intentionally. According to him, I had parked very close to some... *shrubs*. As if this wasn't all bad enough, while I stood there, waiting for him to finish washing his pee off my bumper, he tried very hard to talk me into going home with him, which, although only momentarily, I did consider.

Anyway, by the time I was headed back to Teaneck, between the big five-oh, my foot, the Elk's pee, and the fact that I'd been, once again, so *horribly* underpaid—which, by the way, was a reality I found more and more painful to swallow the longer I did stand-up, the older I got, and the more I watched other, *younger*, people get *big* breaks... the kind of breaks where they didn't have to be fucking *grateful* they'd booked an Elks Lodge for two hundred bucks on a Saturday night—I was miserable. I just felt so lousy, and pissed off, and... *empty*. As I was driving, I began reviewing my career in show business over the last twenty years. Let see, I'd sold six screenplays. None of them were made, but you can make really good money just selling them. I'd written for two sitcoms. I'd spent six months writing that book proposal that that literary agent and I both couldn't believe nobody wanted. I'd been on *Late Night with Conan O'Brien* and *The View*. I'd headlined all over the country, opening for Lewis Black, Colin Quinn, Robert Klein, Linda Ronstadt, pretty much *killing* every time I got onstage, and I still couldn't pay my bills, *and* not a week went by that *someone* didn't ask me if I get special treatment because I'm Charles Grodin's daughter. *It didn't seem to have much of an impact on the Elk who urinated on my car*, I thought, pulling up to the light.

Flipping on my right blinker, about to turn onto my street, I looked to my left, entranced by the Dunkin' Donuts.

—

It's all coming back to me: the pint of Baskin-Robbins Jamoca Almond Fudge...the box of Munchkins. *Omigod, the donut holes*, I gasp. The ice cream–Munchkin casserole I'd whipped up! And, yes, those first few bites did lower the volume on all the noise in my head—*Will I ever be able to fully support myself as a stand-up? Will I ever be able to make enough money to stop nannying? Will I ever be able to stand up in a bigger life—a life where I don't feel smaller than I really am?*

And you know what...all the emptiness I was feeling...not *one* of those donut holes made a dent in filling that hole in my soul.

—

Following Eddie and Snuggs into the living room, I stop, stunned. *God, I can't believe how empty it looks*, I think, even though it's been like this for a week. I was two months behind on my rent, so I'd had an open house the Saturday before and sold almost all my furniture. The only things I kept were the desk my mother made me in high school, the computer on top of it, and one of those tiltboards you lie upside down on to stretch out your back. My dad gave it to me right around the time we agreed I really had to stop taking money; and as much as we both knew it had to happen and was so overdue, we also knew it would probably send my lower back into spasms—which it did, immediately.

I sat down in the middle of the room as Eddie walked over to me, licking my hand with his little sandpaper tongue. "I wish someone would rescue me, the way I rescued you," I say as I stroke his head.

You're kidding, right? I mean, look how great that turned out, some other part of me says to me as I look around at my empty apartment. *That's* why *you're in the position you're in today. You tried to get everyone to rescue you. Dem days is over,* this other part of me, suddenly sounding like Bo Diddley, says. I shut my eyes tight, shaking my head from side to side, wrestling with what I know is true.

"Why can't I fucking rescue *myself*?" I scream, so loudly, I scare Eddie, who charges across the room, diving into the closet across from me. He leaps up on top of the boxes that sit right behind my wedding dress, which is just hanging there. It used to be in a dry cleaner's bag, but Eddie pulled it off so many times, I finally threw it away. So now it just *hangs* there. My eyes still closed, I think back to the day Christopher and I got married at the Boathouse, and how happy we all were.

Eddie meows as I open my eyes to see him peeking out from behind my wedding dress, just his face, shoulder, and arm exposed, so it looks as if he's wearing an off-the-shoulder number for his big day.

"God, my wedding dress," I say out loud, staring at it. It's all so weird. I was a *Mrs.*, and now I'm a *Miss*. It's just a difference of a couple letters, but it feels like a whole alphabet. Eight years, a Mrs.... Eight years, a Miss. Sixteen years together. Letters and numbers, letters and numbers. Ten years cancer-free next Tuesday. Wow. Stage-four brain cancer—what my mother died of when she was fifty-three. Twenty-eight years old, the age I was when I got clean. D&C—the name of the procedure I had to have, twice, when I miscarried. PTA, something I'll never be a part of...

Oh, please, like you'd ever *join the PTA... maybe PETA*, that part of me that always tries to save me with a laugh says to me, making me chuckle.

HP—higher power... the relationship I've been working on since I got sober. *I know sometimes I'm not speaking to you, or not enough, but I always come back no matter how shitty things seem... probably when I need to talk to you even more. But seriously, God, I really do need some better numbers... some better letters.*

What about all my years clean and sober?

"That's true," I say, pushing myself into a standing position. *But what a fuckin' year this has been... What a fuckin' life this has been*, I think as I lie down on the tiltboard. *Maybe I'll see something different from this position*, I think, hanging upside down.

A couple minutes later Snuggles jumps onto my chest, positioning her face about an inch from mine, purring so loudly, she makes me laugh out loud. "You know how much I love you," I say, cupping her face in my hands as I kiss her nose. "But I think we both know we've taken this relationship as far as it can go. We both need to branch out." We lie there like that for about ten minutes, when, all of a sudden, my computer starts beeping loudly, scaring the shit out of Snuggles, who leaps off my chest and onto my computer keyboard. "Ow…Snuggles! You have to stop doing that!" I yell, glancing down at the red claw marks on my chest as I pull myself up. "Get down from there. No one's e-mailing you," I shout, shooing her off the keyboard as I lean over, clicking open my new e-mail….

Dear Ms. Grodin,

We have just received an offer on your book, "Standing Up." It's a good one! I think we should take it.

Look forward to hearing from you.

Your favorite literary agent

"Omigod, thank you," I say, starting to cry as I scoop Snuggles up from my mother's desk, carrying her over to Eddie, who is still in his wedding dress. Great letter. Great number. "Happy Birthday, Mar," I say, this time meaning it wholeheartedly.